More Praise for The

"*The Party Girl Cookbook* is outrageous—outrageous fun, spirited thematic ideas, irreverent entertaining tips, and solid, easy-to-prepare recipes. I want to be a party boy!"

　　　—Sid Goldstein, author, *The Wine Lover's Cookbook*, Director of
　　　　Communications, Fetzer Vineyards

"Sparkles with wit, spunk, and priceless advice on the essentials of demystifying and creating the smashing bash. The key word is fun; the goal—an unforgettable good time for all, especially the hostess! You will literally find yourself planning your next party as you turn the pages."

　　　—Margie Lapanja, Party Girl and author of *Goddess in the Kitchen* and
　　　　The Goddess' Guide to Love

"A book filled with delightful, creative, and festive ideas. Three cheers!"

　　　—Celia Barbaccia, owner, Celebrations Party Company

The Party Girl CookBook

The Party Girl Cookbook

Nina Lesowitz

Lara Morris Starr

Foreword by Gideon Bosker
Afterword by Anneli Rufus

Conari Press

First published in 1999 by
Conari Press
Distributed by Red Wheel/Weiser, LLC
York Beach, ME
With offices at:
368 Congress Street
Boston, MA 02210
www.redwheelweiser.com

ISBN 1-57324-167-9
Cover photography and hand tinting: Kelly Povo
Art direction: Ame Beanland
Cover design: Suzanne Albertson
Book Design and typesetting: Jaime Robles
Illustration page 288: Joan Carol

Library of Congress Cataloging-in-Publication Data

Lesowitz, Nina.
      The party girl cookbook / Nina Lesowitz, Lara Morris Starr.
         p.   cm.
      ISBN 1-57324-167-9
      1. Entertaining. 2. Cookery. I. Starr, Lara Morris. II. Title.
TX731.L418   1999
642'4.—dc21   99–16035
                                        CIP

Set in Joanna Roman and Italic with Miro titling.

Printed in the United States of America on recycled paper
  04 05   VG 10 9 8 7 6 5

To the Party Girls of my family, Meredith Morris and Ruthy Weil
—**Lara Starr**

To my resident kindred Party Girls, Mara and Jaime
—**Nina Lesowitz**

The Party Girl CookBook

foreword

by Gideon Bosker, author of Patio Daddy-O

Ever since my recent sex change operation converted me to the double-X chromosome state of mind, I feel eminently qualified to write a foreword to *The Party Girl Cookbook*. "Party" is my middle name, and the journey from a kitchen Casanova to a kitchen Renova has been remarkably painless. Even before my walk on the femme side, I spent hundreds of hours discussing the pearls of partymaking with women from all walks of life.

And party girls Nina Lesowitz and Lara Morris Starr know how to party, from January to December, in rasta rags or goddess garb. Forget about architecturally significant canapés or scouring the globe for that rare and rarely tasty treat. Too much effort and expense is a sure-fire route to party peril. Remember: "Party girls don't sweat, they glow."

I'd party with cookadelics Nina and Lara any time. They dress to excess, have attitude to spare, and know the ten reasons why trick or treating is better than sex. They will turn your kitchen into a party hall and the rest of the house into a pleasure palace. So shag me with a spoon and let the good times roll, indeed!

introduction

Parties? How I love to give parties!

—Hostess Lily Pons, who was famous in the '40s for throwing "pink parties," where the decor and all the food, even mashed potatoes, were pink

What could be better than a party? The anticipation, the break from the routine, the free food and drinks, catching up on gossip— parties are the best way we know to have fun in public.

Okay, so you think of yourself as a girl who loves to party. You can wear the clothes, drink the drinks, make the small talk, and dance the dance steps. But, if you want to keep the invitations flowing, sooner or later it's going to be your turn to throw a party. When it is, you are going to want to make sure everyone—including yourself—has the time of her or his life.

Start by visualizing. Imagine a brightly lit entry with eager guests arriving in festive attire. Picture your favorite people laughing and enjoying each others' company. The food is scrumptious, the music is just right, and your house or apartment never looked better. No one wants to leave, and the next day your phone doesn't stop ringing with all the post-party analyses and kudos. It's entirely possible. All you need is the desire to have fun and *The Party Girl Cookbook*. We've supplied the ideas, timesaving tips, and easy-to-prepare recipes that will help you unleash your Party Girl powers.

★ 1

Party Girl Basics

1. The Number 1 rule for a Party Girl is HAVE FUN! Your guests will be looking to you to set the tone, and if you're a freaked-out stress bag, you'll bring the whole party down. This is especially true of dinner parties and sit-down luncheons and brunches. You'll turn your guests into nervous wrecks if you're constantly popping up from the table to do this or that. The party recipes in this book are designed for minimal "up from the table" fuss. No fancy salad or dessert platters, or directions that read, "Deep fry and serve immediately."

2. Pick a theme and stick with it! Parties make the biggest impression when the theme is carried out from invitations to party favors. Even if you have dozens of leftover pastel napkins from your Easter brunch, don't put them out at your Halloween party! Get off the dime and get some black, orange, or Halloween novelty napkins!

3. Choose your date carefully. Make sure the day you choose for your party doesn't conflict with a major sporting event or religious holiday. If few of your guests can make it, reschedule the event.

4. Carefully consider your guest list. If you choose to throw a party with a wild theme, make sure you've invited people who like to dress up and party! Mix and match people. Don't invite just people from work or just from your social activities. Invite people from different areas of your life, but try to make sure everyone will know someone. When people arrive, make sure to greet them and introduce them to others.

5. Plan ahead! Do as much of your cooking, cleaning, shopping, and decorating as possible before the day of the party. Carefully read through each recipe you plan on using to see what can be made ahead of time. Nina recommends that you

plan a big theme party months ahead. This will give you time to create an invitation and get it in the mail, and prevent last-minute running around for theme-related decorations. With months to plan, you can borrow items from friends or pick up stuff while you're doing routine errands or exploring distant towns. (Shopping this way has the added bonus of spreading the expense over a longer period of time.) Chill out before the party begins, and fix yourself a drink. Relax, if at all possible. For Lara, this pre-party anticipation "is usually the period of time when I drive my husband most insane," but it's better than last-minute rushing.

6. Boogie! Music is a critical element of a good party. Make tapes or buy new CDs. Don't rely on the radio. Don't ever turn on the television (unless you're throwing the Oscar Party). If you don't have a thirty-CD changer, ask a friend to stand in for you and help change tapes or CDs. You want variety. In the theme parties that follow, we've recommended musical selections that fit together perfectly with each theme. The songs will definitely bring smiles to your guests' faces and enhance the overall event. Plan to play soft music as your guests are arriving and the dancing tunes midway through.

7. Say "Yes!" People like to help out for parties—to bring food, set up decorations, or clean up afterward. It makes them feel involved, and they're more likely to have a good time if they have a sense of participation in the event. Even if you've planned your meal to the last detail, you can always use a loaf of bread or bottle of wine, so accept offers to bring them.

8. Make sure you've emptied the trash before a party! Your guests will be lookin' to lose their paper plates, plastic cups, chicken bones, and whatever else. Put out a few extra trash cans during an outdoor party and set out clearly labeled recycling containers for bottles and cans.

9. Clean up right after the party! There's a strong temptation at the end of even the most successful of parties to climb into bed and leave the dishes for the morning. Don't do it! Muster another two hours of energy, take up offers of help, and clean up before you go to bed. You'll be glad you did in the morning. The job won't be as onerous if you plan ahead. Start the evening with an empty dishwasher. Have an extra bucket next to the sink filled with soapy water. You can dump flatware and dishes in this bucket during the evening, which will save you from scraping and scrubbing during the wee hours of the morning. If you are having a large party, hire help! You can ask friends who own catering companies and restaurants to recommend waiters or waitresses who are willing to work on their night off. Or you can hire a responsible teenager from your neighborhood. This person can take coats, refill glasses and platters of plates, help clean up, and even take photographs.

10. The more food you make yourself, the better! It shows people they are worth the effort it took (and they'll always think it took more effort than it actually did). We've all been to so-called parties where all the so-called host did was unlock the door and toss a bag of chips on the coffee table. This is not a party. When you use pre-prepared or store-bought food, at the very least, dress it up a bit. Put the chips in a pretty basket, pour the hummus into a ceramic bowl and sprinkle a little paprika on top, and please, for heaven's sake, take the Rondele cheese out of the plastic tub and put it in a nice bowl. This rule applies when you're a guest as well. While it's very nice of you to bring a homemade dish to a party, you're not doing anyone any favors by showing up with a casserole in a nasty-looking baking pan or without the proper serving utensils. If you're bringing a store-bought salad or some other pre-fab delicacy, stop at home on the way to the party and

empty it into one of your own bowls, and bring along a serving spoon. It's simply too un-chic to just rip the lid off a plastic deli tub and plop it down on a buffet table, no matter how casual the party is!

11. Don't forget the bathroom! Make sure there's toilet paper loaded in the holder and plenty of spare rolls in an accessible location. Stash your more unattractive toiletries under the sink—this includes toothbrushes and cups with toothpaste film clinging to the rim. Do a quick check of the medicine cabinet. Anything in there you don't want to share with the world? Hide it! People *do* look. (Admit it, you do too!) Carry your party theme into the bathroom. Coordinating candles, flowers, and other decorations helps bring the party into the powder room. It's also a nice touch to infuse the air with a scented candle or potpourri. Pay attention to your towels, too. Just one little ol' hand towel won't do for a large party. Roll up several and arrange them in a basket, or put out large paper napkins in your theme color; just make sure you provide a conspicuous basket to dispose of them.

12. Take photos! Bring out your Polaroid or borrow one for the evening. You can give away copies right then, or make double prints as mementos and send copies to your friends.

13. Have the number of a taxi service handy. Ask a responsible friend to drive home any guests who have overimbibed, or offer them the option of sleeping on your sofa.

14. To be a true Party Girl, you should not only give great parties, but also be a good guest! R.S.V.P. promptly to other people's invitations. Arrive at dinner parties on time, and at other types of parties within half an hour of when it starts. Offer to bring something, and stay late to help clean up. Phone the hostess the next day and tell her how much fun you had.

15. Cater everything! You can create a reputation as a walking party by always providing a bit of a nosh. Attending a long business meeting? Bring a plate of cookies. A friend dropping by to borrow the lawn mower? Offer him a brownie and a glass of fresh iced tea. Meeting your sister for a game of tennis? Pack an extra water bottle and a bag of orange slices. Any ordinary gathering of two or more people can be improved with a tasty treat.

Invitation Basics

◎ The Party Girls recommend that you send invitations. These days it's rare for anyone to get "real" mail, and your hand-addressed invite will stand out in the sea of bills and junk mail. Invitations create a sense of anticipation, and set the tone for the theme. If you don't have the time to develop custom invitations, you can handwrite the details on store-bought cards, or create a flyer announcement that you can color-copy onto jazzy paper. Brighten invitations up with a splash of color from a Magic Marker, a sticker or two, or some of that cute shaped confetti. We've provided you with creative invitation ideas throughout the book.

★ Be aware of what the timing for your party implies. A cocktail party usually has both a starting and ending time and only nibbles and drinks are served—no dinner is expected. If your party starts at 6 P.M. and no ending time is stated, your guests have a right to expect dinner. Parties starting at 9 P.M. or later are in the dinner-free zone. 7 and 8 P.M. are more ambiguous—you'd better be explicit about what you plan to serve, so your guests aren't either surprised by a meal when they've already eaten, or need to scarf peanuts, chips, and dainty hors d'oeuvres into their empty stomachs.

All of your invitations must include:

Name of host or hosts
Date
Time (include an ending time for cocktail parties, usually held from 5 P.M.–7 P.M. or 6 P.M.–8 P.M.)
Address (include a cross street and directions)
R.S.V.P. instructions, phone number, e-mail address, and cut-off date
Dress or costume suggestions

. . . and *can* include:

Menu, if you know it
Planned games and activities

Plan to send out invitations three to four weeks before the party.

Here's a tip for folding letter-sized invitations: Make sure you fold the invitation so that the guest can see the top line of text as soon as he or she opens the envelope. Here's an easy method: Put the invitation face-up on a flat surface. Fold from the bottom third of the page. Turn the invitation over, then fold from the top down bringing the top edge even with the first fold.

Don't forget the neighbors! Notify them of your party date so they can schedule a night out, or invite them as insurance against visits from the police.

Buffet Basics

★ People love to know what they are eating! Label each item on your buffet with a little folded card, or post the whole menu.

✵ Put food at different heights—it looks so dramatic and makes food easier to self-serve. Phone books make great risers—put them on the table before you cover it with the tablecloth.

✵ Put plates at the start of the buffet line and forks and napkins at the end, this way people won't have to juggle everything while they're loading up their plates.

◎ If you do make napkin-wrapped bundles of knives, forks, and spoons, put out extra napkins as well!

✵ Don't set up the bar in the kitchen or on the buffet table. You will need the space in the kitchen, and most kitchens turn into bottlenecks anyway. Keep white wine and beer chilled in ice buckets, coolers, or the bathtub.

Random tips that will make your life as a Party Girl easier:

★ Invest in a desktop publishing program for your computer, such as Printmaster Gold or Printshop. You can create invitations, placecards, menus, and lots of decorations with just a click and a drag, and then run them off on a photocopying machine for next to nothing.

✵ "A few years ago," says Lara, "I found myself with a huge bag of odds and ends—paper plates, cups, napkins, and flatware. I decided I was through buying all new party gear each time I had people over, and brought the whole lot of it to the office. I invested about $50 in reusable plastic 'china' in dinner and dessert sizes, stackable plastic coffee cups, and gigantic-sized packages of forks, knives, spoons, and large beverage cups. All this stuff fits into a large paper shopping bag, and easily stores in the back of my closet. I've got service for about forty guests, which is more than I could ever fit into my house at one time, and I never have to buy paper again. Each time I throw a party, all I have to buy is co-ordinating themed napkins and my table is set. I do have to wash everything after each party, but you'd be surprised how quickly it goes at the end of the night, and this way I'm saving money, the environment, and impressing the guests all at once."

☀ Though for some they conjure up images of drunken frat parties, we're huge fans of Jell-O shooters. They're inexpensive, easy to make, tasty, and, because of the array of colors available, adaptable for almost any party. We make them in what the local restaurant supply houses call "soufflé cups," sort of like fluted muffin cups with a rolled-over top. You can buy them by the hundreds. Dixie cups work too, but they usually are only available in dopey flower patterns or with cartoon images only suitable for kid's parties. We've made black and orange Jell-O shooters for Halloween, red and blue for Fourth of July, and a rainbow of yellow, green, blue, red, and orange for Gay Pride Day. To make Jell-O shooters, simply replace half of the cold water called for in the recipe on the Jell-O box with vodka. Fill the soufflé or Dixie cups about three-fourths full. Fill up a bunch of cookie sheets with these and clear a space in the fridge for several layers. If there will be kids at your party, make a few "virgin" shooters for them.

◎ Stock up on party supplies after Christmas! There's lots of party stuff that can be used all year 'round available cheap, cheap, cheap after the holidays. Skip the Santas and snowmen and head for candles, candle holders, glittery table linens, bowls, platters, and decorations with star or leaf motifs. Get boxes and boxes of Christmas lights in both white and multicolored strings; you can use them for lots of different parties.

❀ Tulle is the Party Girl's power tool! Tulle netting is one of the cheapest and most effective decorating materials available. At less than $1 a yard and available in every color imaginable, you can transform a room with swags, bows, drapes, and braids of tulle for less than $20.

January

We Be Jammin': *A Jamaican Beach Party to Break the Winter Blues!*

An indoor beach party seasoned with a generous shake of island spice is a great way to get in out of the cold. Don't let the nip in the air keep you from having a sun-splashed bash. With the Party Girl's creative tips and twists, you can create a tropical paradise right in your own living room.

Invitations

✳ Green, black, and gold are the colors of the Jamaican flag; use them in your invitations. Buy green cards and gold envelopes and use a thick black pen to write out the party info.

✦ **Headline:** *Hey, Mon—It's a Beach Party!*

Decorating Tips

◎ Once again your colors are green, black, gold, and a bit of red for table coverings, napkins, and paper goods. Buy or gather several 6' 8" bamboo poles (get an extra one for Limbo later!), and tape long ribbons or crepe streamers to the top. Stick them into your potted plants or in buckets filled with sand.

✳ Cover the floors and tables with bright, colorful beach towels. If you've got carpet, secure them to the floor with the hook part of a sticky-back Velcro strip. If you've got wood or other hard floors, use that gummy Fun Tack-type stuff.

✳ Replace your curtains with ocean-blue sheets. Cut lots of fish and other sea creatures from felt and pin them to the sheets.

◎ If you are feeling flush, rent a few palm trees for your party room. Pricey, but effective. String them with Christmas lights, or, as long as you're going for it, fish, beach ball, or other party lights.

✦ Collect seashells if you live near a beach, or buy them from a craft store. Use them to decorate tabletops, or tie them to fishing line and string like garland.

✺ Perfume the room with the scents of the tropics. Light coconut candles or a few sticks or cones of tropical incense. Spray liberally with an Ocean Breeze room spray.

✳ Bring the outside in—replace or augment your current table and chairs with folding beach chairs and lawn furniture.

✦ Hang posters of beach scenes, Reggae bands, and travel posters of Jamaica.

◎ Hang bunches of bananas from plant hooks, the ends of curtain rods, or light fixtures. Pile the buffet table with bananas, coconuts, mangoes, or any other fresh tropical fruits you can find.

✺ Hot, Hot, Hot! Turn the thermostat UP just for one night! You can wear a sweater the rest of the week.

Games and Activities

✳ **Sand Castles:** Set up a corner of the room as a sand castle design studio. Fill a large shallow plastic tub with sand, and set it on a big sheet of plastic—use a painter's drop cloth or a colorful vinyl tablecloth. Next to the tub set out a pitcher of water, a small kids' beach bucket, shovel, and rake. Put a posterboard sign on the wall over the tub that reads, "Build a Sand Castle." Stop by frequently with your camera to take pictures of your guests' creations.

◎ **Limbo:** How low can you go? You remember how this works: Two people hold a pole at either end. They start with the pole held high above their heads, and bring it down lower each time the line of dancers goes under. As the pole gets lower, the dancers have to lean back to clear the pole. Hilarity ensues as the pole goes lower and lower. "Limbo Rock" is the classic song for this dance/game. (See "Musical Selections" for a CD recommendation.) Tie green, black, gold, and red ribbons to the ends of the pole for a festive touch.

✳ **Channel Surfing:** You need to turn the TV on for this game, but you don't need the sound, so the TV won't slow down the other dancing or partying. Divide everyone who wants to play into two teams. Each team has two minutes to flip through the channels to find as many beach-related things as they can: sun, sand, water, swimsuits, surfboards, palm trees. Be sure to establish yourself as the judge of this game, or disputes could turn ugly! Award the winning team a prize.

Costumes

◎ **Rasta Rags:** Those floppy multicolored beret-type things, Bob Marley T-shirts, Erikah Badu-esque headwraps. Award a prize to anyone who shows up with dreadlocks—guests who ALWAYS have dreads are disqualified.

✳ **Bikini Beach:** Swimsuits, shorts, flip-flops, sunglasses, and zinc'd noses

✳ **Calypso Clad:** Ragged-edge jeans cut off at the knee, printed shirts tied at mid-chest, wide-brimmed straw hats, bare feet

✦ Slather yourself with a good coat of fragrant suntan lotion—the scent will bring back instant beach memories! Try one of the new colored sunscreens!

Favors and Prizes

✦ **Dubious Doobie or Gotcha Ganja:** For each favor you'll need plastic wrap, half of a plain white paper towel, a large handful of M&Ms, and a small heap of green paper shreds or excelsior. Start by tearing off a small piece of plastic wrap and laying the M&Ms down on it in a 6-inch row. Wrap the candy tightly in the plastic, tucking the edges under to form a long, thin roll. Place the half-paper towel in front of you. Put a small heap of paper shreds or excelsior in the middle of it. Nestle the candy roll into the shreds. Now tightly roll the towel around the whole thing, and twist the edges to seal. A completely legal joint that offers relief for your guests' next case of the munchies!

✳ A mini-bottle of Jamaican jerk seasoning (storebought or mix your own, see "Food"), is a great favor! Tie the bottle with green, black, gold, and red ribbon and tie on a tag that reads, "Thanks for not being a 'Jerk' and coming to my Beach Party."

◎ Let guests take home a bit of the beach! Glue a pretty seashell to a magnet. Attach a tag that reads, "Thanks for making my life a beach."

✴ **Thank You in a Bottle:** Burn the edges of plain white notepaper for a distressed look. Write a thank-you message on it, roll it up, and put in into a small, pretty bottle. Fill a bowl, tub, or wood box with sand and snuggle the bottles into it. Place the box of bottles by the front door.

◎ Suntan lotion, sunglasses, beach towels, beach bags, or reggae CDs are great prizes or favors.

Musical Suggestions

Roots-Reggae-Rock!! Fill your CD changer with a thumping Caribbean beat: *Hot Hot Vacation Jams*, Various Artists (K-Tel Records). A great collection! Includes

"Limbo Rock," "Hot, Hot, Hot," "The Piña Colada Song," "Iko Iko," "Day'O,"
"The Girl from Ipanema," and a bunch more great songs.

✳ *Reggae Around the World*, Various Artists

🎶 *Calypso from Jamaica*, Harry Belafonte

✦ *Legend: The Best of Bob Marley and the Wailers*

✳ *The Harder They Come*, Jimmy Cliff

Food

"Stroll on The Beach" Salad

Here's a neat predipped crudité that's easy to manage while partying.

4 pounds assorted stick-like veggies: carrots, celery, asparagus,
  green beans, squash spears
2 cups creamy salad dressing—bottled or use Cool 'n' Creamy Dressing
  (recipe follows)
16 plastic drink cups

Put 2 tablespoons of dressing in the bottom of each drink cup. Stand a
handful of assorted stick-veggies in the cup. Makes 16 strolling salads.

Cool 'n Creamy Dressing

1 1/3 cup mayonnaise

2/3 cup buttermilk

2 tablespoons white wine or cider vinegar

1/2 cup green onion, thinly sliced

2 cloves garlic, minced or pressed

2 teaspoons fresh lemon juice

salt and pepper to taste

Mix all ingredients together in a bowl. Cover and chill. Can be made 2–3 days ahead.

Reggae Rounds

1 sheet frozen puff pastry dough, thawed to room temperature

4 ounces (1/2 stick) melted butter

3/4 cup grated Parmesan cheese

1 1/2 tablespoons Jerk seasoning blend (recipe follows)

Roll the pastry sheet into a 10" x 16" rectangle on a floured surface. Brush the pastry with the butter. Sprinkle with the seasoning and cheese. Roll tightly from the 16" end and pinch the seam to seal. Wrap the roll tightly in plastic, and freeze for up to week and at least overnight.

Preheat oven to 375° F. Let the log thaw for 15 minutes before slicing into 1/4-inch rounds. Set the rounds on an ungreased baking sheet 1 1/2 inches apart. Bake for 10–13 minutes, until golden. Let the pinwheels rest on the baking sheet for 5 minutes, then remove to a rack to cool.

Can be baked a day ahead, and stored tightly covered. Makes 64 appetizers.

Jerk Seasoning Blend

1 tablespoon onion flakes

1 tablespoon onion powder

2 teaspoons ground thyme

2 teaspoons salt

1 teaspoon allspice

1/4 teaspoon ground nutmeg

1/4 teaspoon ground cinnamon

2 teaspoons sugar

1 teaspoon black pepper, coarsely ground

1 teaspoon cayenne pepper

2 teaspoons dried chives

Mix together all the ingredients. Store in a cool, dry place in tightly closed glass jar.

Jamaican Chicken Sticks

Yes, we're makin' chicken sticks!

2 onions, finely chopped

1 cup green onions, finely chopped

4 teaspoons fresh thyme leaves or

  1 teaspoon dried

2 teaspoon salt

4 teaspoons sugar

2 teaspoon allspice

1 teaspoon ground nutmeg

1 teaspoon ground cinnamon

2 jalapeño peppers, sliced

2 teaspoons pepper

6 tablespoons soy sauce

2 tablespoon canola oil

2 tablespoons vinegar, any kind

4 whole boneless, skinless chicken

  breasts

Combine all ingredients except chicken in a food processor or blender, and blend until smooth. Place the chicken in a glass baking dish and pour the marinade over the chicken, turning the breasts to coat well. Cover the dish with plastic wrap and chill overnight.

Preheat the oven to 350° F. To make the sticks, first soak 36 bamboo skewers in water for 30 minutes. While the skewers are soaking, slice each half breast into 8 thin slices. Thread each slice onto the pointy end of a bamboo skewer, puncturing the chicken slice 3 times.

Line a baking sheet with tin foil, and set a cooling rack over the foil. Fill the rack with as many of the sticks as will fit. If you've got leftover marinade, brush it over the chicken. Bake until done, about 15–20 minutes. Repeat with the rest of the skewers. Can be served hot, or chilled overnight in a tightly covered container and served cold.

To serve, either set the sticks out on a platter with the chicken ends all facing one way, or cut a piece of fruit, such as a large mango or pineapple, in half and put it cut-side down on a platter. Stick the blunt end of the skewers into the uncut side of the fruit. Makes 36 skewers.

Spinach Spliffs

1½ tablespoons olive oil
large red onion, finely minced
2 cloves garlic, minced or pressed
1 16-ounce package frozen chopped
   spinach, thawed

1 tablespoon red wine or cider vinegar
salt and pepper to taste
48 square won ton wrappers
   (about ⅔ of a 16-ounce package)

Preheat oven to 400°F. Heat ½ tablespoon olive oil in a medium skillet. Add the onion and garlic and cook until tender, about 5 minutes. Add the spinach and cook until heated through and liquid is evaporated, stirring often, about 5 minutes. Season with the vinegar, salt, and pepper, and stir well. Transfer the spinach mixture to a fine strainer, and press out as much liquid as possible.

Moisten half an inch around all of the edges of the wrapper with water. Place about 1 teaspoon of the spinach in the center of a won ton wrapper. Form into a small log about half an inch from each end of the wrapper. Roll tightly from one end, pinch and twist the ends to seal. As each Spliff is made, set it on a lightly greased cookie sheet. When the tray is full, brush the tops with the remaining olive oil. Bake until golden, about 15 minutes. Serve warm or at room temperature.

To make ahead, freeze the unbaked Spliffs on a cornstarch-sprinkled baking sheet and cover with foil. Put them on a greased baking sheet and pop in the oven just before serving. Makes 24 Spliffs.

Rasta Pasta

Pasta Salad with the colors of the Jamaican flag—green, gold, and black—with a bit of red thrown in for pizazz.

1 pound rotini pasta
1 tablespoon olive oil
1 large red pepper, seeded and thinly sliced
1 large yellow pepper, seeded and thinly sliced
1 large green pepper, seeded and thinly sliced
1 16-ounce can black beans, drained
1 garlic clove, pressed
1 teaspoon salt
4 tablespoons fresh lime juice
2 tablespoons white wine vinegar
½ teaspoon freshly grated lime zest
pepper to taste
¾ cup olive oil

Cook the pasta in lots of salted, boiling water until tender, about 6-8 minutes. Drain and rinse with cold water. Heat olive oil in a large skillet. Add the peppers and sauté until tender, approximately 5-8 minutes. Remove from heat and cool to room temperature.

To make the dressing, put all remaining ingredients into a screw-top jar and shake until blended.

In a large bowl, toss together the pasta, peppers, beans, and dressing. Chill for at least an hour or overnight. Serve in plastic drink cups for easy maneuvering. Serves 8-10.

Key Lime Squares

You add the lime to the coconut and bake it all up. . . .

Crust

2 cups flour

½ cup confectioner's sugar

⅓ cup sweetened flaked coconut,
   toasted and cooled (see note)

1 cup (2 sticks) butter, melted

Preheat oven to 325°F. Grease and flour two 8-inch square baking pans. Sift the flour and confectioner's sugar mixture into a bowl. Add the coconut and mix. Pour in the melted butter and mix into a soft dough. Press half of the dough into each pan, and bake for 25–30 minutes, or until golden brown.

Filling

4 large eggs

2 cups granulated sugar

¼ cup flour

1 teaspoon baking powder

5 tablespoons fresh lime juice   2 tablespoons grated lime zest

¾ cup sweetened flaked coconut, toasted and cooled (see note)

While the crust is baking, make the filling. Whisk the eggs and granulated sugar in a bowl until com-bined well (you can use the same bowl you used to make the crust.) Stir in flour, baking powder, lime juice, and zest. Reduce oven temperature to 300°F. Pour half of the lime mixture over each baked warm crust, return the pans to the oven, and bake for 20 minutes. Top the filling with the coconut and bake 5–10 minutes more. Cool in the pans for 10–15 minutes, then chill at least one hour or overnight. Cut each pan into 16 squares.

Before removing the squares from the pan, sprinkle with confectioner's sugar. (The easiest way to get a pretty, light dusting of sugar is to put the sugar into a fine mesh strainer, hold the strainer over the dessert, and gently tap the rim of the strainer. This technique also works for dusting dessert plates with cocoa powder.) Makes 32 squares.

Note: *To toast coconut, spread it in an even layer on an ungreased cookie sheet. Pop it into a preheated 325°F oven. Check and stir after 10 minutes and at 2-minute intervals until the coconut is golden.*

Rum Runners: *Three Do-It-Yourself Tropical Drinks*

Blended drinks are usually a pain in the grass skirt at parties—someone's got to play bar-tender and (wo)man the machine all night. However, you can't *not* have blended fruit drinks at a Jamaican-themed party, so here's what you do: Put out a bar table close to an electrical outlet. Cover it with a plastic table cloth and set it out with:

a blender	coconut cream
rum	superfine sugar
lemon-lime soda	big bowl of ice cubes
bottled lime juice	shot glass
bottled pineapple juice	1-teaspoon measuring spoon
bottled orange juice	1-cup measuring cup
ice cubes	large plastic drinking cups

Garnishes: lemon slices, lime slices, pineapple chunks, maraschino cherries

Flourishes: paper cocktail umbrellas, palm tree swizzle sticks, black, green, and gold napkins

Copy these drink recipes onto a piece of paper, slip it into a lucite holder (available at office supply stores), and let your guests blend their own drinks. Nondrinkers can substitute soda for rum. No need to hover 'round the bar, but do flit by now and then to wipe up spills and replenish ice, juice, and liquor.

Daiquiri

2 shots rum	1 teaspoon superfine sugar
2 tablespoons lime juice	1 cup ice cubes

Runnin' Rum Punch

2 shots rum	1 shot lime juice
1 shot pineapple juice	1 cup ice cubes
1 shot orange juice	

Piña Colada

2 shots rum   4 shots pineapple juice

2 shots coconut cream   2 or 3 ice cubes

Quick Food Ideas

◎ Fresh tropical fruits may be hard to find during winter in some areas, but dried or candied pineapple, banana, papaya, and mango are always available. Chop some up and mix with salted mixed nuts and coconut for a sweet/salty party nibbly.

✳ Skewer chunks of whatever fresh fruit you can find. Serve with "We Be Jammin'" Jam Dip made from 2 cups sour cream and 1 cup of any flavor fruit jam.

Variations on the Theme

✈ **Beach Blanket Bingo:** Throw a '60s-style bikini fling that would make Frankie and Annette proud. Decorate with beach balls and new frontier-era colors: shocking pink, brilliant yellow, lime green, and true blue. Have a steady wave of The Beach Boys, Jan and Dean, and The Ventures coming from your CD player. Serve '60s treats such as Tang, Jell-O molds, and onion soup mix/sour cream dip. Rent a selection of beach movies to have playing in the VCR. Hand out cats' eye sunglasses as party favors.

✳ **Get Lei'd:** Go heavier on the pineapple and coconut in your cooking, edge the buffet table with a costume grass skirt, greet each guest with a lei and a kiss, give out packages of macadamia nuts as favors, stick a Don Ho CD in the player. Fill vases with real or silk birds of paradise, hibiscus, and orchids. A surfboard would be a hard-to-find but one-of-a-kind party prop.

Jamaican Patois Proverbs

Me come yah fi drink milk, me no come yah fi count cow!
Deliver that which you promised, don't just talk about it!

What sweet nanny goat a go run him belly.
A cautionary Jamaican proverb which translated means: What tastes good to a goat will ruin his belly. In other words, the things that seem good to you now, can hurt you later. . . .

Chicken merry; hawk deh near.
Simply means, every silver lining has its dark cloud. Even in the happiest times one must still be watchful.

Mi no come yah fi hear bout how horse dead an cow fat.
Don't bore me with the mundane details.

Wanti wanti can't get it, getti getti no want it.
Have-nots covet what the Haves take for granted.

Trouble no set like rain. Unlike bad weather, we are often not warned by dark clouds on the horizon.

Every mikkle makes a muckle. Similar to "A penny saved is a penny earned."

Every hoe ha dem stick a bush. There is someone out there for everyone.

The higher the monkey climbs the more him expose.

Fire de a Mus Mus tail, him tink a cool breeze. Set a rat's tail on fire and he's thinks there's a cool breeze. Used to describe someone or something that is clueless, usually the upper class.

A new broom sweeps clean, but an old broom knows every corner.

—Adapted from Jamaica: A Land of Roots and People of Culture Web site:

http://www.jol.com.jm/~rvhelm/jamaica.html

Let's Go: *Party on the Town*

Party Girls know how to go places with their parties. We're going to demonstrate just how cosmopolitan and urbane we are when we throw "Party on the Town." Invite your friends for a night out in "The Big Apple" (New York City); "Everybody's Favorite City" (San Francisco); or "The Windy City" (Chicago).

For ideas on throwing a New Orleans "Big Easy Party," see the chapter on Mardi Gras; for a Los Angeles/Hollywood bash, see the "Oscar Night Party;" for a Paris soirée, check out the "Bastille Day Celebration."

Invitations

* ✳ Send guests their "prize notification." Print the outside of the envelope or the back side of a flyer with: *Winner Notification.* The invitation can be a simple letter informing guests of their good luck.
* ◎ **Headline:** *You've Won a Trip for Two (All Expenses Paid)*
* ★ Incorporate your destination theme in the graphics and copy. For instance, use a big red apple for New York.

City Themes

NEW YORK, NEW YORK

New York is popularly called "The Big Apple," a nickname dating from the 1930s, when jazz musicians took the name of a Harlem nightclub and extended it to the whole neighborhood and then to the entire city.

★ 27

Decorating Tips

🐕 Contact the New York City Convention and Visitor's Bureau and request a map of the New York City subway system. Hang it up, along with a poster of the New York City skyline. Send away for "I Love New York" bumper stickers and buttons.

◎ Rent a hot pretzel or hot dog cart from a party rental company.

★ Display copies of the *New York Times*, the *New York Daily News*, the *Village Voice*, and *New Yorker* magazine.

✳ At a local sports store, buy pennants featuring the Yankees, Mets, Giants, Knicks, Jets, or Rangers.

Games and Activities

★ **Guess the New Yorker Cartoon Caption:** Assemble an assortment of favorite cartoons from the *New Yorker* magazine—it's better to have more than you'll need so you don't run out. Cut the captions from the cartoons and keep them in separate envelopes (you may want to photocopy the cartoons first in case you think you won't remember the captions). When guests arrive, each person receives either a caption or a cartoon but not both, as well as a straight pin with which to affix the paper onto his or her clothing. Guests must then circulate and find their "match." Give out three prizes to the first three "couples" to complete their cartoon.

Favors and Prizes

✳ For the *New Yorker* caption contest prizes, give out New York trinkets like an Empire State Building pencil sharpener or a floaty pen of Manhattan.

◎ Give each guest New York subway tokens and an "I Love New York" button.

Musical Suggestions

- ★ "New York Minute," "New York State of Mind," "New York, New York," Frank Sinatra
- ✳ "How About You (I Like New York in June)," "New York City," John Lennon
- ⁙ "The Only Living Boy in New York," Simon and Garfunkel
- ◉ "Daddy Don't Live in New York City No More," Steely Dan
- ★ "I Guess the Lord Must Be in New York City," Harry Nilsson

I LEFT MY HEART IN SAN FRANCISCO

Decorating Tips

- ★ Buy and display posters of the San Francisco skyline, Alcatraz, and the Golden Gate Bridge.
- ◉ If you cannot borrow cable car tschotchkes from friends, contact the San Francisco Convention and Visitor's Bureau and ask them to put you in contact with a retailer that will mail-order miniature cable cars. Display these on your tabletop.
- ✳ Rent a fog machine.
- ⊗ Again, pennants! Find stuff for the Forty-Niners, Giants, and other Bay Area teams.

Favors and Prizes

- ★ Give each guest a map of San Francisco or mini BART guides.

Musical Selections

◎ "I Left My Heart in San Francisco," Tony Bennett
🎵 "San Francisco (Be Sure to Wear Flowers in Your Hair)," Scott McKenzie
☀ "San Francisco (You've Got Me)," Village People
★ "San Franciscan Night," Eric Burdon/Animals

CHICAGO BLUES

Did you know that Chicago's nickname did not come about because of the city's (in)famous weather? In 1893, *New York Sun* editor Charles Dana, tired of hearing Chicagoans boast of the World's Colombian Exposition, dubbed Chicago "The Windy City" because of its denizens' propensity for long-windedness.

Decorating Tips

★ Contact the Chicago Convention and Tourism Board for free brochures and maps. Display the maps on the wall.
◎ Ask friends for Chicago Cubs' baseball caps and prominently display them.
☀ Set out copies of the *Chicago Tribune* and the *Chicago Sun-Times*.
⊗ Once again, pennants! Chicago is home to the Cubs, Bulls, Bears, and the White Sox.

Costumes

Ask everyone to come dressed looking like the Blues Brothers, or at least in nightclub attire.

Games and Activities

"Chicago Trivia" Contest

Questions

1. Where does the term "private eye" come from?
2. What did Chicago gangster Al Capone's business card read?
3. Until the mid-1820s, what was Chicago better known as?
4. What was the original name of the rock group Chicago?
5. The "Whoopee" game found its start in Chicago in 1930; what did it later evolve into?
6. What company introduced the first beer can in 1935, a true innovation for packaging for its day?
7. What military item was first introduced for civilian use in Chicago in 1918?
8. Whose first U.S. album was recorded on the Chicago-based Vee-jay label?

Answers

1. The Pinkerton Detective Agency's trademark eye in its logo. Pinkerton was founded in Chicago in 1850.
2. Alphonse Capone, Secondhand Furniture Dealer, 222 S. Wabash
3. Fort Dearborn (after the army fort that afforded settler protection)
4. The Big Thing
5. Pinball
6. The American Can Company, based in Chicago
7. The armored car by Brinks Incorporated
8. The Beatles, with Meet the Beatles

Musical Suggestions

◎ Classic Chicago Blues artists, including Otis Rush, Jimmy Reed, Muddy Waters, and Buddy Guy. Also Joe Louis Walker, John Lee Hooker, B. B. King, Ruth Brown, and other beloved blues wailers.

✳ "Sweet Home Chicago" is a must, preferably from *The Blues Brothers and Friends, Live From Chicago's House of Blues*.

Food

NEW YORK

Give your guests their beverage choice of an egg cream or a Manhattan. Set out big bowls of kosher dill pickles. Serve baby bagels with cream cheese and lox spreads, Nathan's Hot Dogs, and the following recipes.

Waldorf Salad

This recipe was said to have been created by Oscar Tschirky of the Waldorf before the turn of the twentieth century.

4 large, firm apples, cored and cut into large dice
fresh lemon juice
1¼ cups chopped walnuts
Boston lettuce

4 stalks celery, diced
1½ cups mayonnaise

Place unpeeled apples in bowl and spinkle with lemon juice. Add celery and walnuts. Add mayonnaise, and toss gently. Arrange lettuce on salad plates and spoon salad onto lettuce. Serves 4. Can be doubled.

Potato Knishes

Pastry

4 cups sifted all-purpose flour

1 teaspoon kosher salt

1 cup butter or margarine, cut into pieces

6 tablespoons vegetable shortening

10 tablespoons ice water

Potato Filling (recipe follows)

1 egg yolk

Combine the flour and salt in bowl. In a food processor or with a pastry blender, combine the butter or margarine and the shortening. Add the flour and salt mixture and process until crumbly. Add the ice water and blend together.

Working with half the dough at a time, place on a lightly floured surface and knead for a few minutes. Shape into balls, dust with flour, wrap in plastic wrap, and refrigerate overnight.

Preheat oven to 425°F. On a lightly floured surface, roll out the balls of dough into the shape of a rectangle, one at a time. Cut the rectangle into strips about 8 inches long and 3 inches wide. Place a strip of potato filling in the center and fold over the sides to completely enclose the filling. Cut the pastry into 2-inch lengths and round the ends with your hands.

Place on an ungreased baking sheet and brush with a mixture of 1 egg yolk and 1 tablespoon water. Bake for 20 minutes, or until the knishes are golden brown. These can be made ahead of time and frozen. Reheat in a 375°F oven for approximately 15 minutes. Makes about 70 knishes.

Potato Filling

3 large baking potatoes, peeled
   and cut into quarters

tablespoons butter or margarine

3 tablespoons vegetable oil

2 large onions, chopped

kosher salt and ground white pepper or 3

cracked black pepper to taste

2 eggs, lightly beaten

Boil the potatoes until tender. Melt the butter or margarine and oil together in a skillet. Add the onions and sauté for 5–7 minutes on low heat until soft. Drain the potatoes and mash with a potato masher or mixer until smooth. Stir in the sautéed onions, salt, white and/or black pepper and eggs.

New York Cole Slaw

This is better if made a day ahead. It should be served chilled.

½ cup mayonnaise

½ cup sour cream

2 tablespoons Dijon mustard

2 tablespoons tarragon vinegar

1 teaspoon sugar

kosher salt and ground pepper to taste

1 head cabbage, shredded

Combine first five ingredients and salt and pepper to taste and mix well. Toss with cabbage and refrigerate. Serves 8.

No-Bake New York Cheesecake

Crust

¾ cup graham cracker crumbs
(about 12 single crackers)

2 tablespoons granulated sugar

4 tablespoons butter, melted

To prepare crust: Grease an 8-inch springform pan. Combine all ingredients and mix well, coating crumbs completely with butter. Pat evenly onto bottom of prepared pan. Place in freezer while preparing filling.

Filling

2 packets (1/4 ounce each)
unflavored gelatin

3 egg yolks

2/3 cup sugar

1 cup small curd cottage cheese

8 ounces cream cheese

juice and grated peel of one large lemon
or one medium size orange

1 teaspoon vanilla

2 cups sour cream

fresh berries to decorate

Filling: Sprinkle gelatin over 4 tablespoons cold water; stir and set aside. Place egg yolks and sugar in top of double boiler and beat until thickened and lemon colored. Place pan over (not in) simmering water and cook, until sugar is dissolved, stirring constantly. Mix in gelatin and cook, stirring, until gelatin is dissolved and mixture is thickened. Remove from heat and cool completely. Place cottage cheese and cream cheese in large bowl and beat until almost smooth. Stir in lemon juice, lemon peel (or orange juice and orange peel), and vanilla. Add cooled gelatin mixture and beat together. Stir in sour cream. Pour over crust, smoothe top, and refrigerate at least 4 hours. When ready to serve, run a knife around inside edge of pan before releasing springform pan. Decorate with fresh berries. Serves 8.

New York Egg Creams

Mix equal amounts of vanilla or chocolate syrup and very cold milk. Squirt a hard stream of seltzer into it to make it foam (this will not work with a store-bought bottle of seltzer).

Manhattan

4 ounces blended whiskey

1 ounce sweet vermouth

4 dashes bitters

2 maraschino cherries

Chill two cocktail glasses. In a cocktail shaker, half full of ice cubes, combine all the ingredients except the maraschino cherries. Shake to mix. Strain the mixture into the glasses. Garnish each drink with a maraschino cherry. Makes 2 cocktails.

SAN FRANCISCO

Serve a Monterey Jack cheese platter with grapes and sliced sourdough French bread, wine from Napa Valley, Irish Coffee (recipe follows), and these dishes.

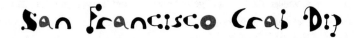

San Francisco Crab Dip

2 packages cream cheese, softened

1 pound fresh cooked crab, shredded, or 2 small cans, drained

1 teaspoon Tabasco, to taste

1 ½ teaspoon ketchup, to taste

½ cup red onion, finely chopped

salt and pepper, to taste

1 cup shredded Cheddar cheese (optional)

Combine ingredients by hand and blend well. Serve at room temperature with crackers or potato chips. For hot crab dip: Place mixture in a Pyrex baking dish and sprinkle with 1 cup shredded Cheddar cheese. Bake at 350°F until cheese is melted; serve immediately. Serves 8 to 12.

Don't Call it Frisco Artichoke Squares

Artichokes are grown just south of San Francisco. California is the world's largest supplier of this vegetable. This dish can be made ahead, covered, refrigerated, and served cold.

2 6-ounce jars marinated artichoke
   hearts
½ cup chopped onion
I clove garlic, minced
4 large eggs
¼ cup fine bread crumbs

¼ teaspoon salt
pepper to taste
½ teaspoon dried oregano
½ teaspoon Tabasco
2 cups shredded sharp Cheddar cheese
2 tablespoons fresh parsley, chopped

Drain marinade from I jar artichokes into a small frying pan. Drain the second jar; set aside marinade for other uses. Chop all artichokes; set aside. Sauté onion and garlic until onion is soft, about 5 minutes.

In a bowl, beat eggs and stir in bread crumbs, salt, pepper, oregano, Tabasco, cheese, parsley, and artichokes. Add onion mixture.

Pour into a greased 7-by-11-inch baking pan. Bake for 30 minutes until custard feels set when lightly touched. Let cool slightly in pan, then cut into 1-inch squares. Cover and refrigerate. Makes 80 squares.

In the window I smelled all the food of San Francisco. There were seafood places out there where the buns were hot, and the baskets were good enough to eat too; where the menus themselves were soft with foody esculence as though dipped in hot broths and roasted dry and good enough to eat too. Just show me the bluefish spangle on a seafood menu and I'd eat it; let me smell the drawn butter and lobster claws. There were places where they specialized in thick red roast beef au jus, roast chicken basted in wine. There were places where hamburgs sizzled on grills and the coffee was only a nickel. And oh, that pan-fried chow mein flavored the air that blew into my room from Chinatown, vying with the spaghetti sauces of North Beach, the soft-shell crabs of Fisherman's Wharf—nay, the ribs of Fillmore turning on spits! Throw in the Market Street chili beans, red hot, and frenchfried potatoes of the Embarcadero wino night, and steamed clams from Sausalito across the bay, and that's my ah-dream of San Francisco. Add fog, hunger-making raw fog, and the throb of neons in the soft night, the clack of high-heeled beauties, white doves in a Chinese grocery window. . . .

—From Jack Kerouac's **On the Road** (1957)

Irish Coffee

In 1952, San Francisco resident Stanton Delaplane, an international travel writer, fell in love with the Irish Coffee drink made by bartender Joe Sheridan at Shannon Airport in Ireland. He brought the recipe home to bartender Jack Koeppler at the Buena Vista Café at Fisherman's Wharf. They tried to recreate this magnificent drink, but the cool cream float kept sinking. So Koeppler flew directly to the Shannon Airport to learn from the drink's creator, and the rest is now part of San Francisco legend.

coffee	1 jigger Irish Whiskey
brown sugar	heavy cream

Fill glass with hot water to preheat, then empty. Pour piping hot coffee into warmed glass until it is about ¾ full. Add 1 tablespoon brown sugar and stir until completely dissolved. Blend in Irish

Whiskey. Top with a collar of slightly whipped heavy cream by pouring gently over a spoon. Enjoy while piping hot.

CHICAGO

Serve bar food, including peanuts and pretzels. The drink, of course, is beer.

Chicago-Style Deep Dish Sausage Pizza

1 packet (2 tablespoons) active dry yeast

¼ cup plus ½ cup warm water

¼ cup plus 1¾ cup unbleached all-purpose flour

2 tablespoons olive oil

½ teaspoon salt

1 tablespoon milk

¾ pound Italian sausage

1 pound shredded mozzarella cheese

10 slices provolone cheese

¼ pound shredded fontinella cheese (not to be confused with Fontina)

⅛ pound grated Parmesan cheese

2 cups tomato sauce

2 cloves garlic, diced

fresh ground black pepper

fresh chopped or dried oregano leaves

Mix yeast, 1/4 cup water, and 1/4 cup flour in a large bowl, and let it rise for about 20–30 minutes (there will be a layer of foam on top). Add remaining ingredients and mix dough with a fork until a ball of dough forms.

Lay down a light dusting of flour on a clean work surface. Knead the dough with the heel of your hand, pushing the dough forward and turning it slightly, then folding it back over. Repeat about 10 minutes until the dough is smooth and stretchy.

Lightly coat a large bowl with olive oil. Gather the dough into a ball, place it in the bowl, and oil the surface with olive oil. Cover the bowl with a towel and put in a warm place to rise until it has doubled in bulk, about 2 hours. When dough has risen, punch it down and let it rise again, about 40 minutes.

Roll out the dough with a rolling pin to about 1/2-inch thickness. Evenly spread out the dough in a well-greased, 14-inch round pan and slowly bring it up along the side, almost to the top. Let the dough rise in the pan for about an hour at room temperature.

Preheat oven to 375°F degrees. Add one cup of sauce to the crust dough. Add sausage in an even layer. Add garlic, sprinkle on the fontinella, and then lay on the slices of provolone evenly. Let cook in the oven for 15 minutes, then remove to add other ingredients.

Add second cup of tomato sauce, sprinkle on the Parmesan, and spread on the mozzarella cheese. Sprinkle pepper and fresh or dried oregano to taste. Place back in the oven and cook for other 30 minutes, or until the crust is a golden brown. Makes one very hearty pizza for 8.

Variations on the Theme

LET'S GO: SURPRISE!

During his college days, Nina's friend Steve Hueston in Canada used to attend parties like this one: First of all, collect a cover charge from your guests a few weeks before the party. The party host or hostess then purchases a round-trip ticket to a secret destination. (So, if you buy two round-trip tickets to Vegas, and a $100 per night hotel room for two nights, and there are 60 people at the party, the cover charge will be approximately $7 per person.) Late in the evening, as close to dawn as possible, draw a winner's name. The winner gets two tickets to somewhere—the catch being that the flight leaves at dawn, so you don't have time to go home and pack. (And this is fun?) You have to bring whatever you think you will need for the trip with you to the party.

february

Eat Your Heart Out:
Valentine's Day Red Party

arty Girls LOVE to dictate dress codes, and this is no exception. Wearing red is mandatory at this party. We don't care if red clashes with your best friend's hair color, she must go out and purchase something flame-red to wear. Don't hesitate to throw this party on Valentine's Day—your coupled friends will be relieved to skip the strain of selecting and securing reservations at a fancy-schmancy French restaurant, and your single friends won't have to pine at home alone.

Be sure to invite plenty of single people. Party hostesses get extra points for matchmaking at this event.

Invitations

◎ **Handmade Valentines:** If you're inviting twenty people or fewer, consider home-made valentines, the kind kids make in grade school. Purchase plain white card stock. Attach a red doily to one side. You can attach stickers with cherubs and hearts, and glue on feathers. The reverse side will contain the invitation details. Put these in red envelopes. Sprinkle some red heart confetti inside.

✦ **Decorate Your Own:** Using your computer laser printer, print out invitations on high-quality white paper, using red ink. After printing them, cut each one into the shape of a big red heart. Ask the invitees to decorate their invitation and bring it with them to the party. You can display the entries on a big piece of foam board at the party, and give an award for the best "valentine."

✳ **Postage Stamp:** The post office sells different versions of a "Love" stamp. You must use these on your envelopes.

◉ **Headline Suggestions:**
Wear Red or Be Dead
You Are Invited to a Heart-to-Heart Party
A Heartwarming Party at (Your Name)'s
For all: Bring something sweet, red, or bubbly. Red attire requested.

Decorating Tips

Valentine's Day brings out the romantic side of the Party Girl. Let your love interest know that this is what we mean when we say we want tangible proof of their love and affection. Valentine's Day is a time to express your deepest longings, revel in the sensuous, savor what's delicious, and bask in the afterglow. With that in mind, think hearts, lace, flowers, candles, and chocolate.

✦ **You Light Up My Life:** To set the mood, you should replace your porch light bulb with a red bulb, which is easily purchased at any hardware store or drugstore. Go wild with candles—buy red, pink, and white candles, and set them aglow throughout the house, including the bathroom(s).

◎ **The Look of Love:** You can purchase lace paper doilies, Cupid cutouts, and red and white crepe paper at your local party supply house. But remember, it is the special touches that your guests will marvel over and remember for all eternity. Be on the lookout for heart-shaped anything, from vases to bowls. You can purchase angel and Cupid statuettes, which look adorable hanging from the wall. Tie red ribbons around your lamps. Purchase tulle from your local fabric store, and swag it around door and window frames, or cover your furniture with it. Cover tabletops with white tablecloths, red overlays, and white doilies, and sprinkle red confetti foil hearts on top, or those little candy hearts with the sayings. Fill bowls with foil wrapped chocolate hearts or Hershey's Kisses.

◎ **Say It with Flowers:** Flowers are an important touch. Red roses are prohibitively expensive during this time of year, so splurge if you can afford it or just buy one or two and display them in bud vases. Six or more red tulips work beautifully when artfully arranged in a central location. Potted bleeding heart plants (Dicentra) in pink and red are magnificent—ask your nursery if they can get these before their typical spring blooming period.

Costumes

Remember, this is a RED party. For a party that Nina threw, she wore a bright red minidress, white pantyhose with red hearts, red shoes, heart earrings, and bright red lipstick. Make sure you take lots of photographs—rooms full of red-garbed guests make for very festive photos.

Games and Activities

★ **Going to the Chapel:** If you have a friend who can act, or a friend who moonlights as a wedding officiate, have him or her wear a preacher's outfit and perform quickie-wedding vows. You can grab people at the party—even if they're complete strangers, and pull them over to the chapel. Stick a bridal veil on the "bride's" head, and take pictures of the "groom" kissing his "bride." Have a boombox playing a taped loop of Billy Idol's "White Wedding," the Dixie Cups' "Chapel of Love," and Frank Sinatra crooning "Love and Marriage."

✳ **Dance with Me:** You *have* to feature dancing at this party. You can give prizes to the best slow dancers at the party. This encourages couples to get on the dance floor.

Favors and Prizes

※ For the Dance Contest prize, you can award Chocolate Body Paint. Order this from Tom and Sally's Homemade Chocolate in Brattleboro, Vermont, (800) 827-0800.

◎ A red "party bag" filled with chocolates.

★ Vessels of massage oil.

Musical Suggestions

★ "Unforgettable," Nat King Cole

※ "For the Love of Him," Bobbi Martin

◎ "The Commandments of Love," Moonglows

✳ "Dedicated to the One I Love," The Shirelles

★ "Sealed with a Kiss," Brian Hyland

⁂ "Do You Love Me," The Contours

◎ "Sweet to be Loved," Marvin Gaye

★ "A Groovy Kind of Love," Mind Benders

✳ "Whisper You Love Me, Boy," The Supremes

※ "My Pledge of Love," Joe Jeffrey

◎ "For Your Love," Yardbirds

⁂ "Love Will Keep Us Alive," Eagles

◎ "Woman" and "Love," John Lennon

※ "Anything for Your Love," Eric Clapton:

★ "You Owe Me Some Kind of Love," Chris Isaak

✳ "Valentine's Day" and "Tunnel of Love," Bruce Springsteen

★ "Crazy Little Thing Called Love," Queen

◎ "Gimme All Your Lovin'," ZZ Top
✳ "The Look of Love," ABC
◎ "Friday I'm in Love," Cure
✈ "Love Shack," B-52's
✳ "Love Is a Drug," Roxy Music
✳ "Bad Case of Loving You" and "Addicted to Love," Robert Palmer
◎ "Cherry O Baby" and "Love, Keep on Movin'," UB40

Food

We are going to have a RED food buffet. Don't worry about overdoing it, we're talking theme here.

Cranberry-Tomato Salsa

2 cups fresh cranberries
½ cup chopped red onion
¾ pound ripe roma tomatoes,
    cored, seeded, and chopped

1 fresh chile (serrano or jalepeño)
2 teaspoons kosher salt
2 tablespoons fresh lemon juice
½ teaspoon ground cumin

Place cranberries in food processor. Pulse until coarsely chopped. Add onion, tomato, and chile, and pulse a few times to combine. Stir in salt, lemon juice, and cumin. Serve with chips. Makes 2 cups dip.

Red Pepper Spread

¼ cup olive oil

1 small onion, chopped

2 large garlic cloves, sliced

1 12-ounce jar roasted red peppers, rinsed and drained

½ cup pine nuts, toasted and cooled

⅓ cup packed fresh basil leaves

2 tablespoons fresh lemon juice

1 slice plain bread, cut up

Place oil in a medium skillet over moderate heat. Add onion and garlic, stirring until softened, about 5 minutes. In a food processor, place onion mixture and remaining ingredients and blend until smooth. Spread over Crostini (recipe follows). Makes about 1½ cups.

Crostini

Slice two loaves of Italian bread or French baguettes into thin (¼-inch) slices. Place on a baking sheet and brush tops with olive oil. Bake in a 350°F oven until edges are light brown.

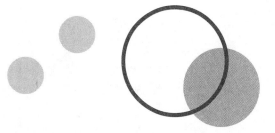

Sun-Dried Tomato Dip

This will keep for weeks!

½ pound sun-dried tomatoes (dry, not packed in oil)
2 cups water
10 medium cloves garlic, smashed and peeled
1¼ cups olive oil
¼ cup vegetable oil
1½ teaspoons dried oregano
1½ teaspoons dried thyme

Cover tomatoes with water in a nonreactive saucepan. Bring to a boil over medium heat, about 8 minutes. Reduce heat to a simmer and cook, covered, for 22 minutes. Allow to cool. Drain. Combine with oil, garlic, oregano, and thyme over low heat, covered, for 20 minutes. Purée in food processor. Serve this dip and the following one with a platter of sliced red bell peppers and cherry tomatoes. Makes 3 cups.

Heart-Stopping Dip

This is a spectacular fuchsia-colored dip!

1 cup (8 ounces) part-skim cottage cheese
1 16-ounce can sliced beets, drained

1 teaspon fresh dill, chopped
salt and freshly ground black pepper, to taste

Combine beets and cottage cheese in a blender or food processor and process until completely smooth. Mix in dill and season to taste with salt and pepper. Makes 1¾ cups.

Two Hearts Are Better Than One Salad

How perfect! Marinate ahead of time, and distribute over lettuce leaves before the party starts.

2 large cloves garlic, minced

4 teaspoons Dijon mustard

4 tablespoons red wine vinegar

¾ cup olive oil

salt to taste

freshly ground black pepper, to taste

2 14-ounce cans hearts of palm, drained, sliced into rounds

2 14-ounce cans artichoke hearts, drained, quartered

1 10-ounce package baby spinach, washed and dried

24 sun dried tomatioes packed in oil, drained and chopped

¼ cup chopped kalamata olives

Combine garlic and mustard in small bowl. Add vinegar and whisk in olive oil until smooth. Add salt and pepper. In a large bowl, combine hearts of palm and artichoke hearts. Pour dressing over and combine well. Marinate at room temperature for half an hour.

At serving time, place spinach in one layer on a tray or large serving plate and arrange the artichokes and hearts of palm on top. Sprinkle with the sundried tomatoes and olives. Makes 12 servings.

Frangipani Tart with Strawberries and Raspberries

1 recipe *Pâte Brisée* dough (recipe follows)

6 tablespoons unsalted butter, softened

½ cup sugar

1 large egg

¾ cup blanched almonds, ground fine

1 teaspoon almond extract

1 tablespoon Amaretto

1 tablespoon all-purpose flour

2 cups strawberries, hulled

2 cups raspberries, picked over and rinsed

¼ cup strawberry or raspberry jam, melted and strained

Make the *Pâte Brisée*. Preheat the oven to 375°F. In a small bowl, cream together the butter and the sugar. Then beat in the egg, the almonds, the almond extract, the Amaretto, and the flour. Spread this mixture evenly on the bottom of the shell and bake for 20–25 minutes, or until the shell is pale golden. (If the filling begins to turn too brown, cover loosely with a piece of foil.) Let the tart cool. Cut the strawberries lengthwise into ⅛-inch-thick slices, arrange the slices, overlapping decoratively with the raspberries, in rows on the tart and brush the berries gently with the jam.

Pâte Brisée

1 ¼ cups all-purpose flour
6 tablespoons cold unsalted butter, cut into bits
2 tablespoons cold vegetable shortening
¼ teaspoon salt

In a large bowl, blend the flour, the butter, the vegetable shortening, and salt, until the mixture resembles meal. Add 2 tablespoons ice water; toss the mixture until the water is incorporated, adding more ice water if necessary to form dough. Form the dough into a ball. Dust the dough with flour and chill it, wrapped in wax paper, for 1 hour. Roll out the dough ⅛-inch thick on a lightly floured surface, fit it into an 11-by-8-inch rectangular or 10- or 11-inch round tart pan with a removable fluted rim, and chill while making the filling. Serves 8.

Chocolate Heart Cookies

1 cup butter, at room temperature
¾ cup sifted confectioner's sugar
1 teaspoon vanilla
2 cups sifted flour

½ teaspoon salt
6 ounces semisweet chocolate
1 teaspoon vegetable shortening

Cream together butter, sugar, and vanilla. Gently stir in flour and salt. Chill until firm enough to roll. Preheat oven to 300°F. Roll dough ½-inch thick on a lightly floured surface or between sheets of wax paper. Using heart-shaped cookie cutters, cut out hearts as close to each other as possible. Re-roll and use the scraps to continue making hearts. Bake on an ungreased baking sheet for 20–25 minutes, or until cookies are dry but not brown. Cool on a rack.

While cookies cool, melt the chocolate in a double boiler or in the microwave. Stir in vegetable shortening. Dip one end of each cookie into chocolate. Place in refrigerator to harden chocolate. You can refrigerate, or even freeze and defrost these until ready to serve. Yield depends on the size of your heart-shaped cookie cutters, up to 4 dozen.

★ Set out a platter of sliced salami and sausages along with Gouda cheese (encased in red) and heart-shaped crackers by Valley Lahvosh Baking Company (available at Trader Joe's and in some gourmet shops and supermarkets).

✳ Set out a beautifully arranged platter of strawberries.

✺ Serve lots of red wine and passion fruit nectar.

Mardi Gras!

Let the Good Times Roll

Nothing says "party" quite like Mardi Gras, and for this party the usual rules do not apply! Forget everything you've ever been told about "flow" and cram as many people into your party space as possible—you want to create that wild, frenzied, steamy, sweaty, Blanche-meets-Stanley-in-a-feathered-mask feeling of Bourbon Street. Turn the music UP! Conversation is not king—dancin' is!

Invitations

◎ Mardi Gras is one of those "floating" holidays that can fall anywhere from mid-February to early March. Have a blowout, ball-type bash the Saturday before Mardi Gras.

✦ January 6, also known as Twelfth Night or the Feast of the Epiphany, marks the official start of the Carnival season that culminates on Mardi Gras—or "Fat Tuesday." Keep up the tradition by sending your invitations out so they arrive on or around this day.

◎ Purple, gold, and green are the official colors of Mardi Gras—choose these colors when buying invitations and envelopes, or paper for making your own.

✳ Include traditional Mardi Gras trinkets in the envelopes—strings of beads, "doubloons" (plastic coins), and masks.

★ Mardi Gras is the ultimate night for outlandish costumes and glad rags—make sure your invitation includes dress suggestions like "Feathers, fringe, and other fabulous finery encouraged."

Decorating Tips

◎ Stick with the Mardi Gras colors of green, gold, and purple, and you can't go wrong! Buy yards and yards of super-cheap nylon netting or tulle in these colors, and drape them over windows and across walls. Cover tables, chairs, and sofas with king-sized sheets, purchased from a discount linen shop or from a just in-the-nick-of-time President's Day white sale, in Mardi Gras colors. Hang lengths of green, gold, and purple ribbon from doorways for dramatic entrances and exits.

✳ Beads are essential to Mardi Gras—they're thrown from floats to eagerly awaiting hands, and the most elaborate and colorful strands are highly prized. Women bare their breasts and men drop their drawers for long strings of the traditional baubles. Decorate with the cheapest plastic beads you can find at a party, costume, or discount store. (Beads can be any color; you don't have to stick with the green, gold, and purple theme.) Pile them on tables, hang them from the rafters, and scatter them on the floor.

★ Masks—especially feathered masks—are also ubiquitous at Mardi Gras. Scour thrift shops for ceramic wall masks—even ugly ones can be tarted up with a bit of green, gold, and purple glitter, or with ribbons in those colors trailing from the sides. Inexpensive silk and lamé half-masks can be found after Halloween at costume or large party shops—better yet, plan early and snap up a bunch on sale after November 1.

◎ Mardi Gras has a lexicon all to itself. Make up banners on butcher paper or posterboard with some of the most common Fat Tuesday phrases:

"Let The Good Times Roll," or in French, "Laissez Les Bon Temps Rouler"

"Throw Me Somethin', Mister" (the traditional plea for beads, doubloons, cups and other "throw" from Mardi Gras Floats)

❋ Make mock street signs for some of the Big Easy's most famous landmarks, such as "Bourbon Street," "St. Charles Avenue," "The French Quarter," and "The Garden District."

◎ In the early days of Carnival parades, flambeaux (gas and oil lanterns), held by dancing and prancing carriers, were the only illumination for nighttime parades. Honor this tradition by placing lots of candles on the tables, mantles, and other safe, stable surfaces. Use inexpensive lanterns, deep glass candleholders, or the plain versions of Mexican prayer candles available at Latin markets and discount stores.

❋ Bras, panties, and other assorted undergarments fly freely at Mardi Gras as the parties get raucous. Start off with some bra-garlands strung about the room or a few pairs each of bikinis, briefs, and boxers hanging from lamps, picture frames, windows, and furniture.

★ Ask your friendly neighborhood travel agent for travel posters of New Orleans.

Costumes

◎ Mardi Gras costumes are more about flamboyant finery than literal character costumes, although you see those too. Flashy colors, fabrics, and accessories in any combination are just right.

❋ Many of the carnival Krewes—the organizations that put on the parades and balls—are named after mythological gods and goddesses: Bacchus, Orpheus, Hermes. Dress as a Greek God or Roman Empress for a night of less-than-holy rollin'.

★ For an elegant party reminiscent of the invitation-only Mardi Gras Ball, throw a black-tie affair, complete with elaborate masks.

✳ Masks are key—have a bunch available for those inevitable party poopers who don't come in costume. Even a "jeans-and-T-shirt-slob" looks like he's in the swing of things with beads around his neck and a mask on his face.

◎ New Orleans' Native American community traditionally marches the streets on Mardi Gras day dressed in elaborately feathered Indian headdresses and costumes. The spangly-sparkley outfits are more suggestive of Las Vegas than true Native American garb, and can inspire great costumes for your party. Start with a cheap Indian headdress from a costume shop and add as many feathers, sequins, rhinestones, and ribbons as your head can handle.

✻ One of New Orleans's most popular parades is the Zulu Parade—traditionally the first parade of the day on Mardi Gras. These African American maskers (paraders) march in blackface and exaggerated "Zulu" dress such as grass skirts, spears, big Afro fright-wigs, and bone necklaces. As with most things at Mardi Gras, rules do not apply, and in this case "PC" rules are definitely out the door! Instead of beads, Zulu warriors award daring bystanders with painted coconuts.

Games and Activities

✳ Greet your guests at the door with one or two strands of "good" beads. These are longer, bigger, more colorful, or more elaborate than the plain beads you'll use for decorating. Encourage guests to trade beads among themselves or to earn them by "dirty" dancing or exposing themselves!

◎ The most precious prizes of the Zulu parade are plastic coconuts decorated with gold paint and glitter. Once thrown from floats, they are now handed to a lucky few who earn them by exposing usually private body parts. Have a few coconuts on hand to award to some of your more daring guests.

✳ Just before midnight, choose a King and Queen of Mardi Gras. Pop a cardboard crown on each of their heads, and invite them to lead a parade around the party.

◎ If you have a balcony, landing, or porch, use it to recreate the action on the balconies of the French Quarter. Partiers hang over the railings and dangle "good" beads before the crowds below. Street revelers must dance or expose their breasts, butt, or other private parts before the prized beads will be dropped from the balcony.

✦ King Cake Baby! A King Cake is a sweet jelly-roll type of cake that has a plastic baby baked inside. King Cake is first served on January 6 (Twelfth Night, which commemorates the day the Three Wise Men or Kings met baby Jesus and delivered their gifts), and is eaten throughout the carnival season. Usually the person who finds the baby has to either host the next party or bring the King Cake. At your party however, the baby-finder should get a prize. (Recipe and ordering information follows).

◎ In New Orleans, the revelry ends promptly at midnight. Mounted police and street cleaning trucks prowl the streets shooing partiers off the streets and use loudspeakers to broadcast "Mardi Gras is over." Midnight may be a bit too early for you to end your party, but you can recreate the experience by turning off the music at midnight and announcing, "Mardi Gras is over—this is now an Ash Wednesday party." Immediately turn the music back on and start dancing again so your guests don't think it's *really* time to leave.

Musical Suggestions

Music is very important at a Mardi Gras party—you'll want it to be loud, constant, and raucous from start to finish. You want your guests to dance, dance, dance, and even if they take a break to eat, smoke, or chat, their toes should be tappin'. Record stores abound with lots of great Cajun and New Orleans jazz music. Get as many CDs as you can fit in your player and hit "shuffle"—you and your guests will!

Here are six great CDs to fill a typical CD changer:

◎ *The Big Easy Soundtrack*, Various Artists
✳ *Mardi Gras in New Orleans, Volumes I and II*, Various Artists
✦ *Live at Tipitina's 1982*, Neville Brothers, Various Artists
❋ *All-Time Cajun and Zydeco Dance Favorites*, Various Artists
◎ *Best of Pete Fountain*
✦ *Mardi Gras!*, Queen Ida and Her Zydeco Band

Food

Food for a Mardi Gras party has to be easy to eat and serve. With so many people and so much space devoted to dancing, there's very little room for sitting and eating. Serve mostly finger foods or one or two "forkable" dishes like Gumbo or Red Beans and Rice. Put out lots of cocktail napkins, but no plates—you don't want to encourage meal-type eating. Gumbo or other rice dishes can be served in paper hot-drink cups that are easy to eat from while standing up.

Spicy Pecans

6 teaspoons salt
4 teaspoons Cajun seasoning

8 cups pecans
4 tablespoons butter, cut into small pieces

Preheat oven to 275°F. In a small bowl, combine the salt and seasoning. Spread 2 cups of the pecans in a shallow baking pan. Dot with ¼ of the butter. Bake 10 minutes. Remove from the oven and sprinkle with 2½ teaspoons of the seasoned salt. Toss well to coat. Return to the oven and bake an additional 5–8 minutes (check frequently to make sure the nuts don't burn). Let the nuts cool on a paper towel. Repeat with remaining nuts.

Store in covered container for up to a week. Freeze for longer storage. Makes 8 cups.

Crescent City Cheddar Crescents

1½ cup all-purpose flour
¼ cup yellow cornmeal
1½ tablespoons Cajun seasoning
½ teaspoon salt
½ teaspoon baking powder
1 stick cold unsalted butter, cut into bits
2 cups shredded Cheddar cheese
4–5 tablespoons cold water

Preheat oven to 400°F and lightly grease two baking sheets. In a bowl with a pastry blender or in a food processor, blend or pulse together flour, cornmeal, Cajun seasoning, salt, and baking powder. Add butter and blend or pulse until mixture resembles coarse meal. Add cheese and 4 tablespoons water and toss with a fork or pulse until water is incorporated, adding enough of remaining tablespoon water to form a soft dough if necessary.

Turn the dough out onto a floured board and kneed roughly 3 or 4 times. Form dough into 4 balls and flatten into disks. Roll out one of the dough disks with a lightly floured rolling pin into a 12-

inch round (about 1/16-inch thick) Cut out crackers using a crescent-shaped cookie cutter. Re-roll the scraps and cut out more.

Place the crescents on prepared baking sheets and prick several times with a fork. Bake until golden, about 12–14 minutes. Switch the placement of the pans in the oven halfway through baking time. With a metal spatula, transfer crackers to racks and cool. Continue rolling, cutting and baking with remaining dough.

Crackers can be kept in an airtight container at room temperature for up to 3 days. Freeze for longer storage. Makes about 12 dozen crackers.

Cajun Shrimp Cocktail

4 carrots, sliced	3 tablespoons salt
2 onions, sliced	3 teaspoons black pepper
6 cloved garlic, sliced	1 teaspoon red pepper flakes
3 bay leaves	2 lemons, sliced
3–4 springs of parsley	3 pounds large shrimp, peeled and deveined

In a large stockpot, bring 9 quarts of water to a boil (if you don't have a big enough pot, divide everything in two and work in two batches).

Add everything but the lemon and shrimp and boil for 10 minutes. Then add the lemon and boil for two more minutes. Add the shrimp and boil until just opaque and tightly curled, about 2–3 minutes. Drain the shrimp and chill. Make the Cocktail Sauce (recipe follows). Can be made the night before the party.

Fill a large bowl about 1/4 full with ice, put slightly smaller bowl over the ice and fill with the chilled shrimp. Place a bowl of the sauce next to the shrimp. Put out toothpicks for spearing the shrimp; a shot glass works well for holding the picks. Makes about 24 appetizer-sized servings.

Cocktail Sauce

1 cup ketchup	2 tablespoons red wine vinegar
1 cup bottled chili sauce	2 tablespoons Worcestershire sauce
4 tablespoons horseradish	4 green onions, thinly sliced
½ tablespoon Dijon mustard	2 teaspoons Cajun seasoning
½ tablespoon lemon juice	a few dashes of Tabasco

Combine all of the ingredients in a medium bowl and stir well. Cover and refrigerate until ready to serve. Make a day or two ahead.

Oysters Rockefeller

You can make the sauce a couple of days ahead and store in the fridge. You should buy the oysters the morning of your party—call the fish counter ahead of time and make sure they'll have enough for you. You can load up several layers of salt and oyster-filled cookie sheets and keep them in the fridge, so you can just pop them into the oven during the party. The rock salt does three things in this dish: 1) anchors the shells so the oysters don't topple over, 2) keeps the oysters hot while they're on the buffet table, 3) makes a tired old cookie sheet pretty and decorative enough to set out on the table. Make sure you have a trash can right next to the buffet table—otherwise you'll be finding shells all over the place!

2 10-ounce boxes frozen spinach, well drained
1 bunch green onions, cut into sections
1 bunch parsley, snipped into sections
3 stalks celery, chopped into chunks
1 cup butter, melted

1 2-ounce can anchovies

1 tablespoon Worcestershire sauce

1 teaspoon anise seed or 4 ounces Pernod
  or other anise-flavored liqueur

2 tablespoons lemon juice

Tabasco to taste

salt to taste

rock salt

8 dozen oysters on the half shell

¼ cup dry bread crumbs

Preheat oven to 450°F. Place first four ingredients in a blender or food processor and chop finely. Add butter, anchovies, Worcestershire sauce, anise, lemon juice, Tabasco and salt, and purée until all ingredients are smoothly blended into a sauce.

Line a large cookie sheet with a 3½-inch layer of rock salt. Place the oysters in half shells in a single layer over the salt. Place 1 tablespoon of sauce on each, and sprinkle with bread crumbs. Bake about 20 minutes or until brown, and serve hot. Makes 8 dozen.

Red Beans and Rice

This is a vegetarian variation of the classic Cajun dish, which can be made a day or two before and stored covered in the fridge. Make the rice at the last minute.

2 cups dry kidney beans, cleaned

3 tablespoons olive oil

6 garlic cloves, minced

4 stalks celery, chopped

1 large onion, chopped	2 carrots, chopped
1 green pepper, seeded and chopped	1 1/2 teaspoon cumin
1 tablespoon salt	1 tablespoon Dijon or country-style
1/2 teaspoon cayenne pepper	mustard
1 teaspoon thyme	1 bay leaf
1/2 teaspoon pepper	1 6-ounce can tomato paste
1 tablespoon oregano	1/2 cup dry red wine
1 teaspoon chili powder	Tabasco to taste
1 tablespoon dried parsley	6 cups cooked white rice

Soak the beans in water in a large covered stockpot overnight or for at least 4 hours. Drain and rinse the beans and return them to the pot with 6 cups of fresh water. Bring to a boil, then reduce the heat to low and simmer while you prepare the vegetables.

In a large skillet, heat the oil and cook the onion, garlic, celery, carrot, and pepper for about 5 minutes. Add the vegetables to the beans along with the spices, tomato paste, and wine. After about 30 minutes of cooking, taste the beans and add Tabasco to taste. Continue cooking for another 30–60 minutes, stirring and tasting frequently, until the beans are tender.

About half an hour before your guests arrive, cook the rice. Keep the pot out on the stove with the lid on—you'll serve right from the pot. While the rice is cooking, heat the red beans on the burner right next to the rice. Set out a stack of paper hot beverage cups and forks, and place two serving spoons on the counter right next to the stove. Let guests serve themselves to rice and red beans. If you've decided your kitchen is off-limits during the party, invest in a couple of hot plates and put the two pots on the buffet table. Makes 20–24 appetizer-sized servings.

Bananas Foster Muffins

Bite-sized muffins infused with the rum and cinnamon flavors of traditional Bananas Foster!

1 ½ cups flour
1 ½ teaspoons baking soda
¼ teaspoon salt
½ plus ¼ teaspoon cinnamon
1 ¼ cups mashed ripe bananas (about 3 large bananas)
¼ cup firmly packed dark brown sugar
½ cup plus 1 tablespoon sugar
½ cup unsalted butter, melted
¼ cup milk
8 tablespoons dark rum
1 large egg

Preheat oven to 350°F. Sift flour, baking soda, salt, and ½ teaspoon cinnamon into large bowl. Combine bananas, brown sugar, ½ cup sugar, butter, milk, 2 tablespoons rum, and egg in medium bowl. Mix into dry ingredients. Fill greased mini-muffin pans ¾ full.

Bake until muffins are golden brown and tester inserted into center comes out clean, about 15 minutes. While muffins are baking, dissolve the remaining two tablespoons sugar and ¼ cinnamon into the remaining 6 tablespoons rum. Brush the glaze onto the muffins while still warm in the pan. Cool the muffins on a rack.

Store tightly covered at room temperature for up to 3 days, or freeze for longer storage. Makes about 36 mini-muffins.

King Cake

½ cup warm water (110°–115°F)

2 packages active dry yeast

½ cup plus 1 teaspoon sugar

4½ cups flour

1 teaspoon nutmeg

2 teaspoons salt

1 teaspoon lemon zest

½ cup warm milk

Icing and Sugar Topping (recipes follow)

5 egg yolks

10 tablespoons butter, cut into slices and softened

1 egg slightly beaten with 1 tablespoon milk

1 teaspoon cinnamon

1 1-inch plastic baby doll

Pour the warm water into a small shallow bowl, and sprinkle yeast and 2 teaspoons sugar into it. Allow the yeast and sugar to rest for 3 minutes, then mix thoroughly.

Set bowl in a warm place for 10 minutes or until yeast bubbles up and mixture almost doubles in volume. Combine 3½ cups of flour, remaining sugar, nutmeg, and salt, and sift into a large mixing bowl. Stir in lemon zest. Make a hole in the center of the flour mixture and pour in yeast mixture and milk. Add egg yolks and, using a wooden spoon, slowly combine dry ingredients into the yeast/milk mixture.

When mixture is smooth, beat in 8 tablespoons butter, 1 tablespoon at a time, and continue until dough can be formed into a medium-soft ball. Place ball of dough on a lightly floured surface and knead. Add up to 1 cup more of flour (1 tablespoon at a time) sprinkled over the dough while kneading until the dough is no longer sticky. Knead 10 minutes more until shiny and elastic.

Using a pastry brush, coat the inside of a large bowl evenly with 1 tablespoon of softened butter. Place dough ball in the bowl and rotate until the entire surface is buttered. Cover bowl with a kitchen towel and place in a draft-free spot for about 1½ hours, or until the dough doubles in volume.

Using a pastry brush, coat a large baking sheet with 1 tablespoon of butter and set aside. Remove dough from bowl and place on lightly floured surface. Punch dough down with one hard whack of your fist and then sprinkle cinnamon over the top. Pat and shape the dough into a thick cylinder about 15 inches long. Twist the cylinder and place on the buttered baking sheet. Pinch the ends together to make a ring. Cover dough with a towel and set it in a draft-free spot for 45 minutes until the cake doubles in volume.

Preheat oven to 375°F. Brush top and sides of cake with eggmilk mixture and bake on middle rack of oven for 25–35 minutes, until golden brown. Place cake on wire rack to cool. Hide the plastic baby in the cake by poking it in through the bottom. While cake is cooling, make the Icing and Sugar Topping. Spread Icing over top of cake. Immediately sprinkle the Sugar Topping in individual rows, alternating green, purple, and yellow. Serves 8 to 10.

Icing

3 cups confectioner's sugar   3–6 tablespoons water
¼ cup lemon juice

Combine sugar, lemon juice, and 3 tablespoons water until smooth. If icing is too stiff, add more water until spreadable.

Sugar Topping

green, yellow, and purple paste food coloring   12 tablespoons sugar

Set out three small bowls with 4 tablespoons sugar in each. Using a different toothpick for each color, drop a bit of paste food coloring in each bowl and stir vigorously until color is even.

Mardi Gras Punch

1 ice ring (giant ice cube made in
   a Bundt or ring mold)
1 40-ounce bottle grape juice
1 48-ounce can unsweetened pineapple
   juice

1 750-ml bottle vodka
2 oranges, thinly sliced
2 lemons, thinly sliced
2 limes, thinly sliced
1 2-liter bottle lemon-lime soda

Place ice ring in bottom of big glass or clear plastic punch bowl. Add liquids in order given. Float slices of oranges and limes on top.

Make an extra batch of this punch and store it in the fridge in two cleaned-out plastic gallon milk jugs or four 2-liter soda bottles.

Makes about 65 one-half cup servings or about 8 quarts.

Variations on the Theme

★ For a more family-friendly Mardi Gras celebration, have a Cajun-style BBQ on the Sunday afternoon before Mardi Gras. Boil crawfish and barbecue oysters, use the same purple, green, and gold color scheme, and make "virgin" Mardi Gras punch.

✳ Fly Down to Rio for a Brazilian-themed Carnival celebration! Switch the Zydeco music for a sexy samba, the punch for Sangria, and serve food flavored with chilies and spices from south of the border.

✳ Throw a mini-Mardi Gras party on the actual Tuesday. Do a simple Cajun/Creole dinner for a few friends and screen a movie set in New Orleans, such as *The Big Easy*, *A Streetcar Named Desire*, or *Tune in Tomorrow*.

★ To order King Cakes, Mardi Gras party supplies, music, and other items, visit Virtual Bourbon Street at **www.mardigrasday.com/shop.html** or call 1-800-642-2912.

Mardi Gras Lexicon

(adapted from the **New Orleans Times-Picayune**)

Ash Wednesday: The day after Mardi Gras and the first day of Lent. In New Orleans, many Catholics attend Mass and receive an ashen cross on their foreheads to symbolize mortality.

Balls: Formal affairs held by Carnival organizations at which their royalty presides. These are invitation-only affairs. The invitations are not transferable and are never referred to as "tickets."

Boeuf Gras: The fatted ox or bull that has, since the Middle Ages, been a part of pre-Lenten celebrations. It symbolizes the last meat eaten before Lent. Until 1901, a real ox, bedecked in garlands of flowers and ribbons, appeared in the Rex parade on Mardi Gras. The ox reemerged as a giant papier-mâché ox on a float that is a traditional part of the parade today.

Callouts: Individuals "called out" from the audience to dance with Krewe members during a ball. They receive small gifts called "favors" from their dance partners. At some balls, general dancing follows the callouts.

Captain: The executive head of a Carnival organization. Captains get to ride in a place of honor in the parade, and, while kings and queens only reign for a year, the captain holds the honor for many years.

While the identity of the king and queen is often revealed, that of the captain almost always remains a secret.

Carnival: The season, stretching traditionally from January 6 (Twelfth Night) to Mardi Gras (Fat Tuesday). All parades, balls, and other events during this period are Carnival events. Technically, only events on Fat Tuesday itself are Mardi Gras events. The word *carnival* means "removal of the flesh," the flesh in this case being the meat that is forsaken for Lent.

Carnival Day: Same as Mardi Gras, the last day of Carnival.

Courir du Mardi Gras: The Mardi Gras run, a Cajun celebration of Mardi Gras in which masked, costumed men ride horses from house to house around the countryside, asking for chickens, rice, sausage. and other ingredients for a gumbo. Afterward, there is dancing and the gumbo.

Court: The king, queen, maids, dukes, and other mock royalty of a Carnival organization.

Doubloons: Silver-dollar-sized commemorative aluminum coins minted for and given out by Carnival organizations.

Flag of Rex: Stripes of purple, green, and gold with a crown on the center stripe. Former kings and queens of Rex are the only ones entitled to fly this flag in front of their home during the season. It is also the flag of Carnival.

Flambeaux: The burning torches—usually kerosene containers mounted on wooden poles—carried in some night parades. Flambeaux carriers are known for their uninhibited prancing and twirling.

"If Ever I Cease to Love": The song of the Carnival season. It dates back to 1872, when the Grand Duke Alexis of Russian visited New Orleans for Mardi Gras. The newly formed Rex organization learned the Grand Duke had fallen in love with singer Lydia Thompson when he saw her in a burlesque show called "Bluebeard." So the group set "If Ever I Cease to Love" from the show to march time, and it has been the song of the season ever since, even though it has absolutely nothing to do with Carnival.

Krewe: A term applied to most organizations participating in Carnival.

Lundi Gras: French for "Fat Monday," the day before Mardi Gras.

Mardi Gras: Fat Tuesday. The Carnival celebration ends at midnight on Fat Tuesday.

Maskers: A term referring to both the float riders, who normally are masked, and those who costume for Mardi Gras.

Pro Bono Publico: The Latin motto of Rex, meaning "for the good of the public."

Rex: Referred to only as "Rex," or as "Rex, King of Carnival," never as the redundant "King Rex" or "King of Rex."

Tableau: A "still life" depiction of a scene by costumed Krewe members, presented at a Carnival ball before the dancing begins. It is based on the theme of the ball. The plural is tableaux.

Throws: Trinkets pitched from a parade float. They include doubloons, beads, cups, and plastic toys.

Sassy Lassies Celebrate St. Patrick's Day

We nice Jewish Party Girls may have qualms about celebrating the life of the fellow who brought Catholicism to Ireland, but ridding the place of snakes? Now that's a reason to party! Here's a Celtic celebration that is the highlight of the otherwise holiday-less month of March.

Invitations

◎ Everyone's Irish on St. Patrick's Day—at least your guests will be! Irish-ize your guests names by adding an "O'" in front of it on the invitation. Akira O'Takayashi and Juan O'Gonzales will no doubt be the first to R.S.V.P.! If you're inviting someone named "Danny," make sure his invitation reads "Danny Boy."

✳ St. Pat's is another "floater" holiday. March 17 could wind up on any day of the week. If it lands on a Saturday night, you've got the luck o' the Irish workin' for ya; otherwise, toss your party the Saturday before. Hit an Irish pub for a pint of green beer on the actual day.

★ **Headline:** *"A Wee Bit of Fun for St. Patrick's Day"*

✸ Use green paper to print out the invites, and plaster lots of shamrock stickers on the envelopes.

Decorating Tips

◎ **It's a Green Scene:** Put green bulbs in your light fixtures, use green table linens and/or papers, and fill flower vases with ferns, baby's breath, and green-dyed carnations.

✦ **Shamrock Schlock:** Blow up green balloons to about 3-inch capacity—use one swift blow! Tie them together in bunches of four with a twist-tie and attach a 12-inch length of 2-inch-wide green ribbon. Hang the balloon shamrocks on all of your doors.

✳ **Heap o' Taters:** Decorate the buffet table with piles and piles of terrific tubers in red, white, brown, or blue. The farmers' market and fancy-schmancy gourmet markets should have a variety of potatoes in lots of colors.

✳ **They're Magically Delicious!:** Set out bowls of "Lucky Charms" cereal for munching. (No, this doesn't count as "food," but it will if you make the Rice Krispies Treats recipe using Lucky Charms instead of Krispies.)

◎ Make sure you've got a bar of Irish Spring by the bathroom sink!

✦ **Pot o' Gold:** Buy long lengths of tulle in red, orange, yellow, green, blue, and purple. Drape them over a curtain rod, over a banister, or from a plant hook in the ceiling. Trail the tulle behind a pot topped with chocolate gold coins. You'll break the bank if you try to fill a whole pot with the chocolate coins, so fill the pot to the rim with crumpled newspaper, then put a layer of coins on top. Though most ubiquitous at Hanukkah, chocolate gold coins can be found year-round at import stores like Cost Plus, in the candy sections of warehouse stores like Costco and Smart & Final, or for the Party Girl with a more discriminating palate, gourmet chocolate shops.

Costumes

Your chances of getting anyone to dress like a leprechaun are pretty slim, but everyone must wear at least a bit of green—or they'll suffer the pinching consequences.

Games and Activities

✳ Wanna get this party started? Limericks will do the trick! Buy several notebooks of ruled paper, with green covers of course. Write on the cover of each notebook: "Limerick Contest—The word is: (BLANK)." Insert an unusual word here, such as *Roadkill, Shoehorn,* or *Anteater.* On the first page of the notebook, explain the game. You can print out several copies of the rules from your computer and paste them into the notebooks so you don't have to write them all out each time:

> **Limerick Contest!** *Make up a limerick using the word on the front of this notebook. Write it down and be sure to sign your name! At 10 o'clock we'll read the limericks and choose one winner for each word. Be creative, be raunchy, be silly, have fun—and leave the notebook out for the next literary leprechaun. Enter as many limericks as you like, and look around for the other notebooks.*

At 10 P.M., turn the music down and gather everyone around. Invite the authors to read their rhyming masterpieces, and award a prize to the favorite from each notebook.

◎ **Kiss the Blarney Stone:** Put a large rock from your yard or local park on your coffee table or on a side table and place a bowl of Hershey's Kisses next to it. Put a sign next to this setup that reads, "Kiss the Blarney Stone and you can help yourself to a Kiss!"

Favors and Prizes

- ◎ Paperback copy of Joyce's *Ulysses*, with Cliff Notes
- ★ Mini-bottle of Irish whiskey
- ✳ Sinéad O'Connor CD
- ✺ Video of a movie set in Ireland like *The Quiet Man* or *The Matchmaker*
- ◎ Irish Coffee glasses
- ★ Notre Dame "Fighting Irish" sweatshirt

Musical Suggestions

Mix traditional Irish tunes with pop music by Irish groups:

- ✺ *The Best of the Chieftains*, The Chieftains
- ✳ *Rock o' the Irish*, Various Artists
- ⁙ *The Joshua Tree*, U2
- ★ *So Far . . . The Best of Sinéad O'Connor*, Sinéad O'Connor
- ✳ *Years May Come, Years May Go*, The Irish Rovers
- ✺ *Watermark*, Enya

Food

One Potato, Two Potato, Three Potato. . . . Keep going, this is an all-potato menu that celebrates the sturdy staple of the Irish table. Although we usually don't encourage departing from a theme, we can't in good conscience recommend any potato beverages. Serve Irish beers such as Guinness and Harp, shots of Irish whiskey, and coffee spiked with Irish Creme.

Sour Cream 'n Onion Potato Dip

1 pound potatoes, peeled and cut into 1-inch cubes
1/2 cup sour cream
3 garlic cloves
approximately 1/4 cup milk or cream
3 green onions, thinly sliced
salt and pepper to taste

Boil potatoes until soft. Mash with the sour cream. Press garlic through a garlic press and mix well into the potatoes. Thin with milk or cream if the dip is too thick. Mix in green onions. Season to taste with salt and pepper.

Can be made a day or two ahead, store covered in the fridge. Stir well and bring to room temperature before serving. Serve with raw veggies, bread, and crackers. Makes 2–3 cups.

Potato Tomato Focaccia

Po-tay-to, Po-tah-to, To-may-to, To-mah-to, let's polish this whole thing off—it's delish!

1/3 cup olive oil
2 garlic cloves, sliced thin
1 teaspoon rosemary
3/4 cup warm water (105°–115°F)
1 1/4-ounce package (2 1/2 teaspoons)
   fast-acting yeast

1/2 teaspoon sugar
2 cups all-purpose flour
1 teaspoon salt
1 12 ounce jar oil-packed sun-dried
   tomatoes, drained and finely chopped
1 1/2 pounds small red potatoes

Lightly grease a 10-by-15-inch rimmed cookie sheet or jellyroll pan. Combine the oil, garlic, and rosemary in a bowl. Cover and set aside.

In a large bowl, stir together water, yeast, and sugar, and let stand until foamy, about 5 minutes. In a small bowl, stir together flour and salt, and gradually stir into yeast mixture until mixture forms a soft dough. Mix in the chopped sun-dried tomatoes. On a lightly floured work surface with floured hands, knead dough 5 minutes, or until smooth and elastic, and shape into a ball. Invert the large bowl you used to mix the dough over dough ball and let rest 10 minutes. Roll out dough into a 13-by-9-inch rectangle on a lightly floured surface and transfer to baking pan, pressing into corners. Let dough rise, covered loosely with plastic wrap or a towel, in a warm place until doubled, about 30 minutes.

Preheat oven to 400°F. Once the dough has risen, make lots of divots all over the dough with your fingers, making sure the dough is pressed to the edges of the pan. Slice the potatoes paper-thin, and arrange them on the dough, overlapping. Brush the potatoes with the oil mixture, but leave the garlic slices in the bowl. Sprinkle the focaccia with salt and pepper and bake for 40–50 minutes, or until golden. Let the focaccia cool in the pan on a rack. When cool, remove the bread to a board and cut into 2-inch squares.

Can be made a day or two ahead, wrap tightly in plastic wrap and then in foil. Makes approximately 35 squares.

Roasted Sage Potatoes

4 tablespoons olive oil	½ cup balsamic vinegar
3 pounds red potatoes, cut into 1-inch chunks	1 tablespoon dried sage
1½ pounds onions, cut into thick chunks	salt and pepper to taste

Preheat oven to 400°F. Pour half of the oil into each of two large rimmed baking pans. Add half of the potatoes to each and toss to coat. Cover the pans with foil and bake for 30 minutes. Increase the heat to 450°F, then take the pans out of the oven and remove the foil. Add half of the onion, vinegar, and rosemary to each pan and toss well with the potatoes. Season each pan liberally with salt and pepper and return to the oven. Roast for 30–40 minutes, or until potatoes are tender, switching the pans halfway through and tossing occasionally.

Can be made a day ahead, store in the fridge in a covered bowl. Bring them to room temperature or reheat to serve. They're delicious either way. Serves 8–10 on a buffet.

Potato Pesto Canapés

1 pound firm, waxy potatoes,
   red- or white-skinned
water to just cover
1 tablespoon salt
1½ cups basil leaves

2 garlic cloves
½ cup olive oil
1 cup freshly grated Parmesan cheese
5 tablespoons mayonnaise

First prepare the potatoes. Place the potatoes, water, and salt in medium saucepan and cover. Place over medium heat and cook for 15–20 minutes or until potatoes are tender. Let the potatoes cool to room temperature.

Place the basil and garlic in a food processor and process until finely chopped. With the machine running, gradually add the oil and process until smooth. Add the cheese and process until well mixed. Scrape into a bowl and blend in the mayonnaise.

Potatoes and sauce can be made a day ahead. To store, slice the potatoes into thin slices and store in a covered container in the fridge. Place plastic wrap directly on top of the pesto and store in the fridge.

To serve, arrange the potato slices on a platter and put a dollop of pesto sauce on each. Makes 20–24 appetizers.

Spud Soup

1½ pounds potatoes, peeled and sliced
1 large onion, chopped into chunks
2½ cups chicken stock
1 cup water
1½ cups milk, buttermilk, or half-and-half
1 cup shredded sharp Cheddar cheese
salt and pepper to taste
couple of pinches of paprika

Put the potatoes, onion, stock, and water in a large stock pot and boil until the taters are tender, 10–15 minutes. Transfer in batches into a blender or food processor and blend until pretty much smooth but with some texture left. Pour back into the pot and add the dairy product of your choice. Bring to a simmer and add the cheese, stirring until the cheese melts. Season with salt and pepper. Cover the pot and chill for overnight.

To serve, place in a large bowl and sprinkle the top with paprika. Serve in plastic or paper beverage cups—much easier than bowls for a party. Makes 6–8 servings.

Spinach Stuffed Potato-ettes

3 pounds teeny, tiny red potatoes

1 tablespoon butter

½ of a large onion, finely chopped

2 cloves garlic, minced

1 10-ounce package frozen spinach, thawed

4 tablespoons grateable cheese—Parmesan, Asiago, Dry Jack

salt and pepper to taste

Preheat the oven to 400°F. Scrub the potatoes and pierce the skin once or twice with a fork. Bake until tender, about 40–45 minutes. Let the potatoes cool until they can be handled; meanwhile, make the filling.

Melt the butter in a large frying pan and add onions. Cook until soft, about 5 minutes, then add the garlic and cook a few more minutes. Add the spinach and cook until liquid evaporates, stirring constantly. Turn off heat.

When the potatoes are cool, slice each in half. Scoop most of the flesh, leaving a thin layer of potato in the skin. Add scooped-out potato to the spinach mixture, and mash until well mixed. Place the potato shells on a baking sheet and fill with the spinach–potato mixture. Sprinkle the cheese over the top. Return to the oven and bake for about 20 minutes, or until golden brown.

To make ahead, fill the potato shells the night before and store covered on a baking tray in the fridge. Pop in to the oven half an hour before party time. Makes about 40 stuffed potato halves.

Sweet Potato Mini-Cheesecakes

2 8-ounce packages cream cheese,
room temperature
¾ cup sugar
1 teaspoon vanilla extract
1 cup mashed cooked sweet potato

2 teaspoons pumpkin pie spice
2 tablespoons flour
3 large eggs
24 ginger snaps

Preheat oven to 350°F. Line 24-muffin pans with paper muffin cups. If you don't have 24-muffin pans (not many people do), then line two 12-muffin pans and bake in two batches.

Beat cream cheese, sugar, and vanilla in large bowl until blended. Add sweet potato, pumpkin pie spice, and flour, and beat on low speed until blended. Add eggs one at a time, beating well and scraping down sides of bowl after each addition. Place a ginger snap each of the muffin cups. Fill each cup ¾ full with batter. Bake cakes until filling is set, about 20 minutes. Cool in the pans for about 10 minutes, then refrigerate overnight. Can be made 2 days ahead. Keep refrigerated. Makes 24 little cheesecakes.

Variations on the Theme

Saints Alive! Saints to celebrate all year long:

◎ **Saint Sebastian:** Patron of Racquet Makers   Feast Day: January 20
Tennis anyone? Gather a group for a game with a picnic lunch to follow, or if you've got a recreation room, your Ping-Pong paddle can count as a racquet in a table tennis tournament.

★ **Saint Amand:** Patron of Winemakers   Feast Day: February 6
Host a wine-tasting party! Ask everyone to bring a bottle of wine wrapped in a
paper bag. Label each bag with a number and ask each guest to taste and rate
each wine on a numbered score sheet. Be sure to include a bottle of
Manischewitz or similar swill, just to keep things interesting. Write each guest's
name on inexpensive wine glasses and boom, you've got your favors.

✳ **Saint Lydwina of Scheidam:** Patron of Skating   Feast Day: April 14
Get an old-fashioned skating party together, either in-line at the park or
ice/roller at a local rink.

✺ **Saint Bernadine of Sienna:** Patron of Advertising   Feast Day: May 20
Use great ads from magazines as decorations. Make a party mix tape that includes
TV or radio commercial jingles, and scour the thrift stores for glasses, plates, and
other props that feature advertising logos and slogans.

◎ **Saint Vitus:** Patron of Actors   Feast Day: June 15
Great day for a charades party, VCR film fest, or pre-theater cocktail party.

✳ **Saint Phocas:** Patron of Gardeners   Feast Day: July 23
Garden Party! Serve an all-vegetarian menu, heavy on the edible flowers. Fill
vases with lots of fresh flowers, and use floral plates and napkins. Give flower
seed packets or small potted plants as favors.

◎ **Saint Lawrence:** Patron of Restaurateurs   Feast Day: August 10
Play restaurant roulette! Gather a small crowd to meet at one place for drinks, another for dinner, and a third for dessert—die-hards will even follow you to a
fourth for a nightcap! Or host a dinner party with food prepared from the cookbook of a famous restaurant. You can also stay home and have restaurant food delivered. Dine while you watch a movie set in a restaurant, like *Big Night*, *Diner*, or
My Dinner with Andre.

✳ **Saint Wenceslas:** Patron of Brewers   Feast Day: September 28
Make your backyard a beer garden with German food and lots of different beers.

✸ **Saint Francis of Assisi:** Patron of Animals   Feast Day: October 4
Pet Party! Invite your friends who have pets for an outdoor party. Set out water
and bowls of food for the four-legged guests and serve animal-themed food like
hot dogs and catfish for the bipeds.

◉ **Saint Cecilia:** Patron of Singers   Feast Day: November 22
Rent a karaoke machine or plan a get-together at a sing-along piano bar.

✦ **Saint Ambrose of Milan:** Patron of Candlemakers   Feast Day: December 7
Decorate any type of party—dinner, cocktail, dancing—with as many candles as
you can. Offer pretty, scented candles as favors.

And The Winner Is ...

Oscar Night on Both Coasts

Every Party Girl fantasizes about sauntering down the aisle to accept her Academy Award. Years of practicing acceptance speeches in the shower will pay off big time when your guests rave about your fabulous Oscar Party.

West Coast Party Girls are at a slight disadvantage when throwing Oscar parties. The telecast usually begins at 6:00 P.M. on a Monday night. Most of the decorating and food prep can be done well in advance, and if you schedule a "doctor's appointment" that'll get you out of the office a bit early, there's no reason you can't throw as festive a fête as your East Coast sisters. East Coasters, with time on their side, can encourage their guests to dress as famous movie stars past and present.

Invitations

★ Make the invitation look like a movie theater ticket. Write "Admit Two to the Show of the Year" on the front and freehand-draw a ticket border.

◎ Gold and silver paint pens will jazz up a plain white notecard or postcard invitation. If you're only sending a few, handwrite all of the party info and include a few freehand stars or stick-on gold star stickers from the office supply store.

✳ Cut out movie ads for nominated films from the newspaper. Paste them up collage-style on an 8½-by-11-inch piece of paper. Photocopy the collage for as many invitations as you'll need, then make a few extra just to be on the safe side.

If you're sending ten or fewer invitations, load the copies into your computer printer and print out the invitation information, or handwrite them. If you've got a lot of invitations to make, print out or handwrite one master sheet with the party info text and photocopy it onto the collage copies. Brighten up the invitations with a few underlines, stars, or squiggles from a silver metallic pen. Send in a black #10 (9½-by-4-inch) standard business envelope and address with the metallic pen.

◎ Postage Stamps: Movie stars! Several are available, including Marilyn Monroe, Humphrey Bogart, and James Dean.

Decorating Tips

✳ Black, white, silver, and gold add glittery glamour to Oscar Night. Trail silver and gold metallic ribbons from black and white balloons. Helium is not necessary; you can tape balloons to ceilings, doors, and the backs of chairs.

✳ The Stars Shine Bright on Oscar Night! Tape tinfoil stars around the room. Scatter star-shaped confetti on the buffet table.

◎ Roll Out the Red Carpet! Set out a "carpet" of red fabric (inexpensive cotton or felt will work) from the TV room through the front door and all the way to the sidewalk.

★ Load up on movie magazines the week of the telecast and put them out on the coffee table. They'll provide lots of background dish during commercials.

✳ More for "atmosphere" than decoration, you'll want to keep the TV tuned in to as much of the pre-show limo-emptying as possible. The E! cable channel provides the best all-day coverage. Move the TVs in your house around so there's one in each room where your guests will be—the living room, dining room, kitchen, even the bathroom! After the Oscar show, ABC usually schedules a Barbara Walters interview special with three top Hollywood stars. The die-hard pop culture vultures in your crowd will want to stay for this always teary gab-fest.

Games and Activities

◎ **Oscar Pools, Movie Stars!** Nothing gets the juices flowin' like healthy competition—except maybe vicious, cutthroat rivalry! Pulling together an Oscar Pool is easy, fun, and, depending on the laws of your state and your ethical perspective, even profitable! There are several ways to conduct an Oscar Pool, but this one's worked successfully for years:

Oscar nominations are usually announced mid- to late February—this is the time to get started! Make up a ballot listing all of the nominees in a dozen or so of the best categories, such as:

Best Picture	Best Original Screenplay
Best Director	Best Adapted Screenplay
Best Actor	Best Original Song
Best Actress	Best Makeup
Best Supporting Actor	Best Visual Effects
Best Supporting Actress	Best Costume Design

The truly obsessed include *every* category in their Oscar pools—from editing to live action short subject. Unless you live in L.A., have friends in "the biz," or are a film student, this is not recommended.

At the top of the ballot, explain the rules of the Pool: "And the winner is . . . You? It's Academy Awards time again! Even if you won't be decked out in jewels and rubbing elbows with the stars, you can still share in the fun by participating in an OSCAR POOL. It's easy! Just fill out the ballot below and return it to me by (DAY OF OSCAR TELECAST) Enter as many times as you like, $2 per ballot. Half of the money collected will go to the (CHARITY OF YOUR CHOICE), the other half will go to the person who wins the most categories. In the event of a tie, the winner will be drawn at random from the high scorers."

Include space for the entrant's name and phone number. Include your fax number if you can receive the ballots via fax. Send, fax, and e-mail the ballots to as many people as possible.

The night of the Oscars, hang up a large piece of posterboard with the categories you included on the ballot. Leave space to fill in the winners as they are announced. At the end of the telecast, score the ballots and declare a winner. If the winner is present, award him or her a mini-Oscar statuette and let them make a teary acceptance speech.

Favors and Prizes

✳ Most major movie-theater chains offer gift certificates in $1 denominations. One or two of these with a star-emblazoned thank-you note make a terrific favor.

◎ Wrap a packet of microwave popcorn in white paper—plain typing paper will work. Write "You're a star—thanks for sharing Oscar Night with us/me" in silver metallic pen. Add a few freehand or stick-on stars.

★ Make up goodie bags of classic movie-theater treats: Goobers, Raisinettes, and Sno-Caps. Add a note that reads, "Thanks for making my Oscar Night shine—your next movie snacks are on me."

Musical Suggestions

You won't have much opportunity for music, since most of the night will be spent watching the show. During commercials or before and after the telecast, you'll want to have a CD of movie theme songs in the stereo.

* ✳ Number One Movie Hits, popular songs from contemporary films
* ★ 100 Hollywood Movie Hits
* ◎ '40s, '50s and '60s Award-Winning Movie Themes, London Pops Orchestra
* ✳ Billboard Top Movie Hits series, titles from the '40s to the '70s

Food

Fruits, Nuts, and Flakes

Mix up a bowl of munchies that describes many of the attendees at the actual awards ceremony—and maybe your party too?

4 cups salted mixed nuts	¾ cup large flaked coconut
I cup golden raisins or other diced dried fruit	

Mix all ingredients together. Set out in a glass bowl on the coffee table or take a tip from hotel cocktail lounges and serve in sturdy little wine glasses scattered about the room. Serves 6–8.

California Roll Salad

Nothing says "L.A." quite like sushi. This dish combines all of the flavors and textures of California Rolls in an easy-to-make salad.

6 cups cooked white rice

3 teaspoons black sesame seeds

1 large cucumber, peeled, seeded, and diced

½ pound cooked crabmeat, picked over

½ cup rice vinegar

6 tablespoons sugar

3 tablespoons salt

2 tablespoons dry sherry

1½ tablespoons wasabi paste or prepared horseradish

1 large ripe avocado

2 tablespoons flying fish roe or salmon caviar

The night before the party, toss the rice with the sesame seeds, cucumber, and crabmeat.

In a small bowl, mix the vinegar, sugar, salt, sherry, and wasabi or horseradish. Pour over the rice and toss well. Store in fridge overnight. Just before serving, peel and dice the avocado and mix into the salad. Sprinkle the roe over the top and serve. Serves 6–8.

Cobb Salad

A classic old-Hollywood favorite—invented at L.A.'s Brown Derby restaurant.

1 head romaine lettuce, rinsed and chopped
½ head iceberg lettuce, chopped
3 ripe avocados
3 skinless, boneless chicken breast halves, cooked and diced
6 slices of lean bacon, cooked crisp and chopped fine
3 large tomatoes, seeded and chopped fine
2 hard-boiled eggs, peeled and chopped fine
2 tablespoons chopped fresh chives or parsley
⅓ cup red wine vinegar
1 tablespoon Dijon mustard
2/3 cup olive oil
½ cup finely crumbled Roquefort or other blue cheese
salt and pepper to taste

Place the lettuce in a large bowl. Halve, pit, and peel the avocados and cut them into ½-inch pieces. Add the chicken, bacon, tomato, avocado, egg, and chives.

In a small bowl, whisk together the vinegar, mustard, and salt and pepper to taste. Add the oil in a slow stream while whisking, and whisk the dressing until it is emulsified. Stir in the Roquefort. Pour the dressing over the salad, and toss the salad well.

You can make most of the salad the night before, just leave out the avocados (they turn brown when exposed to air for too long). Make up the dressing and store it in the fridge. Add the avocados and dressing and toss well just before serving. Serves 6–8.

Barbecued Chicken Pizza

One of the most famous Oscar Parties is held each year at Wolfgang Puck's Spago restaurant. Puck is often credited with starting the gourmet pizza craze. This is an easy version of one of his signature pizzas.

4 tablespoons olive oil

4 large boneless chicken breast halves

1 cup hickory-flavored barbecue sauce

14 ounces smoked Gouda cheese, coarsely shredded

2 16-ounce Bobolis (pre-baked cheese pizza crusts,
  available in the bread section of grocery stores)

1½ cups thinly sliced red onion

2 green onions, chopped

Position rack in center of oven. Preheat oven to 450°F for 30 minutes.

Heat olive oil in heavy medium skillet over medium-high heat. Season chicken with salt and pepper. Add chicken to skillet and sauté until just cooked through, about 5 minutes per side. Transfer chicken to plate; let sit 5 minutes. Cut chicken crosswise into ⅓-inch-wide slices. Using slotted spoon, transfer chicken to medium bowl. Toss with ½ cup barbecue sauce.

Sprinkle half of the cheese evenly over the two crusts. Arrange chicken slices over cheese, spacing evenly. Spoon any remaining barbecue sauce from bowl over each pizza. Sprinkle red onion over chicken. Drizzle with remaining ½ cup barbecue sauce. Sprinkle rest of the cheese and the green onion over.

Place one pizza directly on the middle oven rack. Bake until bottom of crust is crisp and cheese on top melts, about 14 minutes. Remove from oven and bake second pizza. Let each pizza stand 5 minutes before cutting and serving.

To make ahead of time, either bake the night before and reheat just before serving or prepare the pizzas for baking and pop in the oven just before your guests arrive. Makes 8 servings.

A Trio of Popcorn Treats

It's movie house fare all dressed up for Oscar Night. Sweet-talk the kids behind the counter at your local theater into giving you some large popcorn tubs for serving, or buy popcorn boxes at a restaurant supply store.

Caramel Popcorn

3 quarts popped popcorn
  (about 6 tablespoons popcorn kernels)
½ cup butter
1 cup firmly packed brown sugar

¼ cup light or dark corn syrup
½ teaspoon salt
¼ teaspoon baking soda
½ teaspoon vanilla

Preheat oven to 250°F. Coat the bottom and sides of a large roasting pan with a nonstick vegetable spray. Place popped popcorn in roasting pan. In a heavy pan, slowly melt butter; stir in brown sugar, corn syrup and salt. Bring to a boil, stirring constantly; boil without stirring for 5 minutes. Remove from heat; stir in baking soda and vanilla. Gradually pour over popcorn, mixing well. Bake for 1 hour, stirring every 15 minutes. Remove from oven; cool completely. Break apart. Makes about 3 quarts.

Butter Almond Popcorn

½ cup butter

1 cup granulated sugar

¼ cup light corn syrup

¼ teaspoon salt

¼ teaspoon baking soda

½ teaspoon vanilla

3 quarts popped popcorn

(about 6 tablespoons popcorn kernels)

1½ cups whole toasted almonds

Preheat over to 250°F. Melt butter in a medium saucepan. Stir in sugar, corn syrup, and salt. Heat to a boil, stirring constantly. Boil for 8 minutes over lowest heat possible to maintain a boil, stirring only once. Remove from heat; stir in baking soda, vanilla, and butter extract. Combine popcorn and almonds in a large, shallow baking pan. Gradually pour butter-sugar mixture over popcorn, mixing well. Bake 30 minutes, mixing well after 15 minutes. Allow to cool completely. Break apart and store in a tightly covered container. Makes about 3½ quarts.

Chocolate Peanut Butter Popcorn

9 ounces semisweet chocolate

(1½ cups chocolate chips)

2/3 cup smooth peanut butter

⅓ cup margarine or butter

1 teaspoon vanilla

3 quarts popped popcorn

(about 6 tablespoons popcorn kernels)

2 cups powdered sugar

Melt chocolate, peanut butter, and butter in 1-quart saucepan over low heat until melted. Remove from heat, stir in vanilla. Place popcorn in large bowl and pour in chocolate mixture, stirring to evenly coat. Pour the popcorn into large brown paper bag; add the powdered sugar. Fold the top of the bag over a couple of times; shake until well coated. Spread on large sheets of waxed paper to cool. Store in airtight container when cool. Makes 3 quarts.

Sunset Champagne Cocktails

1 quart lemonade	2 bottles of champagne, chilled
1 16-ounce jar Maraschino cherries	

Chill the lemonade overnight in a glass pitcher. Just before setting out on the buffet table, pour the cherries and their syrup into the lemonade. Set out the pitcher and the champagne on the buffet table, guests can add juice to their champagne to taste. Makes 18–20 servings.

◎ Set out chilled sparking water and/or sparking apple cider for the nondrinkers.

Variations on the Theme

★ Create a menu inspired by the top nominated films. Some of the ones we've created in the past include: Bravehearts of Palm Salad, Forrest Gump's "Life Is Like a Box of Chocolate Cake" (square-shaped cake), The Full Monty Cristo Sandwich, Good Will Bundt-ing Cake, Leaf-ing Las Vegas Salad, Four Weddings and a Funeral Pizza (truly inspired—this had four white toppings and one black one!).

✳ Lots of other awards shows make great excuses for a party. Gather friends to watch Broadway's Tony Awards—serve N.Y. food like cheesecake and bagels with lox, and play soundtracks from famous musicals during the commercials. The Emmy Awards honor the boob tube's highest achievers—serve TV dinners on TV trays and send each guest home with a copy of the next week's *TV Guide* as a party favor. The Country Music Awards calls for good ol' rib-sticking country fare like barbecued ribs, biscuits, and pecan pie. For the Grammy Awards, decorate your TV room with the goofiest album covers you can find at the thrift store—you can pick up a whole stack of these platters for just a few bucks. Old 45s can be strung together like garlands and hung from the doorways.

◎ **Film Fest!** Pick a theme and screen two or three related films for your own home video mini film fest. Ideas include:

TECHNICOLOR TEARJERKERS

Imitation of Life	A Summer Place
The Magnificent Obsession	

BITCHFEST

The Women	First Wives' Club
All about Eve	

THE MANY FACES OF BARBRA

Funny Lady	The Prince of Tides
A Star Is Born	

For film parties, check out The Reel List: A Categorical Companion to Over 2,000 Memorable Films **(Delta). This fantastic book groups all kinds of films into fun, offbeat categories and includes dead-on plot summaries. It's great for creating screening parties, movie games, and costume themes.**

Earth Day: *Party for the Planet*

Y ou can be politically correct, and have tons of fun, too, when you throw an Earth Day: Party for the Planet celebration. This event will not only taste good . . . it will be good for you.

Invitation

◎ Create a beautiful handmade invitation. Start by searching for an image of a globe on your computer clip-art program. Set up your invitations so there are two on an 8½-by-11-inch page (one on top, one on the bottom), using the globe image on the left side, and the party specifics on the right side. If you have a color printer, print out your invitation in color, then go to your local photocopy center and make color copies on recycled paper. Using a paper cutter, cut page in half and then fold each invitation. On the (blank) front cover, place a piece of colored homemade paper at an angle. Handwrite your invitation headline. Stamp the back of the invitation with the "recycled" symbol. Insert into recycled envelopes.

★ **Headlines:**
Eco-Party: Help Save the Earth, or
Party for the Planet: Bring Your Own and Go Home with Somebody Else's
Bring an item of clothing, a pair of earrings, or a used book for the Treasure Hunt.

Stick environmental and humane society organization stamps on the outside of your envelopes.

Decorating Tips

◎ **Choose to Reuse:** Line the sidewalk in front of your house with recycling tote boxes. Borrow a few more from your neighbors to line the inside of your rooms. Contact your state's Department of Conservation or Department of Natural Resources for posters to display on your walls. You can also contact your city or county Waste Management Board. They might have a Source Reduction and Recycling Department that provides educational materials, including posters. Go to your local salvage yard or flea market and purchase an inexpensive piece of used furniture. (It makes for a great "conversation" piece.) Buy recycled toilet paper (2-ply natural bath tissue made by Fort Howard in Green Bay, Wisconsin).

Make origami cranes out of newspaper. You can use a thread and needle to string them together and hang from the ceiling.

Create and display collages and sculptures made from recycled materials. For weeks before the party, save up toilet paper and paper towel rolls, egg cartons, burnt out light bulbs, soda can bottles, and milk cartons. Go to your local automotive repair shop and ask for used engine parts like spark plugs. Use your imagination, or ask the kids next door to help you make some art.

On a side table, display brochures for various environmental organizations including Rainforest Action Network, the Sierra Club, the National Wildlife Federation, and others.

Purchase a bunch of recycling buttons featuring the recycling symbol and slogans such as, "Recycle or Die," and "It's a Small Planet, Recycle." Hand these out to people when they walk in.

✳ **Rainforests Forever:** You can create a rainforest environment by placing ferns and palms throughout your house. Purchase mobiles of rainforest birds to hang from the ceiling. Strategically place plastic animals throughout the house and in the foliage. Purchase a green table covering and place small plastic reptiles and frogs near the food dishes. Get things really steamy by running two or more humidifiers to moisten the air. Turn up the heat. Of course, this might make everyone want to escape for some fresh brisk April air—send them into the garden.

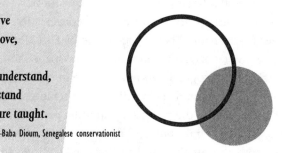

In the end,
We will conserve
only what we love,
We will love
only what we understand,
We will understand
only what we are taught.

—Baba Dioum, Senegalese conservationist

Costumes

Go Green: Request that your guests come dressed in green or brown.

Games and Activities

★ **We Are the World:** Inform your guests that we all need to work together to create beautiful music. Hand out kazoos, handmade musical instruments made from 5-gallon plastic water bottles filled with dry beans or unpopped popcorn kernels and empty popcorn tins and utensils to bang with.

★ **Recycled Treasure Hunt:** One woman's trash is another's treasure. Your guests have been instructed to bring one or more items of clothing, a pair of earrings, or a used book to the party.

When your guests arrive, you should separate their items into designated containers. Make containers from large corrugated cardboard boxes. Line them with recycled paper and label them, "Men's Tops," "Men's Bottoms," "Women's Tops," "Women's Bottoms," "Used Books." Create an earring display by wrapping a piece of green velvet fabric remnant around the top panel of one of the corrugated cardboard boxes. Place the earrings on the display. Near the end of the party, announce that it is time for the treasure hunt, and let your guests go at the containers. Whatever they leave behind, you can donate to your local Salvation Army.

Favors and Prizes

✳ Packets of seeds. These are inexpensive and perfect for this theme!
◎ Redwood tree seedlings
✳ Gardening implements such as small trowels

Musical Suggestions

✳ "Rainforest," Voices of the Earth
◎ "Where Have All the Flowers Gone?," Peter, Paul, and Mary
★ "Save Our Planet Earth," Jimmy Cliff, *Higher and Higher*
✳ "Ecology Song," Stephen Stills, *Stephen Stills 2*
◎ *Rot N' Roll.* Titles include: "I Am an Animal," "Inch by Inch (The Garden Song)," "The Composters," "Put Me in the Compost Pile," "The Landfill Blues," "The

Garbage Blues," "The Recycle Shuffle," "I Am Recycled," "I'm from the Earth,"
"Let's Go Up to the Forest." $10 + $3 postage. Order from Stan Slaughter's All
Species Music, 3517 Virginia, Kansas City, Missouri 64109

Food

Here are the eight rules for a New Green Diet.

1. Eat a variety of foods.
2. Buy locally produced food.
3. Buy produce in season.
4. Buy organically produced food.
5. Eat fresh, whole foods with adequate starch and fiber.
6. Eat fewer and smaller portions of animal products.
7. Choose minimally processed and packaged foods.
8. Prepare your own meals at home.

Don't eat anything that has a face. Don't eat anything that has sexual urges, that has a mother and father, or that tries to run away from you.

—John Robbins, **A Diet for a New America** (1987)

With that in mind, the Party Girls suggest the following delicious vegetarian offerings.

"Give Peas a Chance" Salad

You can make this politically correct salad the day before the party. Wrap it and refrigerate.
Don't forget to label it for your guests!

2 cups shelled raw fresh—not frozen!— peas
  (about 2 pounds unshelled)
I cup finely chopped celery
I cup unsalted dry-roasted peanuts
I 8-ounces can sliced water chestnuts, drained
½ cup sour cream
I teaspoon celery salt
I tablespoon soy sauce
salt to taste

In a salad bowl, toss together peas, celery, peanuts, and water chestnuts. Combine sour cream, celery salt, and soy sauce. Toss with salad ingredients. Makes approximately 8 servings.

Marinated Cheeses with Fresh Herbs

This should be made a day in advance.

I cup olive oil
I cup white wine vinegar
6 tablespoons chopped fresh parsley

6 tablespoons green onions, chopped
I teaspoon sugar
¼ cup fresh basil, julienned

1 tablespoon salt

1 tablespoon pepper

1 pound block sharp Cheddar cheese, chilled

1 pound block Monterey jack cheese, chilled

6 cloves garlic, minced

Combine first nine ingredients in a jar, cover tightly, and shake vigorously. Set aside.

Cut blocks of cheese in half lengthwise and then into 1/4-inch-thick slices. Place in bowl and cover with marinade overnight.

Lay out cheeses, alternating Cheddar with jack on a nice serving platter. Spoon reserved marinade over slices and garnish with fresh herbs. Serve with sliced baguettes. Makes 36 servings.

Garden Spinach Dip with Crudité

1 1/2 pound baby spinach or

  2 bunches spinach, cleaned,

  with stems removed

1 tablespoon olive oil

1 1/4 cup sour cream

1/3 cup mayonnaise

1/4 cup green onion, chopped

1 teaspoon fresh lemon juice

2 tablespoons kosher salt

2 tablespoons fresh minced dill weed

1 8-ounce can water chestnuts,

  drained and finely chopped

In a large sauté pan, sauté spinach in olive oil on medium heat for 2–3 minutes, until wilted. Allow to cool; drain and finely chop.

In a mixing bowl, combine next seven ingredients, stir well. Add spinach and stir well; cover and chill thoroughly.

Serve with assorted fresh cut vegetables. Makes 2 3/4 cups.

Garlic Mushrooms

This is so easy, and so good!

40–50 button mushrooms

½ cup butter

2 tablespoons olive oil

I shallot, finely chopped

8 large cloves garlic, minced

5 stems fresh Italian parsley, finely chopped

Clean mushrooms, and trim off ⅛-inch from the bottom of stem. Melt butter and olive oil together in a large sauté pan. Sauté shallot and garlic for 2 minutes. Add mushrooms and sauté for 5 minutes, or until soft. Lightly sprinkle with chopped parsley, and serve with toothpicks. Serves 15–20.

Zucchini Frittata

2 teaspoons vegetable oil

I small onion, finely chopped

I clove garlic, minced

2 medium zucchini, grated

6 eggs

⅛ teaspoon pepper

¼ teaspoon dried basil

¼ teaspoon oregano leaves

I cup (3 ounces) grated Parmesan cheese

Heat oil in a large sauté pan over medium heat. Add onion, garlic, and zucchini; cook, stirring occasionally until vegetables are soft (about 5 minutes). Remove from heat and let cool slightly. Beat eggs with pepper, basil, and oregano. Stir in cheese and vegetables. Pour into a greased 9-inch pie pan. Bake in a 350°F oven for 25–30 minutes until puffed and brown. Cut into small squares. Serves 10.

Fresh Organic Fruit Salad

Make a fresh fruit salad using grapes, melon balls, strawberries, apple squares, and any other fruits in season.

Serve the fruit salad in this attractive melon basket:

1. Cut a thin slice from the bottom of a large oval melon to stabilize it.
2. Draw the lines of the basket on the melon before you start to cut into it.
3. Use a paring knife to cut out the pieces. Insert the knife halfway into the melon so you will be able to remove the pieces. Be careful not to cut through the handle.
4. Lift out the carved pieces gently. Use a knife to remove the pulp from big pieces so that it can be cut or balled for the filling. Add other cut fruits. Fill the melon.

Mudpie Cookies

2 cups of sugar

2 tablespoons of cocoa

1/2 cup of milk

1/2 cup of butter

1/2 cup of peanut butter

2 cups of oatmeal

1 teaspoon of vanilla flavoring

Mix the sugar and the cocoa together in a bowl. Stir in the milk. Put the mixture in a pot, add the butter, and boil it for 2 minutes. Continually stir the mixture.

Take the mixture off of the stove and mix the rest of the ingredients with the cooked part of the recipe. Drop the mixture by spoonful onto the waxed paper and allow to cool.

Dirt Cups

(taken from the Jell-O Kids' Cooking Fun Book)

2 cups of cold milk
1 3.4-ounce package Jell-O Instant Pudding (chocolate flavor)
3½ cups (8 ounces) Cool Whip whipped topping, thawed
1 16-ounce package crushed chocolate sandwich cookies (like Oreos)
gummy worms or insects

Pour the milk into the mixing bowl and add the pudding mix. Beat with the wire whisk until well blended, about 2 minutes. Let pudding stand for 5 minutes. Very gently, stir whipped topping and ½ of the crushed cookies into the pudding with rubber scraper until mixture is all the same color. Place about 1 tablespoon of the remaining crushed cookies into the bottom of each cup.

Fill 10 paper cups about ¾ full with pudding mixture. Top each cup with the rest of the crushed cookies. Add gummy worms and insects to decorate. Put cups into the refrigerator for 1 hour to chill them—and enjoy! Serves 10.

But unless we all choose to eat fresh, local seasonal food grown by people who are taking care of the earth and practicing sustainable agriculture, we're all going to be undernourished—socially and spiritually, as well as physically. Furthermore, the food won't taste as good.

—Alice Walker, chef and author, from the **Good Food Shopper**

Flourless and Fabulous:
A Party Girl's Passover

Passover is sort of the Jewish Fourth of July, a celebration of independence accompanied by a hearty, rib-stickin' meal. The Passover meal and service is called the "Seder," which means "order." Because so much of Passover is "ordered" by tradition and custom, it's easy for anyone to step in and host one.

Passover commemorates the Jews' exodus from slavery in Egypt. Rent *The Ten Commandments* for a quick refresher course on the story, and to catch a mighty fine lookin' Yul Brynner as the young Ramses.

Can or should non-Jews celebrate Passover? The Party Girls say, "Heck, yeah!" Jewish or not, who can argue that deliverance from slavery isn't a reason to celebrate? Passover is a once-a-year opportunity to reflect on all of the "masters" who "enslave" us as people and as a culture, and to recommit ourselves to fighting for freedom.

Back in the old days (our childhoods), Seders featured long, drawn-out predinner services (often heavy on the Hebrew) that never seemed to end. Once they did end, we were "rewarded" with bottled gefilte fish and canned macaroons. Yeesh, could the ancient Hebrews have had it any worse? These days, you can host a Seder that's serious without being somber, and serve up an unleavened feast fit for a Pharaoh.

Invitations

★ The Seder is a sit-down meal, so only invite as many people as you can accommodate at a table.

◎ Take care with your guest list. Invite people who will bring an open mind and heart to the table, and will treat the event with a certain amount of respect. Lara once hosted a Seder for friends. Two showed up in cutoff shorts, and one brought a dog. Your Seder could and should be fun, but a modicum of formality is called for at any religious celebration, no matter how casual.

✳ Use creamy, ivory-colored notecards and envelopes to make simple, elegant invitations. If you've got kids, ask them to decorate the front with drawings of items from the Seder Plate (more on that later).

★ **Headline:** *Don't Passover (YOUR NAME)'s Seder.*

◎ Because Passover is about creating community, it's appropriate to ask your guests to bring a dish for the meal. People who are not used to cooking for Passover might be intimidated by the "no flour/no leavening" rule. Assign them salads, veggies, boxes of matzoh, Passover wine (it's clearly marked on the label), or grape juice.

Decorating Tips

★ The Seder Plate is the centerpiece of the table and the meal. You can buy an official Seder Plate with sections for each item, or just use a pretty platter or dinner plate.

ITEMS FOR THE SEDER PLATE

Zeroa, or roasted bone—use a shankbone or chicken neck. Vegetarians or the squeamish can use a roasted beet. In a pinch, Lara has used a drawing of a bone cut from a brown paper bag and once, a bone-shaped dog biscuit. ("I was reminded afterward, however, that the biscuit with its cereal fillers was 'wrong-o bong-o' for Passover.") The bone represents the sacrifice made on the eve of the Exodus.

Karpas, a green vegetable. Use enough celery sticks for everyone at the table. If you've got a lot of guests, put one piece on the plate and set out a few small plates of celery on the table. Karpas symbolize the fresh growth of spring.

Charoset, a mixture of chopped nuts and apples. This represents the mortar used by Jewish slaves to build the ancient cities of Egypt. It is tasty so that we are reminded that the security of slavery can be deceptively sweet. (Recipe follows.)

Maror, a bitter herb. Use a dollop of red or white horseradish. Maror is symbolic of the bitterness of slavery.

Baysah, a roasted egg, represents birth, renewal, and the ancient temple offerings. We've also heard that the burned shell represents the heat of the desert. Hard boil an egg, then hold it over an open flame with tongs to scorch the shell.

Matzoh, unleavened bread. You'll need three pieces for the Seder Plate, and more for the rest of the meal. The Isrealites had to leave Egypt in such a hurry that they didn't have time to wait for their bread to rise. Matzoh reminds us of this experience. The three pieces on the Seder Plate should be covered with a cloth napkin.

Some modern Seder Plates also have an orange, representing women's equality. The story goes that an old rabbi, objecting to women becoming full participants in temple services said, "There'll be a woman at the Bimah (altar) when there's an orange on the Seder Plate."

◎ The Passover Table requires a few extra touches. In addition to the Seder Plate, you'll need:

Stemmed wine glasses. Wine is an integral part of the Seder, so use your nicest glasses.

Freshly washed and pressed tablecloth, but don't use starch!

Several bowls of salted water. You'll need this for dipping the Karpas during the Seder.

An extra plate of matzoh. Include two "boards" per person.

The Cup of Elijah. A place is set for Elijah the Prophet at the Passover Table. He's invited in during the Seder to announce the coming of the Messiah. Use one of your regular wine glasses, or a extra fancy goblet. Be sure to leave a window open for Elijah to come through.

Candles. Put two tapered candles in candlesticks at the head of the table.

✳ Fresh flowers are not part of the service, but since this is a rite of spring, it's lovely to have bright blooms on the table.

Games and Activities

◎ **You Gotta Hagaddah!** The telling of the story of the exodus from Egypt is the ultimate party icebreaker—everyone must participate. The Haggadah is a small book that tells the Passover story. It's divided into readings for everyone at the table. The Haggadah tells you when to eat what, how to bless it before you eat it, and has the answers to those famous "Four Questions."

There are Haggadot (the plural of Haggadah) available with widely different points of view, including traditional, feminist, environmental, gay/lesbian, and beyond. Check out a few and find one that fits with you and your crowd. You can get Haggadoth at Jewish bookstores, temple gift shops, and some general bookstores. A great resource is Afikomen Jewish Books in Berkeley, California (510) 655-1977. They carry a huge selection of Haggadot and can help you choose one with a theme that works for your Seder.

✈ **Hide the Afikomen!** This game is usually for the kids, but it's fun for an all-adult Seder too. The Afikomen is half of the middle piece of matzoh from the stack of three on the Seder Plate. At the beginning of the meal, the middle piece is broken in half, and one half is hidden. Every family has their own variation of how the game works, but in general, the leader hides the afikomen and the kids must find it. Lara's family had a slight variation. "Once the middle matzoh was broken," she remembers, "one half was placed between two big, fluffy pillows on a chair next to my Uncle Marty's chair. We kids had to sneak up and steal the afikomen and hide it. At the end of the meal, Uncle Marty would negotiate for the afikomen's release. We were not tough negotiators—the matzoh was his in exchange for a few Baskin Robbins gift certificates."

Favors and Prizes

You Got a Haggadah! Send each guest home with a copy of the Haggadah you used during the meal. Many times Seder guests—very often the non-Jews—are so moved by the story and experience of Passover, they want to refer back to the Haggadah again, or use it to plan their own Seder.

Food

Passover food must contain no *hametz*, or leavening. The hametz food group includes flour, baking powder, cornstarch, and other grains. The rule of thumb for figuring out what is hametz and what isn't: If in doubt, leave it out.

Wine is also integral to the Passover meal. While loganberry swill poured from a screwtop bottle is still tolerated at many Passover tables, there are lots of delish Passover wines available. "Hagafen" is one easy-to-find brand, and any good wine shop can help you find more. For kids and others who don't want to drink wine, provide grape juice.

Many families serve both meat (usually brisket) and poultry (chicken or turkey) for Passover. If this seems extreme, serve one or the other.

Charoset

8 tart apples, peeled, cored,
and finely minced or grated
2 cups toasted walnuts or pecans,
finely chopped

2 teaspoons cinnamon
2 teaspoon ground ginger
1 tablespoon honey
2 cups kosher red wine

Mix all ingredients together in a bowl. Cover and chill overnight before serving. Can be made 2–3 days ahead. Serves 8.

Gefilte Fish

Lara used to have a theory that only non-Jews truly enjoy gefilte fish, and that Jews ate it as part of the whole "suffering" thing. That was until she had homemade gefilte fish, which really is good!

Broth

2 pounds fish bones (ask at the fish
counter of your market)
3 carrots, sliced
2 celery ribs, sliced

2 onions, thickly chopped
3 teaspoons salt
freshly ground black pepper

Put all of the ingredients in a large pot, add enough water to cover. Bring to a boil, lower the heat, and simmer for about an hour. Strain the broth. Use right away to poach the fish, or allow to cool, cover, and store for up to 3 days.

Fish

2 pounds firm white fish, such as
dore or pike
2 eggs
1 medium onion, chopped
1 large carrot, chopped
1 stalk celery, minced
cherry tomatoes

2 cloves garlic, chopped
$1/3$ cup matzoh meal
$1/2$ cup ice water
$2 1/2$ tsp. salt
freshly ground black pepper
lettuce leaves

Process fish in a food processor until finely ground. Once ground, process again while adding in about ¼ cup of the water. Add the rest of the ingredients, except for the rest of the water, lettuce, and tomatoes. Process until smooth. If mixture is too loose, add more matzoh meal. If it is too pasty, add more water. (You're going for fishball consistency.) Chill the mixture for about half an hour. Form the fish into 8 oblong patties, using wet hands.

Bring broth (preceding recipe) to a boil, then lower heat to simmer. Add fish, cover and simmer for 45 minutes. Remove the pot from the heat and let rest for 15 minutes. Remove fish from the broth with a slotted spoon and chill well. Serve on salad plates lined with lettuce leaves and garnished with cherry tomatoes. Serves 8.

"A Little Different" Matzoh Ball Soup

1 cup matzoh meal	6 tablespoon club soda
1 teaspoon salt	4 tablespoons chopped parsley
6 eggs	

Stir the dry ingredients together. Combine eggs, club soda, and parsley slightly with a fork and pour over the dry ingredients. Mix well and refrigerate at least 1 hour. While the matzoh mixture is chilling, make the Tomato/Cabbage Soup (recipe follows).

With wet hands, form matzoh mixture into 16 balls and drop into boiling soup. Reduce the heat and simmer, covered, for 30 minutes. Do not remove the lid while the matzoh balls are cooking. Makes 8 servings.

Tomato/Cabbage Soup

2 large 46-ounce cans tomato juice
8 cups (about 3 pounds) green cabbage, shredded
4 large carrots, thinly sliced
4 stalks thinly sliced celery
2 large onions, finely chopped
salt and pepper to taste

Put all of the ingredients into a large stockpot. Bring to a boil, reduce heat, and simmer uncovered for an hour.

Tzimmes

Pronounced "sih-miss," Tzimmes is a baked vegetable dish. There are as many variations as there are Jewish cooks, but this one is easy and yummy.

12 carrots, peeled and slices
   into 2-inch rounds
3 medium sweet potatoes, peeled
   and sliced into 2-inch rounds
10 pitted prunes

1/4 cup orange juice
2 teaspoons grated orange zest
pinch of nutmeg
3 tablespoons butter
2 tablespoons honey

Preheat oven to 350°F. Boil carrots and sweet potatoes until tender, about 10 minutes. Drain and place in a large casserole dish. Add the rest of the ingredients and mix well. Cover with foil and bake for 30 minutes. Uncover and bake another 8–10 minutes.

Can be made 2–3 days ahead. To reheat before serving, pop into a hot oven white your guests are eating their gefilte fish. Serves 8.

Stuffed Zucchini

8 medium zucchinis, cut in half lengthwise

2 small onions, finely chopped

4 small tomatoes, chopped

4 cloves garlic, chopped

4 teaspoons fresh herbs, such as basil, sage, or thyme

8 tablespoons matzoh meal

Preheat oven to 450°F. Scoop out pulp from each zucchini half with a spoon or melon baller and chop finely. Sauté zucchini pulp, onion, tomatoes, garlic, and herbs until heated through, about 5 minutes. Add matzoh meal to mixture and mix well. Stuff zucchini with mixture. Place in a baking dish with a little water on bottom. Bake for 30 minutes until zucchini shells are soft.

Can be made a day ahead. Cover and chill to store overnight. To reheat, pop into a hot oven while guests are eating their gefilte fish. Serves 8.

Spiced Orange Chicken

½ cup orange juice concentrate, thawed

2 cups chicken broth or water

8 boneless, skinless chicken breast halves

3 teaspoons potato starch

1 large onion, finely minced

1 teaspoon cloves

1 teaspoon cinnamon

salt and pepper to taste

Add the orange juice concentrate and ½ cup of the broth to a large, heavy skillet over medium heat. Brown the chicken in this mixture for about for 5–7 minutes per side. Add the onion, cloves, cinnamon, and 1 cup of the broth. Bring to a boil. Reduce the heat to medium-low, cover, and simmer for 7–10 minutes. Blend the remaining ½ cup broth with the potato starch until smooth. Add this mixture to the skillet and stir until the gravy thickens and begins to bubble. Season with salt and pepper to taste. Arrange the chicken on a platter and cover with sauce.

To make ahead, make the chicken and sauce in a baking pan, cover with foil and chill. Put the pan into a 350°F oven before you sit down to begin the service. It'll be hot but not dry by the time you're ready to eat. Serves 8.

Sweet and Savory Brisket

4–5 pound brisket
2 large onions, sliced
1 cup kosher red wine
1½ cups water or beef broth
2 cups mixed dried fruit (prunes, apricots, apples, pears and/or cranberries)
salt and pepper to taste

Brown meat on both sides in heavy pot over high heat, about 10–15 minutes on each side. Remove the meat to a cutting board. Lower heat to medium, add onions to the pan, and brown over medium heat for about 10 minutes. Return meat to pan, add wine, water or broth, and fruit; bring to simmer. Simmer covered for 2½ hours or until tender. Remove roast from pot to slicing board, let sit for 15 minutes or so before slicing. Skim fat from gravy. Add salt and pepper to taste. Arrange the meat on platter and top with gravy.

To make ahead, cook the meat and the gravy early in the day or the night before the Seder. Arrange the meat on a platter, cover and chill. Save the gravy in a covered bowl. Bring the meat to room temperature before serving. Heat the gravy on a saucepan, and put over the meat just before serving. Serves 8.

Upside-Down Lemon Meringue Pie

Gone are the days when Passover desserts were limited to canned macaroons and dry, chewy sponge cake. With a little creativity, Passover desserts can be just as delish as those at any other meal.

Crust

> 3 large egg whites at room temperature
> 1/4 teaspoon cream of tartar
> dash of salt
> 2/3 cup superfine sugar (you can usually find
>   superfine sugar at the market, or you can make your
>   own by processing regular sugar in the food processor
>   for a few pulses)
> 1/2 teaspoon vanilla

Preheat oven to 275°F. Lightly oil a 9-inch glass pie plate and set aside. Beat the whites, cream of tartar, and salt at high speed until foamy. Add 1/2 of the sugar and beat for one minute. Gradually beat in the rest of the sugar. Add the vanilla and beat until stiff peaks form, about 10 minutes.

Plop the meringue into the pie plate and spoon it over the bottom and sides of the plate. Bake for about 1 hour and 15 minutes, until crisp, dry and buff-colored. If the crust isn't crisp, turn off the oven and leave the crust in there for another 45 minutes. Cool on a wire rack. Can be made a day ahead—leave uncovered at room temperature.

Filling

5 egg yolks	6 tablespoons cold sweet butter
1/2 cup sugar	1/4 cup lemon juice and the zest of one lemon

Whisk egg yolks together with sugar. Add lemon juice and zest and whisk again. Cook in heavy non-reactive saucepan over low heat until thickened, stirring constantly. Remove from heat and add butter, stirring until blended. Pour into a glass dish and chill, with plastic wrap directly on the lemon curd. Can be made a day or two ahead.

About half an hour before your guests arrive, pour the lemon curd into the shell and chill uncovered in the fridge. Serves 8.

Mocha Almond Fudge Torte

1 cup butter	1 teaspoon vanilla extract
1 cup sugar plus 2 tablespoons sugar	16 ounces semisweet chocolate
1 cup brewed espresso or very strong coffee	6 eggs, plus 6 egg yolks
1 teaspoon almond extract	1 pint whipping cream

Preheat oven to 325°F. Grease 9-inch springform pan. Place a circle of wax paper on bottom of pan. Grease the paper and the sides of the pan and set aside. Place butter, 1 cup sugar, and espresso in the top of a double boiler and heat until sugar dissolves; add extracts and stir. Place the chocolate chips in a large bowl and pour hot liquid over chocolate. Stir until chocolate is melted; set aside. In a medium bowl, beat eggs and yolks until frothy; add to chocolate mixture and mix well. Pour batter into the prepared pan. Bake for 1 hour; edges will crack slightly. The torte may not look done, but it will set when chilled. Remove from oven and cool. Cover and refrigerate at least 12 hours. Early in the day of your Seder, remove the cake from the springform. Whip the cream with 2 tablespoons sugar. Pipe or spread on top and/or sides of cake. Chill until ready to serve. Serves 10–12.

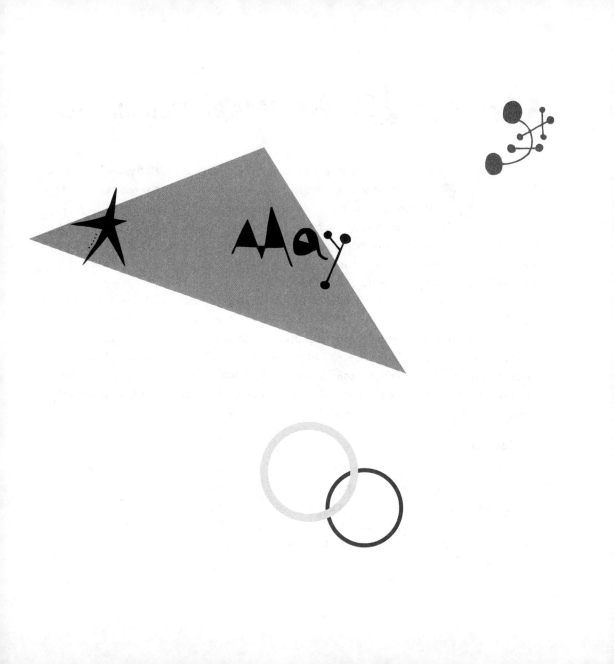

Cinco de Mayo: *Fiesta Méxicana*

Viva México! We're going to have the fiesta to end all fiestas! Who needs to travel, when we can recreate Acapulco and Puerto Vallarta right here at home?

Before we start, let's acquaint ourselves with the historical significance of this holiday. We'll use this information to quiz our guests at the party. It will serve as a conversational icebreaker and prove that Party Girls do their research before propagating broad cultural stereotypes for the sake of the Theme.

Did you know that Cinco de Mayo marks the victory of the Mexican Army over the French at the Battle of Puebla? Although the Mexican army was eventually defeated, the "Batalla de Puebla" came to represent Mexican unity and patriotism. In the United States, the "Batalla de Puebla" is referred to as "Cinco de Mayo." Many people wrongly equate it with Mexican Independence, which was on September 16, 1810, nearly fifty years later. Here in the United States, Mexicans celebrate their heritage by enjoying mariachi music, folklórico dancing, and other types of festive activities.

Invitations

◎ **Wish you were here:** Get some Mexican travel brochures from your local travel agency and insert your party details inside. Or obtain postcards from Mexico (ask your travel agency to get you in contact with the front desk of a popular hotel and have them sent directly to you). You can write out the entire invitation in Spanish. People will figure out how to translate it.

Headlines: *Va a una Celebración del Cinco de Mayo, or*
Fiesta Méxicana
a la Casa de (your name here)
El 5 de Mayo
Margaritas will be served [This is important information.]

★ **Postage Stamp:** If you want to get really authentic, send your invitations to a trusted friend in Mexico, and ask him or her to mail them from there.

Decorating Tips

✳ Light up your entry walkway with luminaria. Make these by placing sand in paper bags with the edges folded down. Place small candles upright in the sand.

✳ String red chile pepper lights in your bushes.

◎ Make or buy lots of big, brightly colored paper flowers for decoration. Put potted palms or other tropical potted plants all around the room. (You can rent these from a plant nursery). Purchase live potted chile plants for your kitchen window. Hang strings of dried chiles from the sides of your windows. Hang serapes (woven rugs for wall hanging), sombreros, and Mexico travel posters on the walls. Swag red, green, and white (the colors of the Mexican flag) crepe paper around chandeliers and across door frames. Orange, red, green, and bright yellow work, too. Display colorful papiér-mâché vegetables inside a big Mexican pottery bowl. Borrow colorful pottery, painted candelabras, earthenware, and hand-carved wooden masks from friends who have shopped their way through Mexico.

★ On your dining room table, diagonally overlay several woven serape-type cloths on the table. For your centerpiece, place a large sombrero upside down with paper flowers and maracas inside.

Costumes

Men should wear sombreros, panchos, and huaraches. Women can wear embroidered dresses and sandals.

Games and Activities

◎ Piñata!

Here's how to make your own piñata in the shape of a Mexican hat:
What You'll Need:

one newspaper	strips of newspaper
scissors	wheat paste or liquid starch
stapler	aluminum wire
rubber cement	mailing tape
3 sheets of green tissue paper	4 sheets of red tissue paper (about 20-by-30-inches)
1 sheet of white tissue paper	metallic ribbon in red, green, gold, and silver

one 12-by-12-inch sheet of aluminum foil
one round balloon inflatable to 11 or 12 inches
plastic sheeting or newspaper for surface protection while covering the balloon

1. Use a pattern as a guide to make the 5 points of the star. The points should be made from 4 thicknesses of newspaper. Each one should measure 7 inches on the straight sides.
2. Staple the layers of newspaper together so that they do not shift when forming the points.
3. Use the tip pattern as a guide to make the tips of the points from aluminum foil. Each one should measure 3 inches on the straight sides. Use rubber cement to glue the tips to the still-flat points.
4. Once the tips have dried, roll the stapled layers of paper together to form the 5 points. Use the rubber cement to glue them together, overlapping the straight edges. Allow to dry.

5. Inflate the balloon to 11 or 12 inches and knot. Dip the newspaper strips in the paste/starch one by one and apply 5 full layers, leaving a 3- to 4-inch bare circle around the knot of the balloon.

6. Make cuts around the bottoms of the points (about 1-inch deep). Fold back the flaps formed by the cuts and glue the points onto the wet balloon, starting at the opening and gluing the first 2 points on each side of it. The remaining 3 points should follow a straight line down the piñata.

7. Allow the piñata to dry thoroughly. Deflate the balloon and remove it.

8. Run wire around the widest part of the piñata. Attach another strand of wire (perpendicularly) to the wire running around the piñata to form a handle, pressing the wire close to the piñata surface. Secure all of the wire (except the actual handle) with the mailing tape. The handle should come up over the opening in the piñata enough to allow it to be filled and so that the rope can pass through easily when the piñata is hung.

9. Make ruffling with the tissue paper and glue it to the outside of the piñata in layers, alternating between colors. Cover the parts of the points not covered in foil as well.

10. Make tassels with the foil ribbon and attach to the tips of the points with rubber cement.

11. Fill with treats. Hang on a hook or a pulley. Two people should handle the rope, pulling it to move the piñata around.

12. Each person who attempts to break the piñata with a long stick or plastic bat should be blindfolded. The piñata is struck until broken.

✳ Dance the Macarena and the Mexican Hat Dance

Favors and Prizes

Favors are a traditional component of a Mexican party, so be sure to provide some. You can make big crepe paper flowers and give one to each guest. The guests can go home with party bags filled with the treats they've collected from the piñata, along with a bottle of hot sauce.

Musical Suggestions

✳ Preferably live mariachi players. Contact a company that books musicians in your area to find out if there are any mariachis for hire. Mariachis are strolling musicians who look like Mexican cowboys dressed up for a special occasion. Another fact to impress your guests: Mariachi costumes—tight spangled trousers, fancy jackets, and big floppy bowties—date back to the French occupation of Mexico in the mid-nineteenth century. The term "mariachi" is believed to be the Mexican mispronunciation of the French word for marriage since mariachi bands were often called upon to play during wedding ceremonies.

◎ *Mariachi—Folklore De Mexico*, various artists

✦ *Conjunto!*, Texas-Mexican Border Music

✺ *Volume 1—Ultimate Mexican Party*, Brazada

◎ *Great Hits—Tequila*, The Champs (1994). Includes "Tequila," "El Rancho Rock," "Limbo Rock," "La Cucaracha"

✦ *Just Another Band from East L.A.*, Los Lobos

Food

Serve these dishes buffet style, so guests can help themselves.

Mexican Salsa

You can make this the day before the party. Wrap well and refrigerate. Sprinkle fresh cilantro leaves on top before serving.

12 ripe Roma tomatoes, cored, seeded and chopped

1 cup onion, finely chopped

4 serrano or jalapeño chiles, finely chopped

1/2 cup chopped cilantro

1 1/2 teaspoons kosher salt

1 1/2 tablespoons fresh squeezed lime juice

Combine the tomatoes, onions, chiles, cilantro, salt, and lime juice in a sauce dish. Stir well. Serve with tortilla chips. Makes 2 1/2 cups

Guacamole

This recipe uses a lot of lime juice, which will prevent the dip from turning brown as the fiesta progresses. Make it up to three hours before the party, wrap well in plastic wrap, and refrigerate.

5 cloves garlic

3 small fresh, hot jalapeño or serrano chiles, stemmed and seeded

1 tablespoon kosher salt

5 tablespoons lime juice

3 large ripe Haas avocados (1 ½ pounds)

2 tablespoons chopped fresh cilantro

Mince garlic, add peppers and salt and mash together to form a paste. Scrape into a bowl, stir in 2 tablespoons of the lime juice and set aside. Just before serving, scoop meat from avocado and mash it with a fork. Stir in the garlic and pepper paste, remaining lime juice, and chopped cilantro.

Nachos

Prepare this in advance, and broil it before serving.

1 dozen stale corn tortillas

corn oil

salt

16 ounces Monterey Jack cheese,
  shredded

5 canned pickled jalapeños,
  stemmed and sliced

lime wedges

Tear each stale tortilla into 8 pieces. Pour 1/4-inch oil in frying pan and turn on high. Fry tortilla pieces 2–3 minutes and salt lightly. Chips should be crisp, but chewy, too. Add more oil if necessary. Drain on paper towels. Spread chips, with some overlapping, on baking sheet and lay cheese and chile slices on top. Broil until cheese melts. Serve on a platter with lime wedges. (You can skip the frying part by using packaged tortilla chips.) Serves 10–20.

Tomatillo, Tomato, and Mozzarella Salad

This salad is inspired by the Mexican flag. You can make this 2 hours in advance, then cover it with plastic wrap and store in the refrigerator.

1 pound tomatillos
1/2 cup orange juice
1/2 cup lime juice
salt and pepper to taste
1 pound firm, ripe tomatoes, thinly sliced
1/4 pound mozzarella cheese, thinly sliced
2 tablespoons chopped fresh cilantro leaves

Pull off and discard the tomatillo husks. Rinse tomatillos and thinly slice into a bowl. Add orange juice, lime juice, salt and pepper, and mix gently. Arrange tomato slices on top of festive serving plate in a circular, overlapping fashion. Arrange cheese slices on top of tomatoes. Spoon tomatillo mixture over top. Sprinkle with cilantro and season with freshly ground black pepper.

Refritos (Refried Beans)

3 cups dried beans (kidney, black,
  or pinto)
9 cups water
1 large onion, chopped

5 cloves garlic, mashed
3 pieces bacon, diced
1/2 cup vegetable oil
salt and pepper to taste

Rinse and pick over beans. Soak overnight in the water. Bring the beans and soaking water to boil in a large pot, cover and simmer for one hour. Add onion, garlic, and bacon and simmer, covered, for another hour. Add salt to taste. Drain and reserve water from cooked beans. Heat oil in a heavy skillet and fry the beans. Mash well with a potato masher as you fry them and add a little of the cooking liquid if they get too dry. Add salt and pepper to taste.

Chicken Fajitas

6 boneless, skinned chicken breasts
1 cup orange juice
1/2 cup lemon juice
1 tablespoon black pepper, ground

5 cloves garlic, minced
1 teaspoon salt
1 tablespoon olive oil

Cut chicken breasts lengthwise. Mix remaining ingredients and marinate chicken for 2 hours or overnight. Barbecue or cook on a gas grill over high heat, turning once, until meat is lightly seared on the outside and cooked through. Cut into pieces. Transfer to a platter.

Serve with warm corn tortillas (warm by placing in microwave oven for a minute, and then into a bowl covered by a cloth napkin), and any or all of the following:

grated cheddar or Monterey Jack cheese
chopped onions
chopped tomatoes
sour cream

coarsely chopped cilantro leaves
sliced chiles
sliced avocado

Serves 16–20.

DESSERTS

Fried Bananas

6 large, soft, black skinned plantains
    (firm green bananas can be substituted)

flour
oil

Peel plantains and slice in ½ inch lengths. Roll in flour and fry in hot oil until golden brown. Serve with vanilla ice cream. Yummy!

DRINKS

Margarita

This recipe makes 8 servings. You can triple it, and store it in the refrigerator. To serve, salt the rim of a glass by dipping the inverted rim in water and then in a saucer of kosher salt.

1 ½ cups tequila

2/3 cup Triple Sec

1 cup fresh lime juice

cracked ice

Mix tequila, Triple Sec, and lime juice with ice. Stir, strain into a Margarita glass, and serve. Salud!

Red Wine Sangria

Since you can't make Margaritas all night, direct guests to this refreshing sangria and let them help themselves. Serve it in a large punch bowl.

12 orange and 12 lemon slices, halved

2 10-ounce bottles chilled sparkling water

½ cup Grand Marnier or Cointreau

½ cup orange liqueur or orange juice

2 bottles red wine

2 peaches, cut in wedge slices

Combine all but sparkling water in a pitcher. Cover and chill to blend flavors. Add chilled water and serve over ice.

Party All Night Long:
Pajama Rama

Remember how much you loved slumber parties when you were a kid? We bet your friends feel the same way. Surprise one of your longtime buddies with a pajama jam in honor of his or her birthday. Do whatever it takes to fool your friend into believing you have planned a quiet evening for just the two—or four—of you. Then be sure to have an extra toothbrush on hand.

Invitations

◎ You don't want to spoil the surprise by sending written invitations, so this time, we are going to e-mail everybody.

Copy: Shh . . . Join Us for a Surprise Pajama-Rama

In honor of _____

Friends don't let friends drink and drive,

so plan on staying overnight for a surprise slumber party.

Wear your pajamas and join us for an evening of games, videos, and surprises.

Decorating Tips

✳ Set up your living room area to look like a big shelter. Put mattresses and sleeping bags on the floor, and set out lots of pillows and quilts.

✶ Drape bed sheets over your tables and chairs.

◎ Tack sexy negligees on the wall.

★ Set out copies of *Goodnight Moon* and *The Runaway Bunny*. (Any family with young children should be able to lend you copies).

✳ Go to **http://HappyBirthday.com** online. Click on their "Time Capsule." Enter the birth date of your friend. This is a free site that contains information like Top News and Sports Headlines, Top Songs of the Year, Academy Award Winners, and famous people born on that date, not to mention the price of a car, a gallon of milk, and a loaf of bread. Print it out, frame it in a plastic box frame, and hang it on the wall. Give it to the guest of honor after the party is over.

Costumes

Nights in White Satin (or Flannel): Everyone should wear pajamas. These can range from nightshirts or lingerie to footsie pajamas.

Games and Activities

✳ **Surprise Masks:** Make masks using a blown-up color copy of a full-face photo of the guest of honor. When the birthday honoree shows up, have everyone don his or her mask and yell, "Surprise!"

◎ **Pass the Orange:** Players stand in a circle, in their jammies of course, with their hands behind their backs. They have to pass an orange from chin to chin without dropping it. Players who drop the orange drop out of the game, and the last person left is the winner.

★ **Pin the Mustache on the Birthday Boy or Girl:** Blow up a photo of the honoree at the one-hour photo store. Make a bunch of "mustaches" out of black construction paper and stick a circle of scotch tape on the back. Blindfold the guests, turn them around three times, and have them attempt to place a "mustache" in the right spot. Award a prize to the person who comes the closest.

◎ **Twister:** You can buy this game at any large toy store. Follow instructions, and have fun.

✳ **Pillow fights and sack races:** Pillow fights are self-explanatory. Use the pillowcases for sack races across your living room!

✦ **Shadow puppets:** Turn off the lights and shine a flashlight on the wall. Use your hand to make silhouettes of animals and have the others guess what it is.

◎ **Videos:** Toward the end of the evening, gather everyone together for videos and popcorn. Or simply run videos all night long. Suggested rentals: *The Pajama Game* (1957), available from Warner Home Video; *Pillow Talk* (1959) with Rock Hudson and Doris Day; *Sleepless in Seattle*; or any cheesy horror movie.

"Happy birthday to you. Happy birthday to you.
  Happy birthday dear [name], Happy birthday to you!"

The melody for this ubiquitous song was written over a hundred years ago by kindergarten teacher Mildred J. Hill and her sister Patty, who later became head of the Department of Kindergarten Education at Columbia University's Teacher College. Published in 1893 as "Good Morning to All," the original song did not have the happy birthday part until the 1920s when Robert H. Coleman published the song with "Happy birthday to you" added as a second verse.

Favors and Prizes

- ✳ Aromatherapy eye masks
- ◎ An overnight kit containing toothpaste, a toothbrush, ear plugs, and a travel pillow
- ✳ Mini-flashlights

Musical Suggestions

- ✳ "Happy Birthday" (we suggest you sing this one)
- ◎ "Birthday," The Beatles
- ✳ "Happy Birthday," Steppenwolf
- ★ *Lullabies for Little Dreamers*, Various Artists, featuring lullabies by James Taylor, Emmylou Harris, Aretha Franklin, The Manhattan Transfer, and others.

Food

What do you eat at a slumber party? Popcorn, of course. Here is a grownup version.

Spicy Garlic Popcorn

Make the spice mixture in advance, and pour it over store-bought bags of plain popcorn right before the party.

¾ cup vegetable oil

6 medium cloves garlic, minced

2 teaspoons chili powder

¼ teaspoon cayenne pepper

1 4-ounce bag unsalted, air-popped popcorn

salt to taste

Place oil, garlic, chili powder, and cayenne in a small saucepan over very low heat. Cook, stirring occasionally, for 5 minutes. Put popcorn in a large bowl, pour the spice mixture over it and toss to coat. Season to taste with salt. Makes 14 cups.

Party Fondue

Fondue is what the Swiss eat when they having a gathering of close friends. Here's an easy recipe that won't get stringy, separate, or become gummy.

1 cup dry white wine

1 large clove garlic, minced

1 pound Swiss cheese, cubed or shredded

¼ cup flour

1 11-ounce can Campbell's Condensed Cheddar Cheese Soup

French or Italian bread cubes

In a fondue pot, simmer wine and garlic. Combine cheese and flour; gradually blend into wine. Heat until cheese melts; stir often. Blend in soup. Heat, stirring, until smooth. Spear bread with fondue forks and dip into fondue. Makes about 4 cups. Serves 8.

Pigs in Blankets

24 cocktail frankfurters, boiled and drained
1 10-ounce package pizza dough
2 egg yolks beaten with 2 tablespoons of water
vegetable spray

Allow frankfurters to cool completely. Preheat oven to 400°F. Roll out dough on a lightly floured surface to a 12-by-15-inch rectangle. Cut crosswise into 6 equal strips, and then cut each strip crosswise into quarters. Place one frankfurter across each piece of dough and roll up; seal the end with a light brush of egg wash. Place on a baking sheet that has been lightly sprayed with vegetable spray. Bake for 15–20 minutes until lightly browned. Serve with an assortment of mustards. Makes 24 pieces.

Chocolate Birthday Cake

Just like Mom made! This can be made up to 6 hours before serving. Don't forget the candles and the milk.

3 1/2 cups sifted cake flour
1/2 tablespoon baking soda
1/2 teaspoon baking powder
1/2 tablespoon salt
6 ounces unsweetened chocolate
1 cup water
1 cup unsalted butter, softened

2 cups granulated sugar
1/2 cup firmly packed light brown sugar
1 1/2 tablespoons pure vanilla extract
6 extra-large eggs at room temperature
1 cup buttermilk at room temperature
Chocolate Frosting (recipe follows)
Piping (recipe follows)

Preheat oven to 350°F. Grease the bottoms of three 9-by-1 1/2-inch round cake pans. Smooth a round of waxed paper into each, and then butter the papers. Sift the flour, baking soda, baking powder, and salt together. In a medium double boiler over lightly simmering water, melt the chocolate in 1 cup of water, stirring occasionally until smooth. Set aside.

In a large mixing bowl or food processor, beat the butter on medium speed until creamy. Continue beating while sprinkling in both sugars a tablespoon at a time. Add the vanilla and beat until very light. Add the eggs one at a time, beating until thoroughly blended after each, then beat until very light and creamy. Blend in the chocolate. Add the flour in three parts, sprinkling it over the bowl and alternating with buttermilk in two parts, and beat on low speed. Fold the batter with a spatula to finish blending.

Divide the batter among the 3 pans, smoothing the tops, then pushing the batter slightly up against the sides. Bake 2 layers on the middle rack and 1 on the lower rack—stagger them so the top layers are not directly above the bottom one. Bake until a toothpick inserted in the center of the cakes comes out clean, 30–35 minutes. Cool in the pans on racks 15 minutes, then turn out onto the racks, top sides up, to cool completely.

Make the Frosting and the Piping. To assemble the cake: Set the thickest layer of cake on a platter, bottom side up. Spread with 2/3 cup of the frosting. Set on the second layer, also bottoms-up, frost it, then set on the top layer, top side up. Frost the top and sides of the cake, making big sweeps of curls in the frosting with your knife. Smooth over the top, so you can pipe "Happy Birthday" on it using Dark or White Chocolate Piping. Serves 12.

Chocolate Frosting

> 5 cups confectioner's sugar
> ¾ cup unsweetened cocoa
> 7 tablespoons whole milk
> 14 tablespoons unsalted butter, softened
> 14 ounces (2 giant bars) milk chocolate, melted
> 2 tablespoons pure vanilla extract

In a food processor or mixing bowl, blend the sugar and cocoa. Melt the butter with the milk at half-power in the microwave or over low heat. Add while hot to the sugar with the chocolate and vanilla. Process or beat until smooth. Spread at once.

Dark or White Chocolate Piping:

> 2 ounces dark or white chocolate

In the top of a double boiler or a heatproof bowl over barely simmering water, melt 2 ounces of dark or white chocolate. Turn into a cone, and pipe while warm. It will harden almost immediately.

To make a paper cone, take two 8½-by-11-inch sheets of parchment paper. Holding the two sheets as one, fold one corner up to form a right angle at the center of one long side, then wrap the other corner around your hand, making a cone. Adjust until the tip is closed, then tape in place. Fill half-full with Piping. Gather the top of the cone and snip the tip to make a round opening the size you wish. Press the frosting out of the cone smoothly with one hand. If you make a mistake, lift it off with a knife tip.

If you prefer to buy a cone, you can mail order it, as well as an assortment of baking supplies, from Williams Sonoma by calling (800) 541-2233.

Between The Sheets

Try this classic cocktail.

2 ounces light rum

2 ounces brandy

2 ounces Cointreau

2 teaspoons lemon juice

In a cocktail shaker, half-full of ice cubes, combine all the ingredients. Shake to mix. Strain the mixture into two highball glasses, filled almost to the top with ice cubes. Makes 2 cocktails.

Party Waffles

Make these up to a week before the party, wrap well and freeze. The morning after the slumber party, reheat party waffles, serve champagne brunch punch, and send everyone home.

2 cups whole wheat flour

1 tablespoon baking powder

4 teaspoons sugar

1/2 teaspoon cinnamon

salt and pepper to taste

1 1/2 cups plain yogurt

3/4 cups water

3 tablespoons oil

4 egg whites

maple syrup

orange slices

In a large bowl, sift together flour, baking powder, sugar, cinnamon, salt, and pepper. Set aside.

Whisk together yogurt, water, and oil. Blend with flour mixture. In a small bowl, beat egg whites to form stiff peaks. Fold into batter mix. Ladle onto heated waffle iron, cook according to waffle iron directions. Let waffles cool, then freeze. Can be reheated in oven directly on rack at 350°F for 5 minutes. Serve with maple syrup and garnish with orange slices. Makes 16 waffles.

Champagne Brunch Punch

This is easy and serves lots of people.

4 cans frozen orange juice

1 bottle white wine

1 cup curacao or triple sec

ice

3 bottles of champagne

Pour first three ingredients over ice in punch bowl. Just before serving, add the champagne.

Variations on the Theme

◎ **Same Time, Next Year:** It doesn't have to be someone's birthday to throw a slumber party—any excuse will do. A gathering of girlfriends from college, a celebration when a group finishes a project. Rent a hotel suite and invite some close girlfriends for a "Gab Fest." Lara's friends do this every year, to catch up on gossip and news. In their most recent one, the organizer created nametags and attached them to champagne glasses. This way, no one misplaced their glass, and they got to take them home as a favor.

Pumps and Circumstance:
A Graduation Prom

What better way to celebrate a grownup graduation than with an adolescent prom party? Commemorate the commencement of law school, med school, business school, beauty school, traffic school, or clown college with the ultimate dance of teen romance!

Proms may carry the most emotional baggage of any single party outside of a wedding reception. Some of us were prom queens, some of us double-dated with a pint of ice cream and a box of tissues. The Party Girl prom party offers those who loved their own prom an opportunity to relive the experience, and for those who didn't, this party is the second chance they never thought they'd get!

Invitations

◎ Make a prom ticket or "bid" with your desktop publishing program. Include two in each invitation.

Sample Headline: Class of (YEAR) Prom

A Night to Remember

Celebrating the graduation of Jane Doe from Barber College

Decorating Tips

✳ You'll need a big open space for this party—either clear out all the furniture from the biggest room in your house, consider an "under the stars" outdoor prom, or investigate off-campus locations, like hotels or community centers.

✳ High school proms tend to have some kind of theme that seems poignant at the time and pretty goofy in retrospect. The theme is often based on a top-40 favorite of the graduating class, such as "Two Tickets to Paradise" or "Stairway to Heaven," or a generic theme like "A Night to Remember." In the '50s, ideas like "Under the Sea" were popular. You can choose a theme like this and use it on your invitations, welcome banner, and photo backdrop.

✶ Use butcher paper or posterboard to make a welcome banner. Hang it in the first spot your guests will see when they walk into the room. Write "Welcome Class of (YEAR)" with poster paints, a huge marker, or glue and glitter.

◎ Prom decor is based on a seventeen-year-old's idea of elegant. Think black, white, and red as a color scheme, cheapie flower arrangements with daisies and carnations, and crepe paper streamers.

✳ A disco mirror ball is a necessary luxury for a prom, and can be rented from party rental places.

✴ Haul out those Christmas lights again and drape them around the room. Tape them to the ceiling for a starry night effect, and down the walls for all-over glamour.

◎ Splurge a little on limo rides. A limousine will run you about $50 per hour, and most companies have a three-hour minimum. Have the driver take groups of promgoers on fifteen-to twenty-minute rides through the neighborhood or down a nearby crowded street.

Costumes

✳ **Tacky Tuxes!** Ruffle-front shirts, pistachio-colored jackets, and white shoes—the badder the better for the fellas.

✳ **Dress to Excess!** The girls can wear big, poufy thriftstore frocks in rainbow colors or dresses from their own prom eras.

◎ **True to Type!** Every graduating class had "The Nerd," "The Jock," "The Cheerleader," and other stereotypes. Incorporate these elements into prom costumes by donning thick glasses, wearing a sports jersey under a tux jacket, or accessorizing a prom dress with pom-poms.

Games and Activities

✦ Set up an area for "official" prom photos. You can make your own backdrop with a few sheets of butcher paper or posterboard. Decorate with stars, fish, or other icons of your theme. Make sure you've got the area staffed for the whole party. Enlist friends to work in shifts or hire a neighborhood teen. Experiment with lighting, distance, and flashes on a roll of film a week before the party, so you know the photos will turn out okay.

◎ Ask your guests to bring their own prom photos—put them up on a bulletin board or posterboard with double-sided tape so that your guests can gawk during the party. Give a prize to anyone who shows in their original prom clothes!

✳ On a small side table, set out two crowns (paper or plastic), a fish bowl, slips of paper and pens, and a sign asking everyone to vote for King and Queen of the prom. Set a cutoff time for nominations. At the designated time, crown the King and Queen and invite them to share a royal spotlight dance. (Pass out a flashlights to a few enlisted helpers to create the spotlight effect.)

Favors and Prizes

✳ Of Course, a corsage! Made or bought, real or fake, have corsages available for all the female guests.

✴ Send each guest their prom photo with a thank-you note as soon as possible after the party.

◎ Give yourself a month or so to hit lots of thrift stores to collect imprinted prom souvenir wine glasses—the shelves of Goodwills and Salvation Armys are full of 'em. Wash them well, and fill with jelly beans or other candies in your theme colors. Cover the top with a square of tulle and tie at the stem with ribbon. Hand one to each guest as they leave.

✳ Dove makes little wrapped chocolates called "Promises." (Get it? Prom-ises. . . .) Gather a few of these into a square of tulle, and tie with a ribbon. Include a condom in case anyone decides to go "all the way" on prom night.

Musical Suggestions

◎ Take into account the ages of your guests and play music from the era of their proms. Include a slow dance after every four or five fast numbers.

★ Make several long mixed tapes so there's no break in the dancing. Keep an eye on the clock so you can change the tape before it's finished.

✳ Ask guests to R.S.V.P. with one or two songs they remember from their prom, or would have *wanted* to hear at their prom.

◎ A few "prom" songs to add to the mix:

"It's Raining on Prom Night," Leslie Gore, on the *Grease* Broadway or movie soundtracks

"At the Prom," The Flamingos

"Junior Prom," Joni James

"Primping at the Prom," Duke Ellington

"Queen of the Senior Prom," The Mills Brothers

"Prom Night in Pig Town," Trout Fishing in America
"I Can't Get Invited to the Prom," The Queers

Food

Proms usually have an entirely forgettable sit-down rubber chicken dinner. No one remembers the dinner, so for this prom, skip it. Start your prom at a post-dinner hour and set out a few platters of finger foods and a huge bowl of punch, and you're ready to go.

"Rubber" Chicken Dippers

Reminiscent of the dreary chicken breasts served at proms—but much tastier!

8 boneless, skinless chicken breast halves

2 cups dry bread crumbs

1 cup grated Parmesan cheese

1/2 teaspoon paprika

4 tablespoons chopped parsley

1 teaspoon salt

1/2 cup butter

2 cloves garlic, peeled and "bruised"
   (press down on them with your thumb so that they are split
   and smashed a bit, but still intact)

Preheat oven to 350°F. Slice each half chicken breast into 6 pieces; set aside. Mix bread crumbs, cheese, paprika, parsley, and salt in a bowl. Melt the butter and the garlic together in a saucepan over low heat. Remove the garlic. Dip the chicken strips in the butter, then in the bread crumb mixture, pressing down to cover completely with crumbs. Bake the strips on a slightly greased baking sheet for 45 minutes. Cool to room temperature. Serve with Honey Dijon Dip (recipe follows).

Can be made a day ahead; wrap loosely in foil and chill overnight. Serve cold or at room temperature. Makes 48 chicken appetizers.

Honey Dijon Dip

1 16-ounce tub sour cream   2 tablespoons honey
⅓ cup Dijon mustard

Mix all ingredients together, cover and chill. Makes 2 cups.

"High School Confidential": Polenta Squares with Sun-Dried Tomatoes and Basil

4 cups water   1 1-ounce jar sun-dried tomatoes
1 teaspoon salt   in oil, drained and chopped
1 cup yellow cornmeal   ½ cup parmesan cheese
2 cup chopped fresh basil

Bring the water to a boil in a large, heavy saucepan over high heat. Add the salt. Slowly add the cornmeal, stirring constantly with a wire wisk. When the mixture boils, turn the heat to low and continue stirring until the mixture is very thick, about 30 minutes. Add the basil and tomatoes and stir well. Pour the polenta into a lightly greased 10-by-15-inch jelly roll pan, spreading evenly. Chill until firm.

Sprinkle the top with the parmesan cheese and bake in a 350°F oven for 15–20 minutes, until lightly browned. Cool to room temperature. Cut into 1½-inch squares.

Can be made a day or two ahead. Cover with plastic wrap and chill; bring to room temperature to serve. Makes approximately 60 appetizers.

Dip-Lomas

2 packages large flour tortillas	chili powder to taste
2 8-ounce packages cream cheese, softened	2 bunches green onions

Working with one tortilla at a time, spread the tortilla with a thin layer of softened cream cheese. Sprinkle with a little chili powder. Cut the tortilla half. Cut each half into 4 strips crosswise. Tightly roll each piece from the curved end. Tie each little roll with a piece of green onion.

Can be make a day ahead. Cover and store in the fridge; bring to room temperature to serve. Makes almost 200 little dippers. Serve with Senior Beanier Dip.

Senior Beanier Dip

3 garlic cloves, minced	¼ cup fresh lemon juice
3 15-ounce cans cannellini (white kidney beans), rinsed and drained	½ cup olive oil
salt and freshly ground pepper to taste	3 teaspoons ground cumin
	chili powder for garnish

Place all of the ingredients except chili powder into a processor and mix until smooth. Make a day or two ahead, cover and chill. Sprinkle the top with a little chili powder to serve. Makes about 3 cups.

Graduation Caps

*Marinated mushroom caps on top of a slice of melba toast look kind of like a graduate's
mortarboard turned upside-down.*

2 pounds small, white mushrooms

1 cup olive oil

2 tablespoons red wine vinegar

4 tablespoons chopped fresh basil

2 tablespoons chopped fresh Italian parsley

3 cloves minced garlic

2 teaspoons Dijon mustard

2 1-ounce packages melba toast

Brush mushrooms well. Remove stems and save them for another use (salad, pizza, spaghetti sauce,
you can think of something. . .). Put the mushroom caps in a large bowl. Shake all of the remaining ingredients except melba toast together in a jar. Pour the marinade over the mushrooms. Cover and
marinate the mushrooms for at least two hours, preferably overnight.

Arrange slices of melba toast on a platter. Top each with a marinated mushroom, open side up.
Makes about 48 canapés.

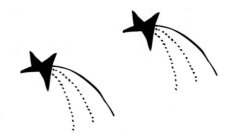

Pie Beta Kappas

Serve these bite-sized pies, and you'll graduate with honors!

1½ cups vegetable shortening
4½ cups flour
2 teaspoons salt
10–12 tablespoons water
2 tablespoons olive oil
1½ large red onions, minced

2 garlic cloves, minced
¾ pound chopped smoked salmon
3 tablespoons chopped, fresh dill
¾ cup sour cream
salt and pepper to taste

First, make the dough: Using fingertips, pastry blender, food processor or two knives, cut the shortening into the flour and salt until the mixture resembles coarse crumbs. Add the water one tablespoon at a time, fluffing with a fork or pulsing for a second or two after each addition. The dough should stick together, but not be sticky. Knead the dough a few times on a floured surface. Roll and cut out 3½-inch rounds; you should have at least 36.

Preheat oven to 450°F. Heat the olive oil in a heavy skillet, and cook the onion and garlic for about 5 minutes, until wilted. Remove from heat, add the salmon and combine well. Add the dill and sour cream and mix well. Season with salt and pepper.

Place a tablespoon of filling to one side of a dough round. Moisten all around the edges of the dough round with water. Fold the dough over the filling and press down on the edges with the tines of a fork to seal. Prick the top two or three times with the fork. Bake on an ungreased cooked sheet for about 20 minutes, or until golden. Serve warm or at room temperature. Makes about 36 mini pies.

From Date Truffles

2 cups packed pitted dates, very coarsely chopped
4 tablespoons bourbon
½ cup whipping cream
4 tablespoons maple syrup
¼ cup unsalted butter
½ teaspoon ground cinnamon
2 cups (12 ounces) semisweet chocolate chips
3 cups finely chopped toasted pecans

Line a cookie sheet with foil. Mix dates and 2 tablespoons bourbon in bowl; set aside. Bring cream, syrup, butter, and cinnamon to simmer in heavy medium saucepan, stirring frequently. Remove from heat. Add chocolate and whisk until smooth and melted. Stir in date mixture and remaining bourbon. Freeze mixture until firm enough to mound on spoon, stirring occasionally, about 20 minutes.

Drop chocolate mixture by rounded tablespoons onto foil-lined sheet. Freeze until almost firm, about 10 minutes. Roll each mound in pecans. Chill until firm. Can be prepared 2 weeks ahead. Cover and keep refrigerated. Serve cold. Makes about 36 truffles.

Spiked Punch

48 ounces cranberry juice
(made from frozen concentrate)
48 ounces orange juice
(made from frozen concentrate)

2 2-liter bottles 7-Up
3–4 pounds ice cubes
1 quart vodka

Mix the first four ingredients together in a huge punchbowl. Give the bottle of vodka to two of your male guests and ask them to "spike" the punch throughout the evening.

If you don't have a bowl big enough, fill two bowls, and funnel the contents of the second bowl back into the two-liter bottles. Put these extra bottles in the fridge and replenish as necessary.

Make sure you label the punchbowl "spiked" so that no one is surprised by the alcohol. Makes about 50 6-ounce servings.

Shower Power! *First Comes Love, Then Comes Marriage, Then Comes the Party Girl with a Baby Carriage!*

ven the most competent Party Girl may panic when called upon to hostess a shower. Her best gal-pal/sister/relation is facing a life-altering event—and she's got to mark to occasion with a sufficiently significant soirée. This party will live in the heart and mind of the guest of honor for her entire life, so there's a bit of party pressure—but nothing a Party Girl can't handle.

"Couple showers" for both weddings and babies are currently in vogue, but we think these occasions are much more fun when they're chicks-only parties. Let's face it, men are more involved both as grooms and fathers than ever before, but can any guy honestly say he'd enjoy playing games and opening gifts in front of assembled family and friends? We thought not!

Showers—both bridal and baby—work best when they follow a basic formula:

1. Gathering and greeting
2. Game 1
3. Lunch
4. Game 2
5. Dessert
6. Opening Gifts

7. *Maybe just one more sliver of that cake...*
8. *Thank yous and farewells!*

Start a shower at about noon on a Saturday or Sunday, and allow about two and a half to three hours for the festivities. The party should take place a month or so before the big day. The trick is to strike a balance between slightly silly games or icebreakers and total humiliation. It should be fun, not torture. You also want to make sure the bride or mama-to-be gets her share of the traditional trappings—bow bouquets, pink and blue for baby decor, white or silver for bridal, not to mention gifts galore—while still keeping things fresh, fun, and flowing. These ideas will help you do just that.

Invitations

✳ **For Bride:** Find a photo of a bride from a bridal magazine and replace the model's face with a photo of your guest of honor—try to find one where she's making an especially goofy face. Play around with it on the copy machine until you've got it reduced enough to place on a plain folded card. Make enough copies for all of your invitations and paste them on plain store-bought notecards. Write all the party dates inside.

◎ **Headline:** *Look out!... Here Comes the Bride!*

✻ **For Baby:** Get a baby photo of the guest of honor from her mother, husband, or other relative. Make copies and paste it onto folded pink and blue notecards. Place in contrasting pink and blue envelopes (put a blue notecard in a pink envelope and vice-versa).

★ **Headline:** *Oh Baby! (HER NAME)'s Having a Baby!*

Decorating Tips

FOR BRIDE

※ **Tack-O-Rama:** Hit the party supply store and get a bunch of the worst decorations you can find—the cheaper and uglier, the better! Accordion-pleated centerpieces with cardboard brides and grooms, posterboard wall decorations, garlands with bells and doves, and plastic gold rings are just a few of the superbly shlocky finds to be found.

◎ **Power Flower for the Shower:** Pick a single flower—one that will be featured in the bride's bouquet or at the reception—and use that as your decorating theme. If your flower is, say, a rose (ooh, how original), you can use invitations with photos of roses, fill vases with roses, put rose-scented soaps in the bathroom, and give rose-scented lotions and candles as game prizes. For the buffet table, buy bunches of fluffy air ferns and spread them around, stick freshly cut roses and sprigs of baby's breath among the ferns. The roses will stay nice for the duration of the party. Offer mini rose plants or chocolate rose pops (available at fancy chocolate shops) as favors. This works for any flower: daisies, sunflowers, tulips, whatever.

✶ **It's a Nice Day for a White Wedding (Shower):** Every bride—whether or not she's technically pure of body and spirit—can choose to wear white these days. An all-white scheme is a pretty and easy way to decorate for a shower. White flowers, white tablecloths, white paper plates and plastic forks. White ribbon bows on the stems of glasses, and white balloons. If your bride-to-be has chosen "wedding colors," accent with those colors, or with silver, gold, or black for an elegant look. You can incorporate accent colors by scattering colored confetti on a white-topped buffet table, tying colored ribbons on stems of glasses or flower vases, or using colored napkins.

✳ **Have This Cake—But Don't Eat It:** Make a three-tiered floral wedding cake-like centerpiece. You'll need twenty-three white plastic, paper, or foam drink cups. The center of the centerpiece will be three cups high. Start with a cup set right-side up, then glue a second cup on top of it—rim to rim. Glue the third cup to the bottom of the second—bottom to bottom. Now make five two-cup pieces glued bottom to bottom. Snuggle the two-cup flower holder pieces in a circle right up against the three-cup piece. Finally, circle the whole thing with ten single cups. This may look a little like the result of a kindergarten craft day as is, but when you fill each of the sixteen openings with flowers, it's truly stunning. At the end of the party, you can dismantle the whole thing and give the flowers away as favors—a real double-duty beauty!

FOR BABY

◎ **Think Pink (and Blue):** Baby blue and powder pink are *de rigeur* for a baby shower. Pink and blue balloons add instant color to a room for just a few dollars. If you don't want to bother with the expense and trouble of a helium tank, blow up pink and blue balloons and tape them to the ceiling. Tie blue ribbons to the pink balloons and pink to the blue, and cut them off just at head level. Put a few of the balloons on your front door as well.

✈ **Showers Bring Flowers:** A pastel floral theme is pretty and oh-so-feminine for a baby shower. Use pastel table coverings (paper or cloth) in a variety of shades. Fill vases with mixed, colorful flowers in soft shades. A white watering can filled with flowers is a perfect centerpiece.

✳ **Kid Stuff:** Decorate with baby items that the guest of honor can take home at the end of the party. A jumbo-size box of diapers can make a great ottoman for the pregnant lady to prop up her feet on while opening presents. Use children's books from a used bookstore or thrift shop as serving trays, trivets, or writings tablets for games. Use pretty plastic-tipped diaper pins as "confetti" to scatter on the buffet table. Take the top off baby bottles to use as mini flower vases. Make a "garland" by stringing a clothesline across the living room and hanging baby clothes on it from clothespins. "Tommy Tippy" cups make great cream and sugar holders; use a feeding spoon as a sugar spoon. Prop a few stuffed animals on couches and chairs. Hang a mobile over the buffet table.

FOR BOTH

◎ Set aside a special chair for the guest of honor to sit in while she's opening her gifts. Make sure you've got an especially comfortable one for the mother-to-be; a rocking chair is perfect! Decorate the chair with ribbons, bows, and/or flowers. Of course, the day's "queen" must wear a crown while she's on her throne. For the bride, glue or sew a length of white tulle to a comb or barrette for an instant veil. For Mama, make or buy a paper crown and glue a few plastic babies or pictures of babies to the front.

✳ Have a large trash bag handy for the discarded gift wrap, and one or two extras for the guest of honor to haul home her loot.

Games and Activities

FOR BRIDE

✦ **Couple Quiz:** As each guest arrives, pin a card to her back with the name of a famous married couple. She must ask the other guests questions to try to figure out who's on her back. The questions must have a "Yes" or "No" answer. There are no winners or losers in this game, but it's a great icebreaker. Some fun couples to use:

George and Martha Washington	Barbie and Ken
Ricky and Lucy Ricardo	Bill and Hillary Clinton
Julius and Ethel Rosenberg	Antony and Cleopatra
Nicholas and Alexandra	Fred and Wilma Flintstone
Steve Lawrence and Edie Gormé	Adam and Eve

◉ **Toilet Paper Brides:** Divide the guests into groups of four or five and supply each group with a few rolls of toilet paper. Send each group to a separate room and give them twenty minutes to fashion a bridal gown—one person in each group must act as model. Let the bride-to-be choose the winner and award the members of each group a prize—a copy of a fashion magazine would be a great prize for the budding designers.

✳ **Our Love's in Jeopardy:** Get together with the groom-to-be and grill him for information about the bride for categories such as: Favorite Foods, Pet Peeves, Hobbies and Leisure, At Work, Childhood Days, Likes and Dislikes. Just like the TV game show, you'll be writing up five "answers" in each of these categories, and challenging the guests to answer them in the form of a question.

Make up a game board using sheets of butcher paper or four pieces of posterboard taped together. Draw a grid on the game board with five columns and six rows. Put the names of the categories along the top, and dollar amounts: $100, $200, $300, $400, and $500 along the left side. Write the "answers" in the squares, then cover each one with a piece of paper cut to size and secure with a small piece of tape at the top.

The game board will look something like this:

Jane Jeopardy!

	Food and Drink	Pet Peeves	At Work	Childhood Days
$100	Jane's favorite cocktail	Jane runs screaming when this song comes on the radio	This woman was the worst boss Jane ever had	The name and occupation of Jane's imaginary friend
$200	Jane burned this dish at her last dinner party	Don't step on Jane's carpet without first doing this	This was Jane's first job after college	Jane had this special name for her favorite stuffed animal
$300	Jane will break out in hives if you serve her this vegetable	Jane hates it when Jack does this with his hands	What Jane would do if she could have her dream job	What Jane said the first time she saw her little brother
$400	Jack proposed to Jane at this restaurant	Jane would rather open a vein than see a movie starring this actor	Jane gets to work promptly at this time every morning	Though Jane would probably rather forget it, this was her nickname at camp
$500	Jane's favorite junk food	This is the worst thing you can do to Jane while her back is turned	This is the "little white lie" on Jane's resume	Jane was the schoolyard champ at this game

Tape the board to a wall that's visible to the whole party and let the game begin! Randomly choose someone to start the game—the person sitting to the right of the bride is a good place to start. Let the guests answer questions and collect "money" until all of the answers are revealed. Hand out play money as people win to help keep score. In the event of a tie, either ask a "Final Jeopardy" tiebreaking question or award two prizes.

✳ **Bridal Bounty Bingo:** This is a great game to play while the gifts are being opened to keep people's attention where it should be—on the bride! Make up bingo cards with five rows and five columns for each guest with different gift categories written in each square, such as:

Bathroom Items	**Home Improvement**
Really for Him	**Books**
Appliances	**Gourmet Gifts**
Really for Her	**Home Decor**
Bed Linen	**Kitchenware**
Heirloom Gift	**Wedding Supplies**
Lingerie	**From the Registry**
Gag Gift	**Cash-ola**

As the gifts are opened, the guests can put an X in the square in the category in which it fits. The first guest with five X's in a row wins a prize.

✳ **Bow Bouquet:** A classic! Save the bows from the gifts to make a "bouquet" for the bride to use during her rehearsal. Assign a bouquet-maker before gift-opening begins—give her a paper plate, scissors, and scotch tape. Make a hole in the center of the plate to push the long ribbons through. Arrange the bows on the plate and secure with tape.

FOR BABY

★ **Name the Baby:** This works the same as the bridal shower "Couple Quiz," above, but use famous babies:

Baby Jesus
Baby Jessica (the one who fell down the well in Texas)
Baby Huey
Louise Brown (the first "test tube baby")
The Lindberg Baby
Rosemary's Baby
The Gerber Baby
The "Dancing Baby" (of Ally McBeal and Internet fame)
The Dionne Quintuplets
Baby New Year

◎ **Feed the Baby or "Eeew, They Eat This Stuff?"** Buy about ten different types of jarred baby food in a variety of colors. Number the lids of each jar and write down the flavor that goes with each number. Soak off the labels of the jars and set them out on a table with slips of paper. Also set out plastic spoons. Each guest tries to guess the flavors of the baby food—she can do so by sight, smell, or, for the brave, taste. For an extra challenge, include one or two jars that have more than one type of food, like Apple/Banana or Carrot/Pea.

★ **Baby Price Is Right:** Buy five baby items—diapers, baby powder, baby shampoo, to name a few—and put them out on a table. Play "Vanna" and describe each item in your best spokesmodel detail. Have each guest write down her guess at the retail price of the items. The one who comes closest on each item wins a prize.

FOR BOTH

* **First Things First:** Write down the first thing the bride or mama says as she opens each gift, such as, "Oh my gosh," "How sweet," and "What have you done?" When the gifts are all open, repeat them back to her, but say that this is what she will say either on her wedding night or when she first sees her new baby!

◎ **Making Memories:** Especially appropriate for second-time brides or mothers. Ask each guest to bring a special photo to give to the bride or "expectant one." Gather everyone around a table set up with scrapbook pages, markers, pens, colored paper, glue sticks, old magazines, and other craft supplies. Each guest shows the photo and tells the story of why she chose to share it. Then each guest makes a scrapbook page for the photo, which includes writing down the story. The guest of honor can make a cover page while the others are working. She then has a beautiful and personal keepsake of the day.

Favors and Prizes

FOR BRIDE

◎ **Love, Sweet Love:** The world needs more of both: love and sweetness. Wrap up a single truffle in a bit of tulle, or rejacket a chocolate bar with your own custom wrapper honoring the bride.

✦ **Love in Bloom:** Send each guest home with a small potted plant or flower.

* **Picture Perfect:** An inexpensive picture frame is always a great favor. Slip a piece of paper into the photo slot saying that you'll send the guest a copy of a photo of her with the bride from the shower—then do it!

FOR BABY

✸ Do the new mother a favor and declare that no thank-you notes are expected for any of the shower gifts! She's got a lot to do to get ready for the baby, and you know she appreciates what you've given her. This does NOT apply to brides! The Mrs.-to-be must write her thank-you notes!

◎ A cellophane bag of pink and blue jelly beans will give the guests something to munch on the way home.

★ Something "baby"-sized: a goody bag of miniature Hershey bars, a demitasse coffee cup, tiny bottles of scented lotion, a small picture frame—you get the picture.

Musical Suggestions

Music is not strictly necessary for a shower, but a little background music is nice while folks are eating. Either play soft jazz or easy listening, or mix a tape of songs with "Baby" or "Wedding" themes. Here's a dozen of each covering a variety of styles and eras to get your brain goin'.

FOR BRIDE

✳ "Chapel of Love," Dixie Cups

◎ "Wedding Bell Blues," Fifth Dimension

★ "White Wedding," Billy Idol

✴ "Wedding Day," Bon Jovi

◎ "Love and Marriage," Frank Sinatra

✳ "I Went to Your Wedding," Patti Page

◎ "Hawaiian Wedding Song," Andy Williams

✦ "Will You Marry Me?" Paula Abdul

✦ "I Wanna Marry You," Bruce Springsteen

✳ "The Prayer of a Happy Housewife," Basia

◎ "Beloved Wife," Natalie Merchant

✦ "The Secret Marriage," Sting

FOR BABY:
- ✳ "Baby Love," The Supremes
- ✳ "You're Having My Baby," Paul Anka
- ★ "Baby I'm-a Want You," Bread
- ◎ "Be My Baby," The Ronnettes
- ★ "Love to Love You, Baby," Donna Summer
- ✳ "Somebody's Baby," Jackson Browne
- ★ "Maybe Baby," Buddy Holly
- ✳ "Baby What a Big Surprise," Chicago
- ◎ "Baby, Baby, Don't Get Hooked on Me," Mac Davis
- ✦ "(It's All Right) Baby's Comin' Back," The Eurythmics
- ◎ "Scream Like a Baby," David Bowie
- ✳ "Walkin' My Baby Back Home," Nat King Cole

Food

A shower spread should have lots of fresh, light foods with bright flavors. Chances are the bride is watching her calories so she can fit into the dress of her dreams, and the mama doesn't need a heavy lunch to make her feel bloated—she's already there! Spend your culinary energy and your guests' caloric concentration on a fabulous dessert.

Herbed Yogurt Dip

Make the night before or up to two days ahead to allow the flavors to blend. Serve with the usual crackers, and veggies. Use lots of "baby" veggies for a baby shower: baby corn, baby carrots, baby squash, baby artichokes.

1 cup lowfat cottage cheese	1 tablespoon chopped fresh mint
1 cup plain lowfat yogurt	2 tablespoons chopped fresh chives
2 tablespoons minced green onion	2 garlic cloves, minced or pressed
2 tablespoons chopped fresh parsley	salt and pepper to taste

Combine all ingredients in a food processor or blender and process until smooth. Cover and chill until ready to serve. Makes 2 cups.

Citrus Salmon Finger Sandwiches

1 pound fresh salmon filet
3 tablespoons fresh lime juice
3 tablespoons fresh lemon juice
1 small red onion, minced
6 springs of fresh dill
a few dashes of white pepper
2 8-ounces packages light cream cheese, softened
1 long, seeded sourdough baguette

Freeze the salmon for about 15 minutes, then slice paper-thin. Lay the slices in a single layer in a glass baking dish. Sprinkle the fish with the lime juice, lemon juice, onion, and pepper. Lay 5 of the dill springs over the fish. Cover the fish with plastic wrap and refrigerate at least 1 hour or overnight. To serve, slice the bread into thin rounds, top with a bit of cream cheese and a slice of salmon. Chop the remaining sprig of dill and sprinkle over the sandwiches. Makes approximately 30 finger sandwiches.

Endive Scoops with Salsa de Fruta

1 cup pineapple chunks, drained and chopped

1 medium apple, red or green, peeled, seeded and chopped

1 orange, peeled, segmented and sliced thin

1 tablespoon fresh lime juice

1 tablespoon fresh lemon juice

2 tablespoons fresh mint

2 tablespoons minced sweet, red onion

24 endive leaves, about 3 large heads

1 cup lowfat sour cream

Put the pineapple, apple, and orange in a medium glass or ceramic bowl and mix. Add the lemon juice, lime juice, mint, and onion and stir to combine. Cover and refrigerate overnight or at least 1 hour. To serve, arrange the endive leaves in a circular pattern on a large platter. Put a small dollop of sour cream on the inside-end of each leaf. Put a spoonful of salsa over each dollop of sour cream. Makes 24 appetizers.

Chilled Asparagus with Lemon Garlic Sauce

2½ pounds fresh asparagus
2 large garlic bulbs
1 tablespoon olive oil
1 teaspoon dried rosemary
1 cup low-fat sour cream
½ cup low-fat mayonnaise
2 tablespoons fresh lemon juice
2 green onions, minced
salt and pepper to taste

Trim the woody end off of the asparagus. Boil in lots of salted water until just tender, about 5 minutes. Drain and chill. To make the sauce, first roast the garlic bulbs. Preheat the oven to 375°F. Trim about half an inch off the top on each of the garlic bulbs. Place them on a square on aluminum foil, drizzle with the oil and sprinkle with the rosemary. Wrap tightly in the foil and bake until soft, about 45 minutes. When done, set aside to cool. Stir the sour cream, mayonnaise, and lemon juice together in a medium bowl. Squeeze the garlic cloves into the bowl and mash by pressing them up against the side of the bowl with a rubber scraper. Stir in the green onion and mix well. Season with salt and pepper.

The dressing can be made up to a week ahead. Store tightly covered in the fridge. To serve, arrange the asparagus on a platter—pointy ends all facing one way. Pour the dressing cross-wise over the middle of the asparagus. Serves 8–10.

Pasta Salad with Tomatoes, Peas, and Tuna

1 pound bowtie pasta

1/3 cup white wine vinegar

2 tablespoons water

1/2 teaspoon sugar

1 large garlic clove, minced

1/2 teaspoon Dijon mustard

1/2 cup olive oil

salt and pepper to taste

1 10-ounce package frozen peas,
   boiled until tender and drained

2 pints cherry tomatoes, halved

2 6.5-ounce cans water-packed tuna, drained

1/2 cup shredded fresh basil leaves

Cook the pasta according to package directions. While the pasta is cooking, make the dressing. Put the vinegar, water, sugar, garlic, mustard, and olive oil in a jar. Screw on the lid and shake well. Drain cooked pasta in a colander, rinse with cold water, and drain again. Toss the pasta with the dressing. Add the peas, tomatoes, tuna, and basil. Toss well. Makes 10–12 servings.

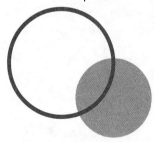

Orange Tarragon Butter

Dress up a basket of store-bought rolls with this flavorful butter.

1 1/2 cups unsalted butter, softened

4 tablespoons fresh tarragon or
   1 tablespoon dried

2 tablespoon fresh minced parsley

1 tablespoon minced or pressed garlic

2 tablespoons grated orange zest

2 tablespoons fresh orange juice

salt and pepper to taste

Mix all ingredients with an electric mixer until well blended. Dump the butter onto a large sheet on plastic wrap. Form the butter into a 12-inch log and roll tightly in the plastic, twisting the end to seal. Roll the plastic log to form an even cylinder. Chill the butter at least half an hour or overnight. To serve, slice the butter into 1/2-inch rounds and arrange on a plate. Garnish with a few springs of tarragon. Makes 24 pats of flavored butter.

Lemon Poppyseed Cake

A showy dessert is one of the highlights of a shower. No one should be intimidated by making a frosted cake—it's easy if you take your time. But for those who want to make things a little easier, this recipe can also be used to make about 24 cupcakes.

1 1/2 cups sugar

3/4 cup unsalted butter, softened

2 tablespoons grated lemon peel

3 large or extra-large eggs

1/4 cup fresh lemon juice

2½ cups flour

1 teaspoon baking soda

1 teaspoon baking powder

½ teaspoon salt

1½ cups buttermilk or sour milk

   (to sour milk, put 1½ tablespoons white vinegar

   in a 2-cup measuring cup. Add enough milk to

   measure 1½ cups)

4 tablespoons poppy seeds

Preheat the oven to 350°F. Grease and flour two 8-inch or 9-inch cake pans. Beat sugar, butter, and lemon peel in a large bowl until light and fluffy. Add eggs one at a time, beating each one in well before adding the next one. Sift the dry ingredients together into a medium bowl. Add a third of the sifted dry ingredients—mix in well. Then add half of the buttermilk and mix in well. Add another third of dry, the other half of the milk, and then the final third of dry—mix well after each addition. Add the poppy seeds and mix well. Pour half of the batter into each pan and smooth the tops with a rubber spatula. Bake until a toothpick poked into the center comes out clean, 35–45 minutes. It's a good idea to switch the placement of the pans halfway through baking time to make sure they're both done at the same time. Let the cakes cook in their pans for about 15 minutes, then turn out onto cooling racks. When completely cool, wrap tightly in plastic for overnight storage or in foil for freezing up to one week.

Frost with Cream Cheese Frosting (recipe follows). To dress up the cake, add a layer or fresh fruit such as sliced strawberries, thinly sliced peeled peaches, or a single layer or raspberries. Makes 10–12 servings.

For cupcakes: Line muffin pans with cake cups. Fill about ¾ full. Bake until golden brown on top and a cake-tester comes out clean, about 20–25 minutes.

White Chocolate Cream Cheese Frosting

We like to make a lot more frosting than we'll need so we can play around with decorating. This makes enough frosting to fill and frost a two-layer 8-inch or 9-inch cake, plus plenty left over for decorating. You can freeze leftover frosting practically forever.

12 ounce white chocolate	2 8-ounce packages cream cheese, softened
(two packages of Baker's is the easiest	1 cup unsalted butter
to find at the grocery store)	2 tablespoons freshly squeezed lemon juice

Break up the white chocolate and melt on top of a double boiler set over very low heat, stirring constantly. To melt in the microwave, place in a glass bowl or measuring cup and zap at 15-second intervals. Stir between zappings. Remove before totally melted, and stir vigorously until smooth. Set aside to cool.

Beat the cream cheese until smooth and creamy, slowly add the cooled white chocolate in a steady stream while beating constantly. Add the butter and lemon juice and beat until blended. Use right away, or store covered one day at room temperature, covered two weeks in the fridge, or for months in the freezer. (Bring to room temperature and rebeat to use chilled or frozen frosting.)

Cake Decorating Tips

◎   Cake layers are easier to work with if they are baked, frozen, and thawed before assembling and decorating.

◎   Invest in a long, flat pastry spatula. It works much better than a butter knife or rubber spatula for frosting cakes. If you don't have one and don't want to get one, a small, long-handled rubber spatula is the second-best option.

◎   Assemble the cake on a flat cake platter or a piece of stiff cardboard or foamcore covered with tinfoil or wrapping paper. A regular dinner plate has a "bowl" to it that makes it difficult to work with when frosting cakes.

◎   If you love to bake and plan to make layer cakes often, invest in "straight-sided" professional cake pans. The ones that most people use have tapered sides and fit into one another for easy storage, but it's hard to get smoothly iced sides with the slope-sided layers.

◎   Cakes look much better when the layers are even. First cut a strip of paper 27 inches long and $1\frac{1}{2}$ inches inches wide. Wrap the paper around the cake, with the bottom of the strip flush with the countertop or cutting board you're resting the cake on. Secure the paper with tape. Score about half an inch into the cake with a serrated knife around the top edge of the paper. Remove the paper strip. Fit a length of dental floss into the $\frac{1}{2}$-inch cut, and bring the ends together in front of you. Cross the ends of the floss over each other, and slowly pull until the floss has cut off the uneven top layer of the cake.

◎   Brush the layers with a pastry brush to get rid of most of the crumbs.

◎   Put a dollop of frosting on the cake platter before you set down the first layer to help anchor it.

◎   Arrange the layers like this: Put the first layer on the frosting dollop "baked" side down and cut side up. Frost first layer and add fruit, if desired. If you're using fruit, only place it to about half an inch from the edge of the cake. Set the second layer cut side down on top of the filling.

◎ Spread a very thin layer of frosting all over the cake. This is called a "crumb coat" and will keep the cake crumbs from showing up on your finished cake. Stick the thinly frosted cake into the fridge and chill until the frosting is set. Now you're ready to frost the cake.

◎ Plop a large dollop of frosting onto the top of the cake. Smooth it over the top and let it mush over the sides. The trick for frosting both the top and sides is to never let your spatula touch the cake—it should only touch the frosting. Scoop up mounds of frosting onto the tip of your spatula and frost the sides of the cake.

◎ To "clean up" the bottom of the cake, stick your little finger against the cake board at the base of the cake, with the tip just touching the cake layer. Turn cake platter counter-clockwise while keeping your finger in place.

◎ A freeform frosting treatment is informal and pretty—swirl the frosting around on the top and sides. If you want a smooth bakery-perfect look, it's easy to do, but only if you have a long, flat metal spatula. Here's how: Put the thickly frosted cake into the fridge and chill until set. Put very hot tap water into a tall glass, and quickly dip your spatula into the water and wipe dry. Working quickly, lightly run the spatula over the top of the cake—the "heat" will slightly melt and smooth the frosting. Imagine that the spatula is a feather and that you're lightly brushing the cake to get the right "feel" for the motion needed. Do the sides of the cake by holding the heated spatula in one place and turning the cake platter counter-clockwise. Reheat the spatula in hot water as needed.

◎ If you've got a pastry bag, chances are you know how to use it, so I'm not going to get into the finer points of piping decorations. If you don't, decorate the top, sides, and base of the cake with fresh fruit or organic edible flowers such as roses, daisies, nasturtiums, or violets.

◎ **For cupcakes:** Frost the tops with a generous slathering of frosting. For a bridal shower, a cute presentation is to stick a "bride and groom" pick in each one and arrange in tiers in a pedestal cake plate, creating a "wedding cake" of individual cupcakes. For a baby shower, color half of the frosting pink and half blue—regular liquid food coloring works fine. Frost half the cupcakes with each color and arrange on a platter.

Variations on the Theme

✳ **Round the Clock Shower:** Assign each guest a time of day and ask her to bring a gift that the couple can use at that time. Continue the "time" theme by giving small clocks, novelty watches, or calendars as prizes, and decorating the top of the cake with a clock face.

◎ **Gourmet Shower:** For the bride who loves to cook, ask guests to bring gifts of gourmet food and kitchen items. Use cookbooks or fancy flavored olive oils as prizes and favors, or hire a cooking teacher to do an in-house cooking class.

✶ **On Location Shower:** Especially appropriate for second-time brides, older brides who have "everything," or a bride who's having a series of showers in her honor. Go "on location" to a paint-your-own pottery studio, ceramics class, or cooking school for an afternoon for girlie gabbing while you create.

FOR BABY

◎ **Queen for a Day:** Treat the mother-to-be like royalty before the little prince or princess is born. Add royal titles like "Lady" or "Duchess" when addressing the invitations. Have the guest of honor wear a paper crown throughout the shower. Drape the chair in which she'll sit to open her gifts in royal purple fabric for an instant throne. Have the guests bring gifts for the mama rather than the baby—such as gift certificates for baby-sitting, housecleaning, manicures, massages, or meal-delivery services. Decorate the party room with royal-hued balloons in rich blue, gold, emerald, and purple. Don't let mama do a thing for herself all day—appoint someone to "escort" her to and from the shower, fix her a plate of food, and hand her the gifts. Add "name the queen" to your game line-up. Copy photos of well-known and obscure queens from an encyclopedia and challenge your guests to ID them.

Even Party Girls Get The Red, White, and Blues: *A Fourth of July Spectacular*

Wherever the Party Girl goes, there's bound to be fireworks of some sort. But on the Fourth of July, the skies of our nation light up with real-life rockets' red glare, and the Party Girl is at her dazzling best.

The Fourth of July is all about beaches, backyards, and barbecues, and showing your true colors: red, white, and blue, of course. This is your chance to revel in all that is uniquely American, from corn dogs to Coca-Cola.

You'll want to schedule your party for late afternoon, allowing folks to fill up on food and fun before heading out to catch the big light show.

Invitations

✳ Find an image of Uncle Sam for the front of the invitation. Write "We Want You" on the front and "To join us for the Fourth of July" on the inside. Include all of the party details.

◉ If you're planning a beach party, edge a plain white panel invitation with glue and sprinkle with sand. Let dry and fill in the party details with red and blue markers.

★ Write the invitation on the white stripes of a small American flag.

Decorating Tips

☀ Be shameless with the red, white, and blue. Balloons filled by either helium or lung power should be tied to every available surface. Swag away with crepe paper streamers and bunting.

✳ School supply stores are a great source for large cutouts of presidents, American flags, the Declaration of Independence, and other patriotic symbols.

◎ Make a firecracker centerpiece for the buffet table by wrapping an oatmeal or coffee can in red wrapping paper. Drape a piece of thick black yarn or cord from the top to look like a fuse.

★ Buy small American flags at a party, drug, or discount store and use them to label the food at the buffet table. Write the names of each dish on a flag with a laundry pen or sharpie. Use half of a Styrofoam ball or a small red apple as a base.

Games and Activities

◎ **Dead Presidents:** Dig up some dirt on our past chief executives and make up quiz sheets. Award a "bag of Dead Presidents" (assorted coins, go easy on the pennies) to the winner. If more then one person gets them all correct, draw a winner at random from the tying high scorers. Here are a few to get you started:

Who was the first president born in the United States of America? (Martin Van Buren—the presidents before him were born before the Revolution)

Who was the only bachelor president? (James Buchanan—rumor has it he may have been gay)

Which three presidents died on the Fourth of July? (John Adams, Thomas Jefferson, James Monroe)

Which president had a dog named Fala? (FDR)

◉ **Bombs Bursting in Air:** Line up the players in two lines facing each other. Give everyone in one line a water-filled balloon (red, white, or blue). The balloon holders toss their balloon to their partners directly across from them in the other line. Each line then takes one step backward and tosses the balloons back across. Keep tossing and moving back—soon balloons will begin bursting. Continue until only one pair of balloon tossers is left high and dry.

✳ **Star-Spangled Star Search:** You might get a few more takers for this game after the beer has been flowin'! Our national anthem is notoriously difficult to sing, but that can be half the fun. Challenge your guests to sing the "The Star Spangled Banner" before the Supreme Court (a panel of three judges). Award extra points for anyone who knows ALL of the verses (reprinted here)—award "Jackson Certificates" ($20), "Hamilton Certificates" ($10), and "Lincoln Certificates" ($5) to the top three winners. Make sure you let folks know on the invitation that you'll be holding this contest, it'll give them time to get psyched up!

The Defense of Fort McHenry
Francis Scott Key
20 September 1814

> Oh, say can you see, by the dawn's early light,
> What so proudly we hailed at the twilight's last gleaming?
> Whose broad stripes and bright stars, through the perilous fight,
> O'er the ramparts we watched, were so gallantly streaming?
> And the rockets' red glare, the bombs bursting in air,
> Gave proof through the night that our flag was still there.
> O say, does that star spangled banner yet wave
> O'er the land of the free and the home of the brave?

On the shore, dimly seen through the mists of the deep,
Where the foe's haughty host in dread silence reposes,
What is that which the breeze, o'er the towering steep,
As it fitfully blows, now conceals, now discloses?
Now it catches the gleam of the morning's first beam,
In full glory reflected now shines on the stream:
'Tis the star spangled banner! O long may it wave
O'er the land of the free and the home of the brave.

And where is that band who so vauntingly swore
That the havoc of war and the battle's confusion
A home and a country should leave us no more?
Their blood has wiped out their foul footstep's pollution.
No refuge could save the hireling and slave
From the terror of flight, or the gloom of the grave:
And the star spangled banner in triumph doth wave
O'er the land of the free and the home of the brave.

Oh! thus be it ever, when freemen shall stand
Between their loved homes and the war's desolation!
Blest with victory and peace, may the heaven-rescued land
Praise the Power that hath made and preserved us a nation.
Then conquer we must, for our cause it is just,
And this be our motto: "In God is our trust."
And the star spangled banner forever shall wave
O'er the land of the free and the home of the brave!

Favors and Prizes

◎ Send your guests off to watch fireworks with a snack bag of all-American treats, such as Cracker Jacks, salted peanuts, Hershey bars, and bubble gum.

★ While many counties have outlawed consumer fireworks, sparklers are sometimes still available. Hand each guest a box labeled, "Thank you for bringing sparkle to the Fourth."

Musical Suggestions

✳ If you can wire your backyard for playing tapes and CDs, choose music from the golden age of the American century, '40s swing and big band, '50s doo wop and rock, and '60s Motown. If you have time to make some mixed tapes to play, include patriotic classics like:

"Star Spangled Banner," Jimi Hendrix
"Back in the USA," Chuck Berry
"Living in the USA," Linda Ronstadt
"(Comin' to) America," Neil Diamond
"America," from *West Side Story*
"Surfin' USA," The Beach Boys

✳ If you can't wire your backyard to play tapes or CDs, haul out your loudest boombox and tune it to an oldies station. Many of them play greatest hits countdowns over the Fourth of July holiday—a fine backdrop for your partyin' fun. Make sure you have plenty of extra batteries. If you use an extension cord, tape the cord down to the ground with duct tape or secure it to the grass with heavy wire. It's easy for running kids and other revelers to trip on an exposed cord.

Food

While a Party Girl usually honors her guests with an array of homemade gourmet treats, on the Fourth of July it's perfectly acceptable to put on a spread of classic consumable Americana—the more processed, the better. Load your buffet with Spam, Velveeta, Twinkies, Moon Pies, Wonder Bread, and Tang. The kids will love it, and more than a few adults will admit a weakness for the mass-produced munchies of their youth. Serve American beer like Sam Adams' American Patriot, and wine from the Napa Valley. However, you don't want your reputation as the hostess with the mostest to go down like a bomb bursting in air, so do add a few of these recipes to the bill of fare as well.

Barbecued Peanuts

3 cups unsalted dry to roasted peanuts
¼ cup smooth bottled barbecue sauce
½ teaspoon season salt or Cajun seasoning

Preheat oven to 300°F. Mix all of the ingredients together in a bowl. Stir to coat peanuts evenly. Spread the nuts in an even layer on a lightly greased baking sheet. Bake for 10 minutes, stir, then bake another 10 minutes. Cool completely and store at room temperature in an airtight container. Makes 3 cups.

Stars and Stripes forever Salad

4 large cucumbers	I large jicama
4 large carrots	I large head iceberg lettuce

Shred the lettuce into a large bowl. Using a vegetable peeler, peel the carrots and cumbers lengthwise into long strips. Peel them right into the bowl of lettuce. Peel the jicama and slice into 1/4 to inch slices. Lay each slice on a cutting board. Using a small star to shaped cookie cutter, cut out as many little jicama stars as you can. Add the stars to the salad. Make the salad early in the day of your party and stick it in the fridge until ready to serve.

Dressing:

1/4 cup seasoned sesame vinegar	salt and pepper
1/2 cup canola oil	

Put all the dressing ingredients into a jar and shake well. Can be made up to a week ahead. Toss the salad with the dressing just before you put it out to serve. Serves 6–8.

Amber Waves of Grain Salad

2 cups wild rice	I cup chopped mushrooms
I tablespoon olive oil	2 minced garlic cloves
I cup minced onion	salt and pepper

Dressing:

½ cup apple cider vinegar	1 tablespoon mustard
¾ cup canola oil	1 teaspoon salt
2 tablespoon honey	½ teaspoon pepper

Rinse the wild rice in a strainer until the water runs clear. Drain well. Bring 5½ cups of water to a boil in a large heavy saucepan. Add the rice. Return to a boil, give it a couple of stirs, cover and reduce the heat to low. Cook for 40 minutes, or until the rice is tender and the outer shells of the grains have cracked. Remove the rice from the heat and let stand covered, for 10 minutes. Put the rice in a bowl and let cool while you prepare the veggies and dressing.

Heat the olive oil in a skillet. Add the onion and cook for 5 or so minutes until it is tender. Add the mushrooms and cook another 2 or 3 minutes. Add the garlic and cook for 1–2 minutes more. Season to taste with salt and pepper. Add the veggies to the rice and toss to mix. Put the dressing ingredients into a jar and shake well; toss with the rice. This salad can be made a day or two ahead. Cover and refrigerate, bring to room temperature to serve. Serves 6–8.

Corn Dog Muffins

An easy-to-make variation of a carnival classic.

5 hot dogs	1 teaspoon salt
1 cup corn meal	½ teaspoon pepper
1 cup all to purpose flour	1 cup milk
¼ cup sugar	⅓ cup vegetable oil
1 tablespoon baking powder	1 egg

Preheat oven to 400°F. Line 12 muffin pans with paper muffin cups. Cook the hot dogs in boiling water until done. Remove from the heat and allow to cool while you prepare the muffin batter.

Combine all dry ingredients in a large bowl. Measure the milk into a 2-cup or larger measuring cup. Add oil and then crack the egg right into the measuring cup. Whisk the liquid ingredients until well blended. Add the liquid ingredients to the dry and mix until just combined. Slice the hot dogs cross-wise into thin discs and add to the muffin mixture. Mix with a few strokes until dispersed. Spoon batter into the prepared muffin pans. Fill each pan ¾ full. If any cups are left empty, fill them with water to ensure even baking. Bake for 20 minutes or until golden on top. Can be frozen up to two weeks ahead of time. Cool and freeze in freezer bags or airtight containers. Thaw at room temperature before serving. Makes 10–12.

Uncle Salmon Spread

12 ounces cream cheese at room temperature
9 ounces smoked salmon
1½ teaspoons prepared horseradish
3 teaspoons lemon juice
1½ teaspoons fresh dill

Mix all ingredients in a food processor, scraping down the sides as needed. Cover and chill, bring to room temperature before serving with crackers or mini rye bread slices. Makes about 2 cups.

One if by Land, Two if by Sea Kebabs

You can make the kebabs the night before the party and store, covered,
in the fridge in a baking pan.

1 pound steak, cut into 1-inch cubes

2 pounds large raw shrimp

4 pounds assorted veggies: 1 to 1½-inch slices of zucchini,
   thick onion slices, mushrooms, bell peppers

16 bamboo skewers

Honey Glaze (recipe follows)

Soak bamboo skewers in water for about half an hour before you load each one with (in order): 1 piece vegetable; 1 piece shrimp; 1 piece of vegetable; 1 piece steak; 1 piece vegetable; 1 piece shrimp; 1 piece of vegetable. You may want to make some with just veggies, just steak, or just shrimp to accommodate all of your guests' various food quirks.

Honey Glaze

1 cup orange juice

1 cup red wine

¼ cup honey

¼ cup soy sauce

2 tablespoon balsamic vinegar

2 garlic cloves, minced

freshly ground pepper

Bring the orange juice and wine to a boil in a medium saucepan. Boil until reduced by half. Remove from heat. Add remaining ingredients and whisk to combine. Makes 1 cup.

Brush the kebabs with Honey Glaze. Grill until done, brushing with additional glaze while they cook. Makes 16 kebabs.

Red, White, and Blueberry Dessert

This "recipe" is so simple it's a stretch even to call it a recipe, but it's perfect for a backyard barbecue celebration of the Fourth. This is best made the morning of your party and left to chill until you're ready to serve.

3 pints strawberries

3 pints blueberries

2 pints whipping cream

1 teaspoon vanilla

4 teaspoons confectioner's sugar

Rinse the berries in their baskets. Working on a cutting board, hull and quarter the strawberries and put back in their baskets. Set aside. Dump out one basket of blueberries on the cutting board and check for stems and squishy ones, gather them back into the basket and repeat with the second basket. Set aside. Whip the cream by hand or with a mixer until thick and foamy; add vanilla and sugar, and continue whipping until thick and fluffy. Put a layer of whipped cream in a large clear glass or acrylic bowl, add a layer of strawberries. Slather on another layer of whipped cream and a layer of blueberries. Continue layering until your bowl is full or you're out of cream and berries.

If desired, serve with slices of Boston Tea Party Tea Cakes. Makes 10–12 servings.

Boston Tea Party Tea Cakes

2 cups all-purpose flour

1½ teaspoons baking powder

¾ teaspoon salt

1½ cups sugar

¾ cups canola oil

3 eggs

3 tablespoons grated lemon peel

¾ cup milk

Glaze

¹/₂ cup lemon juice   ¹/₄ cup sugar

Preheat oven to 350°F. Butter and flour two 8-by-4-inch loaf pans. Mix the first three ingredients in a large bowl. Combine sugar, oil, eggs, and lemon peel in a mixer bowl, beat for 2 minutes. Add dry ingredients alternately with milk in two batches each. Divide batter between the two pans and bake for 75 minutes, or until a cake tester comes out clean.

While the cakes are baking, prepare the glaze. Stir the lemon juice into the sugar until the sugar is dissolved. Run a knife around the cakes to loosen them from the pan. Brush the glaze over the hot cakes, allowing it to drip over the sides. Cool cakes in their pans. Turn out cooled cakes. You can make these about a week ahead of time. Wrap them tightly in foil and freeze. Thaw and slice to serve. Makes 16 servings.

Quickie Fourth Food Ideas

◎ **Purple Mountain Majesty Potato Salad:** Use those gourmet "Peruvian blue" potatoes in your favorite potato salad recipe.

★ **I Cannot Tell a Lie Cherry Pie:** Buy a cherry pie from a good bakery, but don't lie and say you made it yourself.

◎ **The Redcoats Are Coming:** Set out a cheese tray with those red wax-wrapped Gouda cheeses.

✳ **1776-Bean Salad:** Buy 6 cans of different beans, dump them in a bowl and dress with bottled Italian dressing.

Variations on the Theme

※ **Melting Pot:** Celebrate our nation's cultural diversity by asking each of your guests to bring a dish representing his or her ethnic or national origin. Decorate the party with flags of the world and use this quote from the Reverend Jesse Jackson on your invitation: "Our flag is red, white, and blue, but our nation is a rainbow—red, yellow, brown, black, and white."

★ **Celebrate Your Independence**—Gather your girlfriends for a celebration of individuality. Invite each lady to wear something that reflects her unique personality, a wacky hat, outrageous earrings, or daringly crimson lipstick. Toward the end of the party, have each women write down on a piece of paper one thing that is keeping her from achieving her full independence—ex-husband, student loan, crabby mother-in-law—and then throw the paper into the dying embers of the barbecue.

Let Them Eat Cake: *A Bastille Day Celebration*

If the starving French peasants in 1789 had parties like this one to go to, the revolution would have been abandoned, and Marie Antoinette would have kept her head!

Bastille Day, which commemorates the storming of the Bastille prison by a Parisian mob and the beginning of the bloody French Revolution, is celebrated each July 14 with dancing in the streets, parades, drinking, and eating. That's our kind of partying! So get ready for a soirée that mixes the masses with the upper classes—united by a love of liberty and joie de vivre!

Fascinating Facts about the Guillotine

1. The first evidence of the existence of a guillotine-like machine was one used at an execution in Ireland in 1307.
2. In 1789, during an French Assembly debate about the Penal Code, Dr. Guillotin submitted a proposition recommending that death, without accompanying torture and by means of decapitation, should become the standard form of capital punishment.
3. Marie Antoinette was decapitated on October 16, 1793. After being loaded on an open cart and driven slowly through the streets of Paris for three hours, she mounted the steps to the guillotine platform with her head held high.

4. When Charlotte Corday d'Armont was executed for the murder of Jean-Paul Marat, assistant executioner François Le Gros lifted up the severed head and slashed its cheek, which blushed. Le Gros was sentenced to three months in prison for his breach of scaffold etiquette.

5. In 1932, French prisoner Andre Baillard received clemency after he was already strapped into the bascule at the Santé prison.

6. A law was passed in 1939 decreeing that executions were no longer public.

7. More than 400 applicants applied for the post when the job of executioner became available in France, in 1951.

8. Hamida Djandoubi was the last man executed by the guillotine in France on September 10, 1977.

9. Marcel Chevalier was the last executioner in France. He held the official position from 1976 until the abolition of the death penalty in 1981. Your guess is as good as mine is about how he spent his time after September 10, 1977.

10. In 1981, Philippe Maurice was granted clemency from François Mitterand. Maurice would have been the last person to be guillotined, if the sentence had been executed.

11. A lock of King Louis XVI's hair, harvested just after he was beheaded, sold for $5,536 at an auction in Grenoble, France in 1998.

Invitations

◎ **Headlines:** *Allons enfants de la Patrie*
Le jour de glorie est arrivé!
You won't lose your head at our Bastille Day Celebration . . . unless you really want to.
Celebrate Liberté, Fraternité, and Egalité at our Bastille Day Celebration on July 14.
Respondez, s'îl vous plait.
Dress in your stylish French best.

Decorating Tips

* **Purple Reign:** Marie Antoinette liked the color purple. Use lots of it throughout your house.
* Buy little French flags and use them as decorations.
* Hand-letter or print out banners with a computer graphics program using blue, white, and red ink. One should read, "VIVE LA FRANCE" and the other, "LIBERTÉ, FRATERNITÉ, ET EGALITÉ."
* Display posters of Paris.
* Find Eiffel Tower reproductions. We've spotted inexpensive Eiffel Towel table lamp bases, clocks, blue, white, and red Eiffel Towel candles, and objets d'art made of wire or metal. A great source is the Ballard Designs catalog, (800) 367-2775. In the '80s the trendy shoe store Sasha of London made shoes with inverted Eiffel Towers as heels. These would be the ultimate thrift store find. Use one of your finds as a centerpiece on your blue, white, and red-covered table.
* Order a tin of Madeleines from Dean & Deluca. These come in a "La Tour d'Argent" tin with a view from the famed Paris restaurant. Display these on your table.

Costumes

* Elaborate costumes, à la eighteenth-century French aristocrats with skyscraper coifs and fans
* Culottes and the Revolutionary *cocarde* tricolor pin
* Blue and white striped cotton shirts and tight pants, topped with a beret

Paris wholly has got to the acme of its frenzy; whirled, all ways by panic madness ... into that grand fire-maelstrom which is lashing round the Bastille.

—Thomas Carlyle

Games and Activities

※ **Hire an off-duty French waiter.** Have him look upon your guests with haughty disdain and condescending arrogance and ignore all requests not made in French.

◎ **La Marseillaise:** This holiday is all about nationalism, so have your guests sing along to France's national anthem, "La Marseillaise." Print out the lyrics in French.

★ **Dancin' in the Streets:** Take the party out into the streets. Blast your stereo and create general havoc in your neighborhood.

※ **Set Off Fireworks:** If you have any leftover fireworks from the Fourth of July—that other Independence Day celebration—set them off after dark.

※ **Accent Contest, N'est-ce Pas?:** Have guests compete by speaking in the most outrageous French accents possible. Award a prize to the most elaborate accent. For inspiration, remind guests about the performances of John Cleese in *Monty Python and the Holy Grail* and Kevin Kline in *French Kiss*.

◎ **Play Boules:** Boules (or Pétanque, pronounced "paytonk") is an outdoor bowling game that originated in France and evolved from ancient Greek and Roman games. It is played on any small area of bare ground with small metallic balls and a smaller, wooden ball used as the market ball (cochonnet). It can be played anywhere. The great thing about this game is that it can easily be played with a drink in one hand! If you live on a cul de sac or a street that doesn't have a lot of traffic, set it up outside; otherwise you can play it on your lawn. Here's how to play:

1. The game is played singles, doubles, or triples. In singles and doubles each player uses three boules, but in triples only two boules.
2. The starting team is decided by the toss of a coin. One member of the team chooses the starting place and draws on the ground a circle in which to stand. Both feet of the thrower must remain inside the circle till the boule lands.

3. The first thrower throws the cochonnet between six and ten paces away from obstacles.

4. She then throws her first boule trying to place it as near as possible to the cochonnet.

5. A player in the other team then comes into the circle and tries to throw her boule nearer to the cochonnet, or knock away the leading boule. The boule nearest to the cochonnet leads.

6. Then it is up to a player in the team not leading to throw until her team gets a leading boule, and so on.

7. When a team has no more boules the players of the other team throw theirs and try to place them as close as possible to the cochonnet.

8. When both teams have no more boules the points are counted. The winning team gets as many points as it has boules nearer than the best of the losing team.

9. A player of the winning team throws the cochonnet from where it is, and the game starts again until one team reaches thirteen points.

The only really essential equipment is a set of three steel boules. To be legitimate for competition play, a boule must conform to the following specifications: Weight: 650–800 grams (1 pound 7 ounces–1 pound 12 ounces) Diameter: 70.5–80.0mm (2¾ inches–3⅛ inches).

To purchase Boules: European Sporting Goods, Inc., (800) 68 BALLS, or (305) 591-7060 in Florida.

Throughout the world, there are many outdoor games that have as their central activity the competitive pitching of a heavy ball along the ground so as to arrive closer to a target than one's opponent. The English have their lawn bowling, which is played on a manicured lawn and has several sub-types. The Italians have their bocce; the South Slavs their Balinaje.

Of all these games, the French game pétanque is the most aggressive and is played by more people all over the world than any other.

Favors and Prizes

- ★ Give everyone a bottle of French red wine, tied at the neck with blue, white, and red ribbons.
- ◎ A French-English dictionary.

Musical Suggestions

- ✳ *Songs of Paris and Others,* Yves Montand
- ★ Anything by Edith Piaf
- ◎ *The French Album,* Celine Dion
- ★ "I Love Paris," Michel Legrand
- ✳ "Paris Midnight," Liane and the Boheme Bar.
- ✳ "La Boheme," Charles Aznavour.
- ◎ "Voulez-vous Coucher Avec Moi," Lady Marmalade

According to a report by Benjamin Franklin, Marie Antoinette, King Louis, and their family were very well fed during their imprisonment by the French National Convention in 1792. Here's one repast:
Dinner consisted of three soups, four entrées, three roast dishes, each of three pieces, four sweet courses, a plate of fancy cakes, three compotes, three dishes of fruit, three loaves of bread with butter, one bottle of Champagne, one small carafe of Bordeaux, one of Malvoisie, one of Madeira, and four cups of coffee.

Food

What better way to honor the aristocracy who lost their heads during the French revolution than by serving food with heads and headless food? These French recipes are absolutely heady! Bon Appetit!

Calamari Salad (without heads)

You can make this ahead of time and refrigerate, covered, for one or two days.

¾ pound frozen cleaned squid, tentacles and rings
3 ribs celery, cut into ⅛-inch slices
½ red onion, diced
¼ teaspoon oregano
¼ teaspoon red pepper flakes
2 cloves garlic, minced
⅓ cup coarsely chopped Italian parsley leaves
1 teaspoon salt
1 tablespoon olive oil
1 tablespoon lemon juice
butter lettuce leaves for serving

Mix squid, celery, onion, oregano, and red pepper in pot on stove. Cook over low heat for 5 minutes. In a small bowl, combine garlic, parsley, salt, oi,l and lemon juice and combine well with warm, cooked squid. Place on top of butter lettuce leaves. Serve at room temperature. Makes 2 cups.

Artichoke Heads

These can be steamed ahead of time, and served at room temperature.

8 medium-to-large globe artichokes	1 teaspoon kosher salt
2 teaspoons fresh lemon juice	¾ cup water

Trim artichokes by removing brown outside leaves. Slice ⅛-inch off the bottom and ¼-inch off the top. Slightly fan open the top leaves. Sprinkle with lemon juice and salt. Boil water in a large pan and place artichokes upright in pan. Cover tightly and steam for 45 minutes. Allow to cool. Arrange on a large platter and serve with melted butter. Serves 8.

Roasted Garlic Heads

4 heads fresh garlic, loose outer skin removed	2 sprigs fresh rosemary ¼ cup extra virgin olive oil

Preheat oven to 400°F. Cut off the stem and the top one fifth of the heads of garlic. Place them on a large piece of heavy-duty aluminum foil. Place the rosemary sprigs across the top of the cut heads. Drizzle with olive oil. Close up the aluminum foil and seal the edges tightly. Roast for 1 hour or until the garlic is tender. Remove the package from the oven, open carefully, and let the contents cool slightly. Serve with sliced French baguettes.

The lowly potato was not a popular vegetable in France during the reign of Louis XVI. A French agricul-turalist, Antoine-Augustin Parmentier, was convinced that the potato could play a major role in solving the country's food shortages. How to make potato consumption en vogue? Prior to the French Revolution, he sent Louis XVI a bouquet of potato flowers for his birthday. Marie Antoinette put some in her hair, sparking the trendy practice of sticking these blossoms in one's lapel or hair, and the potato was on its way to becoming a staple in France.

Head of Lettuce Salad

Serve whole butter lettuce heads intact. Have a gravy boat filled with vinaigrette on the side for guests to help themselves.

Vinaigrette

¼ cup balsamic vinegar
1 cup extra virgin olive oil

½ teaspoon Dijon mustard
salt and pepper to taste

Whisk ingredients until well blended.

Quiche Lorraine

Pastry Shell

I cup butter, chilled	I egg, slightly beaten
3 1/2 cups all-purpose flour	1/4 cup vegetable oil
1/4 teaspoon salt	1/2 cup cold water

Filling

4 slices bacon, chopped	1/2 teaspoon salt
I onion, chopped	dash of cayenne
2 tablespoons all-purpose flour	2 cups (8 ounces) shredded Swiss cheese
I 1/2 cups milk	2 tablespoons flour
4 eggs, slightly beaten	

Cut chilled butter into 1/2-inch slices. In a medium bowl, combine flour and salt. Use a pastry blender to cut in butter slices until mixture resembles oatmeal; set aside. In a small bowl, combine egg, oil, and water. Using a fork, stir egg mixture into flour mixture until evenly distributed. Divide dough in half, shape into two balls. Wrap in plastic wrap or foil. Refrigerate at least I hour.

In a medium skillet, sauté bacon and onion until most of fat is cooked out of bacon, 7–10 minutes. Remove from heat, drain. Stir flour into drained bacon mixture.

On a lightly floured surface, roll out pastry to a 17-by-12-inch rectangle. Fit onto an ungreased 15-by-10-inch baking sheet with raised sides. Turn under and crimp edge of pastry.

Sprinkle half of the cheese over the crust. Mix together the remaining ingredients and pour over quiche. Bake until firm, about 45 minutes. To serve, cut into small squares. Makes approximately 50 appetizers.

Whole Poached Salmon (with head)

This can be cooked the day before, and served at room temperature.

3–4 pound whole salmon

2 quarts water

2 cups dry white wine

1 bay leaf

½ teaspoons salt

In a fish poacher or pan big enough to hold the fish, combine the poaching liquid by adding water, wine, bay leaf, and salt. Simmer for 30 minutes. Add the fish on a poaching rack or wrapped in a double thickness of cheesecloth. Measure the fish at its thickest point, and then poach for 10 minutes per inch. When fish is cooked, remove from stock and reserve for another use. Carefully remove skin from the top of fish while it is still warm by taking a sharp knife and cutting through the skin all along the backbone. With the tip of your knife, tease out the dorsal fin (the one along the backbone) and the backbone. With a pair of scissors, cut through the skin at the tail end of the fish and at the head. Gently pull skin off, working from the backbone side toward the belly flaps and from head to tail. Discard skin. Refrigerate.

Serving the fish: When your guests have eaten the top layer, lift the big central bone and the tail end and remove, leaving the bottom portion.

Fruit Gâteau

After all that rich French food, let them eat this light sponge cake decorated to look like—what else—heads!

2 layers of Genoise (recipe follows)

2 cups assorted fresh fruit (peaches, sliced strawberries, apricot halves, grapes)

Glaze (recipe follows)

whipped cream

Makes two "heads."

Genoise

6 large eggs

1 cup sugar

1 cup sifted flour

½ cup sweet butter, melted and clarified

1 teaspoon butter

Preheat oven to 350°F degrees. Grease and lightly flour two 9-inch layer cake tins.

In a large bowl combine eggs and sugar. Stir until combined. Set bowl over a saucepan containing 2 inches of hot (not boiling) water. Place saucepan containing bowl over low heat for 5 minutes, or until eggs are lukewarm, lightly stirring 2 or 3 times to prevent them from cooking at the bottom of the bowl. When eggs look like a bright yellow syrup, remove bowl from heat. Beat with an electric mixer for 10–15 minutes, scraping sides with a rubber spatula when necessary, until syrup becomes light, fluffy, and cool. It should triple in bulk. (If you are beating by hand, it will take about 25 minutes.)

Sprinkle flour on top of the whipped eggs. Fold in gently, adding slightly cooled, clarified butter and vanilla. Do not overmix. Pour batter into prepared pans. Bake for 25–30 minutes, or until cakes pull away from sides of pans and are golden brown and springy when touched lightly on top. Remove from pans and cool on rack.

Arrange fruit to make "faces" on top of each spongecake layer. Spoon glaze evenly over fruit. Let set 30 minutes. Use whipped cream to make "hair."

Glaze

1 tablespoon corn starch	1 tablespoon lemon juice
1 cup apple juice	

In a small saucepan mix together corn starch, apple juice, and lemon juice. Stirring constantly, bring to boil over medium heat and boil 1 minute. Cool. Makes 1 cup.

August

Oh My Goddess, Let's Party!

Make no mistake; this is not a Toga Party. This is an official Goddess Party, sanctioned by the high and mighty. Party Girls *are* goddesses. According to Margie Lapanja, author of *Goddess in the Kitchen*, a kitchen goddess is a luminary; a person who enlightens others through her grace and craft; a woman whose charm and cooking arouses adoration.

Adoration is fine, but worship is even better. So throw this party to honor the immortal Goddess spirit in all of us. When your guests arrive, make sure to greet each one with reverence and graciously welcome them into your Temple.

Invitations

◎ Type the invitation details on a piece of paper, make copies and attach them at an angle onto a parchment scrolls. You can buy parchment paper from an art supply store. Tear rough edges on the top and bottom of the parchment paper by hand. Roll it up and tie gold elastic braid around it. These can be placed in mailing tubes and mailed, or delivered by a hired messenger wearing wings on his Nikes.

✳ **Headline:** *A Party Fit for the Goddesses (and Gods)*

Copy: *Join us at the Temple of the Goddess (your name here) for a Greco-Roman Feast*

Wear Formal Olympian Attire.
Headpieces Will Be Provided.

Decorating Tips

◎ Float rose petals in large cut-crystal bowls.

✳ Place potpourri in bowls throughout the house containing rosemary, lavender, sage, and thyme leaves.

★ Fill your living area with couches, if you can borrow some from your neighbors. If not, place lots of pillows on the floor. Use white, lacy pillowcases.

✺ Use your Cupid statuettes and mobiles from Valentine's Day. Track down statuettes of goddesses and make small shrines by placing flowers at the base of each.

✳ Place lots of potted palms around the party rooms. Buy grapevines and twine the leaves across your fireplace mantle.

◎ Videotape *Xena* episodes and play them throughout the evening.

★ Place lots of white, silver, and gold candles throughout the house. Display lots of vases and urns, preferably ones made of silver, or with Greco-Roman motifs.

✳ Create a low dining table by placing a piece of plywood across sturdy crates. Cover the table with a white sheet or tablecloth. Put lots of candlesticks on the table.

◎ For the pièce de résistance, make a Greco/Roman temple!

Here are the instructions for a tabletop centerpiece-sized temple, but you can make them in any size.

You need:

2 8-by-10-inch sheets of corrugated paper	masking tape
1 6-by-8-inch sheet of corrugated paper	white glue or glue gun
2 7-inch corrugated cardboard circles	newspaper

2 6-inch corrugated cardboard circles

10 2-inch corrugated cardboard circles

3 irregular cardboard shapes in three sizes,
    the largest about 5½-by-3½-inch

white paint

flour and water

First roll the sheets of corrugated paper into thin columns 1½-inches in diameter. Secure with tape. Cut off the top of the 6-inch column at a slight angle—fill in the hole in the slanted opening with newspaper.

Glue each of the cardboard circles together in pairs. Glue the irregular pieces on top of each other.

Now start to erect the temple! Center the 6-inch circle in the 7-inch circle and glue in place. Glue three of the 2-inch circles in a triangle shape on the 6-inch circle. Glue the columns to the three 2-inch circles and secure with tape. Top the 10-inch columns with 2-inch circles. Glue the stacked irregular piece across the top of the 10-inch columns. If you're using white glue, let the whole thing dry overnight.

Paint the temple with white paint—bottled, canned, or spray.

When the paint is dry, mix up a thick paste of flour and water. Smear it unevenly all over the temple.

When the temple is dry, touch it up again with white paint. After the second coat of paint dries, decorate with vines and bunches of grapes.

Costumes

※ Everyone should come dressed as a goddess or a god. The women can wear a draped sheet, tied at the waist with a thin gold rope. Or they can drape the sheet over one shoulder and tie a sash under their breasts. The men can wear "togas."

When guests arrive, place headbands on their heads—gold elastic braid or flower headwreaths for the women, and crowns of bay laurel for the men.

◎ Have guests come dressed as their favored goddess/muse. Artemis, Goddess of the Hunt, would wear leather shorts and a halter top with sandals; Demeter and Persephone would have laurels in their hair and carry baskets of fruit; Aphrodite, Goddess of Love, would be naked (!); and Nike, Messenger of the Gods, would wear her Nikes. (If a lot of guests arrive in Aphrodite garb, you may end up with another type of party altogether.)

Games and Activities

✳ **Serving the Goddess:** Ask male friends to come bare-chested and get them to help serve food and feed the grapes to the goddesses. The Number 1 rule is, No Goddess' request can be refused, or else the person who refuses the request risks severe punishment.

★ **A Toast to the Goddess:** The Romans were famous for their toasts. Ask everyone to take a turn making a toast to one of the goddesses in attendance.

◎ **Goddess Lore:** Test your guests' knowledge of mythology. Ask them to fill out this quiz and give a prize to the person with the highest score.

1. *Venus or Aphrodite is the goddess of* _____ ?
2. *What month is named after the Greek Goddess of spring and rebirth?*
3. *Which goddess searched for her abducted daughter Persephone?*
4. *Who was the God of wine and which festival of drunken debauchery is named after him?*
5. *Who was the Roman Goddess of the forest, the moon, and the hunt?*
6. *What is the name of the beautiful horse with wings?*
7. *Name the nine muses.*
8. *Who was the Greek Goddess of wisdom and justice?*

Answers: 1) love; 2) May/Maia; 3) Demeter; 4) Bacchus; 5) Diana; 6) Pegasus; 7) Calliope (epic song), Clio (history), Euterpe (lyric song), Thalia (comedy), Melpomene (tragedy), Terpsichore (dance), Erato (erotic poetry), Polyhymnia (sacred hymns), and Urania (astronomy); 8) Athena.

◎ **Guess the Number of Grapes:** Place a large bunch of grapes in a glass bowl. Ask guests to guess the number of grapes in the bowl. Record their guesses, and award a prize to the one who comes the closest.

Favors and Prizes

✳ An Olympic metal or trophy.

◎ Each guest can take home a homemade headwreath. Make simple flower and herb wreaths for the women, and bay laurel headpieces for the men.

✦ Copies of books including the Iliad or the *Odyssey* by Homer, *Goddesses in Everywomen* by Jean Shinoda Bolen, and *Goddess in the Kitchen* by Margie Lapanja.

Musical Suggestions

✳ The soundtrack from *The Clash of the Titans*, featuring Laurence Rosenthal conducting the London Symphony Orchestra

◎ "Hymns to the Goddess," Bob Kindler

✳ "Venus," Shocking Blue or the Bananarama remake

✦ "Diana," Paul Anka

◎ "Cupid," Sam Cooke

Food

Watercress Salad with Green Goddess Dressing

The dressing can be made two to three days ahead and stored in the refrigerator.

1 1/2 cups mayonnaise

1/2 cup sour cream

7 anchovy fillets, mashed

1 teaspoon fresh lemon juice

2 tablespoons minced fresh tarragon leaves

2 tablespoons minced fresh chives

1/2 cup chopped fresh Italian parsley

1/4 cup tarragon vinegar

1 clove garlic, minced

1/4 teaspoon kosher salt

freshly ground black pepper, to taste

4 bunches watercress, coarse stems removed, rinsed, spun dry

2 cucumbers, peeled, seeded and chopped

3 cups cherry tomatoes, halved if large.

Combine first 11 ingredients in a food processor and process until smooth. Drizzle on top of tossed watercress, cucumbers, and tomatoes. Makes 2 1/4 cups.

Greek Olive Spread

This can be made up to four weeks in advance.

3 cups Kalamata olives, pitted   ⅓ cup extra-virgin olive oil

Coarsely chop the olives in a food processor. Add the oil in a steady stream until you have a smooth purée. Store in a tightly covered container in the refrigerator.

Roman Crostini

This can be made in advance and served at room temperature.

1 Italian baguette loaf cut in thin slices   4 garlic cloves, peeled
½ cup extra-virgin olive oil

Brush both sides of the sliced bread with olive oil. Lay slices on cookie sheet and bake in oven until golden. Remove from oven and lightly rub the whole peeled garlic cloves on one side of the bread. Serves 10.

Moussaka

A dish fit for Greek Goddesses. Make it early in the day, brown just before serving.

3 pounds eggplant
2 tablespoons kosher salt plus 1 teaspoon
½ cup extra-virgin olive oil

3 cups onions, finely chopped

1 tablespoon finely minced garlic

1 pound ground lamb

¼ cup white wine

1 14-ounce can tomato puree

1 bay leaf

1 teaspoon dried thyme

1 teaspoon crumbled dried oregano

2 tablespoons Italian parsley, chopped

½ cup butter

½ cup flour

5 cups warmed milk (not boiled)

salt and ground white pepper to taste

1 ¼ cup bread crumbs

6 tablespoons Parmigiano-Reggiano cheese

Slice eggplants into ¼-inch rounds. Salt well and set in a single layer on paper towels. Set aside to bleed for 30 minutes. Pat dry. Heat ¼ cup oil in a large skilled and lightly sauté eggplant slices for 3–4 minutes on each side; set aside.

In a large saucepan, sauté onions and garlic in ¼ cup heated olive oil for 5 minutes. Increase heat to high, and add the ground lamb. Cook until well browned, about 10 minutes. Drain fat from pan. Reduce heat to low and add wine, tomato puree, bay leaf, thyme, oregano, chopped parsley, and 1 teaspoon salt. Mix well and simmer, uncovered for 30 minutes.

In a separate saucepan make béchamel sauce: melt ½ cup butter over low heat. Add flour, 1 tablespoon at a time, whisking well after each addition. Cook gently for 2–3 minutes. Add hot milk slowly, whisking constantly, and cook over low heat for about 20 minutes, or until the sauce has the consistency of thick cream. Add salt to taste and ground white pepper.

Butter a 5-quart casserole. Sprinkle ½ cup of the bread crumbs on the bottom of it. Layer half the eggplant slices over the bread crumbs. Cover with half the lamb mixture. Cover with 3 tablespoons of the Parmigiano-Reggiano cheese and ¼ cup bread crumbs. Add the remaining eggplant slices, then top with the béchamel sauce. Sprinkle with remaining cheese and bread crumbs. Dot with remaining butter.

Bake in a preheated 350°F oven for 50 minutes. Before serving, brown the top by setting under broiler for 3–4 minutes. Let sit for 10 minutes. Cut into squares. Serves 8–10.

Glittery Grapes

Use these for the "Serving the Goddess" activity described above. They look really elegant!

1 3-ounce package any flavor gelatin	½ cup ice cubes
½ cup boiling water	12 small clusters seedless grapes

Divide gelatin equally into two bowls. Take one bowl and dissolve gelatin in ½ cup of boiling water. Add ice cubes and stir until ice melts. Dip grape clusters in liquid gelatin mixture and shake off excess moisture. Make sure your hands are dry. Using your fingers, sprinkle remaining gelatin powder over grapes. Place clusters in 12 small bowls. Makes 12 clusters.

Ambrosia

fresh coconut	2 bananas, sliced
5 oranges, peeled and sectioned	½ cup pecans, coarsely broken
1 can crushed pineapple, with juice	sugar to taste

1 can fruit cocktail, with juice

2 apples, chopped

cherries for garnish

Grate coconut in bowl. Add oranges, pineapple, fruit cocktail, apples, bananas, and nuts. Sweeten with sugar, being careful not to add too much as the syrup from the fruit is usually sufficient. Chill before serving. Serve in a crystal bowl. Serves 8.

Angel Food Cake

1 1/4 cup sifted cake flour

1/2 cup sugar

egg whites from 12 eggs (at room temperature)

1/4 teaspoon salt

1 1/4 teaspoons cream of tartar

1 teaspoon vanilla extract

1/4 teaspoon almond extract

1 1/3 cups sugar

Sift flour with 1/2 cup sugar 4 times. Combine egg whites, salt, cream of tartar, and extracts in large bowl. Beat with a flat wire whip, rotary beater, or high-speed electric mixer until soft peaks form. Add 1 1/3 cups sugar, sprinkling in 1/3 cup at a time and beating until blended after each addition, about 25 strokes by hand. Sift in flour mixture in four additions, folding in with 15 complete foldover strokes after each addition and turning bowl often. After last addition, use 10–20 extra strokes. Pour into an ungreased 10-inch tube pan. Bake at 375°F for 35–40 minutes, or until the top springs back when pressed lightly. Invert on rack and cool thoroughly. Then remove from pan and frost. Serve with Heavenly Butter Cream Frosting (recipe follows).

Heavenly Butter Cream Frosting

1/2 cup butter	1 egg
1/8 teaspoon salt	1 teaspoon vanilla
1 pound unsifted confectioner's sugar	2 tablespoons milk

Cream butter and salt; gradually add sugar in parts, blending well after each addition. Stir in egg and vanilla. Add remaining sugar alternately with milk, until of spreading consistency, beating after each addition until smooth. Makes 2 1/2 cups.

Drinks

Serve Greek Ouzo and Italian wines.

Ambrosia Punch

1 20-ounce can crushed pineapple, undrained
1 15-ounce can of Coco Lopez cream of coconut
2 cups apricot nectar, chilled
2 cups orange juice, chilled
1 1/2 cups light rum
1 liter club soda, chilled

In a blender, purée pineapple and cream of coconut until smooth. In a punch bowl, combine the purée, nectar, juice, and rum. Mix well. Just before serving, add club soda and serve over ice. Serves 12.

Variations on the Theme

★ **Midnight Sun Party/Summer Solstice:** Check an almanac to find out when the full moon falls.

✳ Tie your Goddess Party to an ancient celebration. Here are some ideas:

January 8: Midwives' Day. This is the day set aside for honoring midwives—the helpers for ancient goddesses who watched over women in childbirth. A good day to host a baby shower.

January 11: Carmentalia. Carmenta was a goddess of prophecy and childbirth. Pregnant women and new mothers visited her shrine on her festival day, where they would learn of their new babies' fortunes. No males were permitted to enter this goddess' temple. She also didn't permit killing animals for food. On this day, invite new mothers over for a vegetarian feast, and read each child's horoscope.

February 13: Parentalia. A Roman holiday dedicated to honoring those dead and gone. This holiday lasted nine days, during which time people visited their parents' graves with offerings such as milk, wine, honey, oil, and spring water. They decked the graves with roses and violets. On this day, invite your orphaned friends over for a session of remembrance and ceremonial offerings to their departed loves ones.

February 22: Caristia. On this date, ancient Romans honored those still living. Concordia, the peace goddess, ruled over this holiday. Ovid explains that on Caristia, "A crowd of relations comes. . . . Sweet it is, no doubt, to recall our thoughts to the living after they have dwelt upon the grave and on the dear ones departed from us; sweet, too, after so many departed, to look upon those of our blood who are left, and to count kin with them." What an excellent day to have a family reunion! Invite family members, especially any who are squabbling. Set out olive branches and have a feast. Go around the room and ask each person to describe what qualities they appreciate in each other.

March 5: Isis Festival. On this day, honor the goddess Isis, the sailors' patroness and inventor of the sail, by inviting your friends to go sailing. Ancient Roman celebrations included loading a boat with spices and other offerings, and setting it out to sea.

April 12: Cerelia. Ceres was the Roman grain goddess. The poet Ovid explains how to celebrate this holiday. "You may give the goddess splet, and the compliment of salt, and grains of incense. . . . Good Ceres is content with little, if that little be but pure. White is Ceres' proper color; put on white robes at Ceres' festival." You must serve cereal and different kinds of bread.

April 28: Floralia. This is a fun one. The prostitutes of Rome chose Flora as their own personal goddess. She was a goddess of flowers and fertility. Your guests should drape themselves with flower leis. You can rent and show an erotic video, and give away vibrators or sex toys as favors.

June 9: Vestalia. The Goddess Vesta was a fire goddess. Only women were permitted to enter Vesta's temple. There they asked the goddess' blessing on their families and offered her food that they had baked in their own ovens. They were welcomed by the goddess' priestesses: the Vestal Virgins. On this day, have a barbecue and ask each guest to bring a yummy baked dessert.

June 14: Birthday of the Muses. Yep, even the Muses had a mother. She was the Goddess Mnemosyne (memory), who was herself a Muse. Host a "Mother's Night Out" by inviting all the mothers you know for cocktails and reminiscing.

August 19: Vinalia. A wonderful day to host a wine-tasting party in honor of the love goddess Venus. On this day every year, the Roman vintner's fire-ripe grapes were plucked. Ancient Romans invoked Venus on this day. You can have a love fest (see suggestions in "Valentine's Day Red Party" section) and drink lots of wine.

Super Sheroes Extravaganza

Get your girlfriends together for a party celebrating powerful women superheroes. (Boy Wonder sidekicks can be invited, too.) Let's pay homage to all those fearless, crime-stopping females that have helped save the world from evil forces.

Have no fear—this party will rock 'em, sock 'em, and leap over tall buildings in a single bound. (Hopefully your guests won't.)

Invitations

* **Headlines:** POW! KAZAM! Join Us for an Action-Packed Evening
* Create a comic book cover. Write SUPER SHEROES PARTY in perspective lettering across the top of the page. Scan in an image of a super shero from a comic book cover. Replace the shero's face with a same-sized image of your face. Draw a big dialogue balloon, and type the invitation details in the balloon. Make color copies at your local copy store.

Decorating Tips

* Spread copies of comic books around your house. You can buy loads of them for next to nothing at comic conventions.

◎ Draw or paint silhouettes of city skylines at dusk on poster-sized paper and tack to wall.

★ Put up posters of any of the following Super Sheroes (from comics or television): Xena: Warrior Princess; Sheena: Queen of the Jungle; Batgirl; Spidergirl; Wonder Woman; Supergirl; Catwoman; InvisibleGirl; Vampirella; Bionic Woman; Barbarella; Marvel Girl, The Wasp; and Tank Girl.

✳ Place action figures throughout your house—you can purchase these from a local toy store, or better yet, borrow some from your neighbors' children.

★ Purchase spider web material from your local party supply store (this stuff is ubiquitous at Halloween, but you may have to search for it at other times).

◎ In huge black ink perspective lettering, write "POW," "KAZAM," "SPLAT," and "WHACK!" Then pin or tape these exclamations on your walls.

✴ Drape capes, masks, and other disguise paraphernalia around chandeliers, lamps, and other places.

Costumes

◎ Sleeveless catsuits with any and all of the following accessories: long white gloves, thigh high boots, black mask, cape, thick belt.

✳ You can purchase a Supergirl, Catwoman, or Xena costume online or at a local costume store.

★ Superwoman or Superman T-shirts.

✳ Librarian-by-day outfit.

Games and Activities

★ **Super-Match Quiz:** Award a prize to the person who can match each super shero with the actress who first portrayed her on the screen.

1. **Emma Peel**
2. **Barbarella**
3. **Batgirl**
4. **Bionic Woman**
5. **Wonder Woman**
6. **Xena**
7. **Sheena: Queen of the Jungle**
8. **Buffy the Vampire Slayer**

Answers: 1) *Diana Rigg;* 2) *Jane Fonda;* 3) *Yvonne Craig;* 4) *Lindsay Wagner;* 5) *Lynda Carter;* 6) *Lucy Lawless;* 7) *Irish McCalla;* 8) *Sarah Michelle Gellar.*

◎ **Comic Writing Contest:** Ask everyone to write the first paragraph of an imaginary comic (for example, "A long time ago in a galaxy, far, far, away," which comes from *Star Wars*), and then have everyone read hers or his aloud.

✳ **Nominate Your Favorite Shero:** Put out ballots asking everyone to vote for their favorite local shero. Preselect five sheroes, representing beloved women leaders in your community—politicians, activists, teachers, corporate leaders. Develop an award certificate on your computer. The wording can read, "In honor of your accomplishments, you have been elected Shero of the Year." After the ballots are tallied, write in the name of the honoree. Have everyone sign the certificate. Send this to your local shero along with a group photo. We're sure she'll be tickled.

Favors and Prizes

◎ Comic books, of course.

✳ Power Bars! Display a bunch of power bars, and give each Super Shero and Super Hero one to help her or him keep up their strength.

✻ A copy of *Sheroes: Bold, Brash (and Absolutely Unabashed) Superwomen* by Varla Ventura.

✦ Borrow a scanner from one of your freelance graphic designer friends. Take Polaroids of everyone in costume, and ask someone to scan the photos and insert them into a template that looks like the cover of a comic. Then print out a color page and give it to your friends as a favor.

Musical Suggestions

◎ "Heroes," David Bowie

✻ "Superman," Kinks

✦ Music from the *Batman Movie*, U-2.

◎ "Super Heroes," *Rocky Horror Picture Show* soundtrack

✻ "Superman's Song," Crash Test Dummies

Food

This menu is designed to give your powerful guests the strength to make it through the night. If anyone's energy field begins to dim, hand her or him a Power Smoothie with boosters and a Kryptonite Krunchie. You may not conquer the universe this evening, but you'll win the war against boring parties for all time.

Defeat-The-Deviled Eggs

You can make the filling a day in advance, and stuff the eggs up to two hours before the party. For a little additional flavor, top each egg with a thin slice of black olive, or a single leaf of Italian parsley.

12 large eggs, hard cooked and peeled

¾ cup mayonnaise

3 teaspoons mustard, preferably Dijon

salt to taste

pinch cayenne pepper

paprika

Boil eggs for approximately 10 minutes. Place in ice water to cool, and to make them easier to peel. After peeling, slice each egg in half and remove the yolks. Mash the yolks with the mayonnaise, mustard, and a pinch of the salt and pepper until smooth.

You can spoon the filling into the yolks, or pipe it with a pastry bag. Sprinkle with a little paprika and serve at room temperature. Makes 24 pieces.

"Soup-er Woman" Spinach Soup

3 tablespoons butter

1 small onion, chopped

2 pounds spinach,
washed, stemmed, and chopped

2 tablespoons flour

4 cups low-fat milk

4 cups chicken broth

Salt and pepper

½ teaspoon paprika

4 green onions, finely diced

Melt the butter in a stockpot. Sauté the onion for 5 minutes, until soft. Add spinach and sauté for 5 more minutes, until limp. Blend in a food processor or blender until smooth. In the stockpot, add flour. Stir in spinach, milk, and broth and heat until hot. Season with salt and pepper to taste. Sprinkle with paprika and chopped green onions. Makes 10 cups.

Shero Sandwiches

You can make these a few hours before the party starts.

2 loaves sweet French or Italian bread,
   sliced lengthwise
¼ cup extra-virgin olive oil
8 balls fresh mozzarella cheese, sliced

8 ripe Roma tomatoes, sliced
32 whole basil leaves
salt and fresh ground pepper to taste

Spoon a teaspoon of olive oil on each side of the four slices of bread. Slice the mozzarella cheese into ¼ inch slices. Place slices of cheese, tomatoes, and basil leaves on bread slice. Sprinkle salt and pepper on top, cover with top half of bread, and cut into 1½ to 2-inch pieces. Makes 16 servings.

Super Spicy Noodle Salad

Are your super-guests strong enough to handle this dish? Make it in the morning and serve at room temperature.

1 pound soba noodles
½ cup peanut butter
½ cup warm water
⅓ cup soy sauce
4 tablespoons rice wine vinegar
1½ tablespoons dark sesame oil

2½ teaspoons hot chili oil
4 cups fresh mung bean sprouts
2 cucumbers, peeled, cut lengthwise,
   seeded and cut in slices
chopped green onions

Cook the noodles *al dente* in a pot of boiling water. Drain and rinse with cold water. In a blender or food processor, mix the peanut butter, warm water, soy sauce, vinegar, and oils. Toss the noodles with the bean sprouts, cucumbers, and sauce. Top with chopped green onions. Serve on a platter over crisp romaine lettuce leaves. Serves 10–12.

Kryptonite Krunchies

This is an easy-to-make crunchy crisp treat that will help fortify our fighting femmes in their battles against evil.

1 6-ounce package semisweet chocolate pieces
¼ cup super chunk peanut butter
2⅓ cups corn flakes
⅓ cup dry roasted peanuts

In a 1-quart saucepan, stir together chocolate pieces and peanut butter. Cook over low heat until melted. Stir in corn flakes and nuts. Drop by teaspoonfuls onto waxed paper. Cool 15–20 minutes or until set. Makes about 32 1½ inch cookies.

Power Smoothies

Make these two colorful smoothies in advance and store them in pitchers in your refrigerator. On your beverage table, offer a variety of "boosters." You can purchase these supplements in any health food store in powder or liquid form. Put each booster in a small bowl and label it.

Boosters

Bee Pollen	Protein Powder
Wheat Bran	Soybean powder
Brewer's Yeast	Spirulina
Ginseng	Wheat Germ
Lecithin	Vitamin C

Berry Blast

2 cups low-fat strawberry yogurt

1 cup cranberry juice

3 cups fresh strawberries,
  hulled, quartered, and frozen

2 cups fresh raspberries, frozen

6 ice cubes

The fresh fruit should be frozen in plastic storage bags overnight. Crush the ice cubes in a blender, then add the yogurt and cranberry juice. Add the strawberries and raspberries, and blend until smooth. Serves 5.

Wonder Woman Smoothie

2 cups orange juice

2 cups fresh strawberries,
  hulled, quartered, and frozen

4 fresh bananas, frozen and sliced

2 cups fresh mango, diced and frozen

6 ice cubes

Freeze the fresh fruit overnight in a plastic storage bag. Crush the ice cube in a blender, then add the rest of the ingredients. Blend until smooth. Serves 5.

September

Party of the Decade:
A Twentieth-Century Retrospective

The cheese ball is a necessity for modern entertaining.

> —**Mary Meade's Magic Recipes for the Electric Blender** (1956)

This party theme lives up to its billing. Years after Nina threw this event, her friends were still talking about how much fun they had. We are going to turn one hundred years of history into one great party theme—The Greatest Party of All Time. Your friends will appreciate their wide range of choices. Everybody has something in their closet they can wear—that vintage flapper dress or Jacqueline Kennedy sheath they've been saving for a special occasion. Your duller friends can just come dressed as themselves, and run the risk of looking quite goofy.

Invitations

◎ Find a computer art image of an elegantly dressed dancing couple. Design an invitation, with two on a page. Color copy it onto white cardstock paper. Cut in half using a paper cutter. Fold in half and insert in fancy, gold trimmed envelopes.

Headline: *Party of the Decade, or A Twentieth-Century Retrospective*
Copy: *Come Dressed as Your Favorite Decade*

In the background of the recording on your answering machine, play sounds from the past, such as Frank Sinatra or the Supremes. Invitees will immediately get it, and it will add to the anticipation. The uninvited will remain clueless.

Decorating Tips

◎ To set the proper tone, see if you can borrow or rent display cars from previous decades and park them in front of your house. These can be used later as photo props.

✳ Use '50s, '60s, and '70s motifs to decorate three different rooms in your house. For inspiration, rent videos from each era. Here are some ideas:

THE '50S

Borrow "antiques" from your grandmother, or scout out thrift stores for stand-up ashtrays. Display pinup posters.

THE '60S

Hang a wooden bead curtain from one of your door frames. Lava lamps are obtainable almost anywhere these days. Go to your local "head shop" for other '60s paraphernalia, such as water pipes or psychedelic posters. Look around for artwork featuring Peter Max designs, RPM picture sleeves of '60s tunes, or anything featuring antiwar slogans. There is a company online at **http://www.concertposter. com** that sells original vintage psychedelic rock concert posters from Winterland, Fillmore West, the Avalon Ballroom, and more. You can also purchase an original theater poster from the Broadway production *Hair*, and the Woodstock poster is in its second printing. Buy a blacklight from any drugstore. You can also purchase incense sticks and the incense boats to burn them in. Printed Indian or Pakistani bedspreads can be used as tapestries. Tie-dye a plain white top sheet and use as a wall hanging.

THE '70S

You can go the Studio 54 glitteratti route. If you choose to decorate your entry hall or main room in '70s kitsch, start the excitement outside by renting velvet ropes. Ask a friend to play bouncer and keep the guests waiting behind the velvet ropes. Let the guests dressed '70s-style enter first. Purchase glitter fabric remnants from your local fabric store and drape these across the furniture. You can rent a fog machine and a disco light from party rental companies. Set out mirrors on the coffee table with coke spoons and small bottles filled with flour. You can also roll some fake joints using dried parsley and rolling papers and lay them out on candy dishes. Remember macramé? Hang macramé creations from the ceiling along with ferns and other hanging plants. And let's not forget about pet rocks. Get a rock, any rock, and designate it as your special "Pet Rock."

Costumes

- ◎ **Roaring Twenties:** Flapper dresses worn with long beaded necklaces. Cloche (hat) or velvet beaded turban.
- ✳ **Dirty Thirties:** Draped chiffon dresses. Anything with an Art Deco motif. Tuxedos for men. Gangster gear.
- ★ **Swinging Forties:** Suits for women. Long dresses and neck sashes. Zoot suits for men.
- ◎ **Fabulous Fifties:** Dresses with rounded shoulders, full busts, tiny waists, and full skirts. Poodle skirts. Cat's eye frames with rhinestones. Toreador pants. Men's smoking jackets. Thin ties. Hawaiian shirts. Saddle shoes. Spike heels.
- ★ **Psychedelic Sixties:** Tie-dyed anything. Jeans with '60s patches. Batik tops. Mini skirts. Fishnet stockings. Fringed vests. Nehru jackets. Peace symbol earrings. Go-go boots.
- ◎ **Superfly Seventies:** Big Afro wigs. Polyester shirts and leisure suits. Wide belts. Huge wide ties. Hip-hugger bell bottoms. Platform shoes.

◎ **"Upwardly Mobile" Eighties:** Women's shirts with big bows. Big shoulder pads. Madonna-like corsets with pointy bras. Punk rocker dyed and spiked hair. Acid-washed jeans. Bowling shoes. Parachute pants.

☀ **Nirvana Nineties:** Huge pants that fall below your butt. Grunge wear. Body piercing.

Games and Activities

✳ **Costume Contest:** Hand out ballots listing the decades. Ask guests to nominate the "best dressed" guest for each era. If you are not using nametags (and we don't recommend them, since some of your guests will be wearing very special vintage clothing), this will require that people find out whom they're voting for.

◎ **Faded Fads:** Set a time to play "Faded Fads." Do the limbo! Swing those hula-hoops! Pogo dance! Guests will undoubtedly contribute their own ideas.

★ **Jump, Jive, an' Wail:** Swing is the thing. Blast '40s hot jazz and '90s jumping-blues and twirl and whirl to the retro sounds of swing music. Hire an instructor to teach couples "the basic" dance step.

Musical Suggestions

This one is easy. Have you ever watched late night TV? Call that 800 number and send in $19.95 for *The Best of . . . the* '30s, '40s, '50s, '60s, '70s. Record stores sell tapes and CDs of Top Forty hits from every decade. If you want to save money, make your own tapes. Choose artists and songs that make a defining cultural statement for that decade, like Glenn Miller for the '40s; the Village People for the '70s; Nirvana for the '90s.

Here are some suggestions:

✳ '20s: Louis Armstrong

◎ '30s: Woody Herman

- ✳ '40s: Benny Goodman, Glenn Miller (also '90s bands including "new swing" like Big Bad Voodoo Daddy, Royal Crown Revue, Cherry Poppin' Daddies, The Brian Setzer Orchestra)
- ✳ '50s: Elvis Presley, Buddy Holly, Bill Haley, Chubby Checker, Fats Domino
- ✈ '60s: Fifth Dimension, Jimi Hendrix, Janis Joplin, Four Seasons, Monkees, Doors, Beatles, soundtrack from *Hair*
- ◎ '70s: Peter Frampton, Fleetwood Mac, Bee Gees, Carpenters, Cat Stevens, Village People
- ✳ '80s: Cindi Lauper, Duran Duran, Prince, Blondie, Culture Club, MC Hammer
- ◎ '90s: Boyz II Men, Notorious BIG, Tupac, Spice Girls, Pearl Jam, Nirvana, techno music

Food

Go retro as we offer delicacies from the '50s, '60s, and '70s! No one makes and serves food like this anymore. Ask your mother for help. She'll dish out memories along with cooking tips. Leave out the arugula and fancy grilled vegetables. Your guests will enjoy these tastes of yesterdecade. Remember, the '50s and '60s were a time of processed convenience foods.

In 1970, Frances Moore Lappe wrote *Diet for a Small Planet*, which addressed the link between our food choices, the environment, and world hunger. Americans were also beginning to worry about the percentage of fat in their diets and the adverse effects of pesticides and food additives in their meals. Party fare reflected this new consciousness. Consider how Americans switched from Swedish meatballs to vegetable dips galore. Offer your guests a real trip down culinary memory lane.

Jelly Beans

It was reported that over 40 million jelly beans were consumed at various celebrations during the Inauguration of President Ronald Reagan. He kept them on hand in the Oval Office, and dispensed them at Cabinet meetings. Set out jelly beans in various flavors—very festive, and very '80s!

'80s Cheeseball

2 8-ounce packages cream cheese
2 8-ounce cups shredded sharp Cheddar cheese
1 tablespoon chopped pimiento
1 tablespoon chopped green pepper
1 tablespoon finely chopped onion
2 teaspoons Worcestershire sauce
1 teaspoon lemon juice
dash cayenne
dash salt
finely chopped pecans

Combined softened cream cheese and Cheddar cheese, mixing until well blended. Add pimiento, green pepper, onion, Worcestershire sauce, lemon juice, and seasonings; mix well. Chill. Shape into ball; roll in nuts. Serve with crackers. Serves 12.

'50s Party Mix

According to Ralston Purina, this is their longtime, all-time favorite, dating from 1952.

6 tablespoons butter or margarine

1 teaspoon seasoned salt

4 teaspoons Worcestershire sauce

2 cups Corn Chex cereal

2 cups Rice Chex cereal

2 cups Wheat Chex cereal

3/4 cup salted mixed nuts

Preheat oven to 250°F. Heat butter in a 13-by-9-by-2-inch baking pan in oven until melted. Remove. Stir in seasoned salt and Worcestershire sauce. Add Chex and nuts. Mix until all pieces are coated. Heat in oven for 45 minutes. Stir every 15 minutes. Spread on absorbent paper to cool. Makes 6 3/4 cups.

'50s Cocktail Meatballs

You can shape, brown, and refrigerate these hours before the party. Then reheat and serve out of an electric frying pan.

1 pound ground beef

1 egg, slightly beaten

2 tablespoons fine dry bread crumbs

½ teaspoon salt

½ cup finely chopped onion

⅓ cup finely chopped green pepper

2 tablespoons butter or margarine

1 10¾-ounce can condensed tomato soup

2 tablespoons brown sugar

1 tablespoon vinegar

1 tablespoon Worcestershire sauce

1 teaspoon prepared mustard

dash hot pepper sauce

Mix thoroughly beef, egg, bread crumbs, and salt; shape into 50 small ½-inch meatballs. Arrange in shallow baking pan (12-by-8-by-2 inches). Broil 4 inches from heat until browned; turn once. Pour off fat. Meanwhile, in saucepan, cook onion and green pepper in butter until tender. Add meatballs and remaining ingredients. Cover; cook over low heat for 10 minutes. Stir occasionally. Makes about 3½ cups. Serves 20.

Onion Dip

Everyone made this in the '60s.

1 envelope Lipton Onion Soup Mix   2 cups (16 ounces) sour cream

In a small bowl, combine ingredients chill. Serve with plain potato chips. Makes about 2 cups.

Tuna Casserole

This dish can be prepared and baked ahead. Put it back in the oven for the last five minutes during the party. (You can spare five minutes!) Your guests will appreciate the extra effort you've made to carry out the theme. You can stick it in the microwave later in the evening for the midnight munchies. WARNING: This casserole is very salty. Have lots of water on hand.

2 cups egg noodles   1 cup cooked peas
1 10¾-ounce can condensed cream   1 7-ounce can tuna, drained and flaked
   of celery or mushroom soup   ½ cup slightly crumbled potato chips
¼ cup milk

Cook egg noodles until firm, approximately 10 minutes. Place drained noodles in a 1-quart buttered casserole dish. Blend soup and milk; stir in tuna and peas. Place on top of noodles. Bake at 400°F for 25 minutes or until hot; stir. Top with chips; bake 5 minutes more. Makes about 6 cups.

'70s Vegetable Dip

¼ cup chopped watercress

1 tablespoon chopped chives

½ teaspoon dried tarragon leaves

3 flat anchovy fillets, chopped

2 teaspoons drained capers

2 tablespoons vegetable oil

1 teaspoon Dijon mustard

1 tablespoon lemon juice

⅛ teaspoon salt

1 egg

1¼ cups vegetable oil

2 carrots, peeled, cut in sticks

2 celery sticks, cut in thin sticks

1 medium turnip, peeled, sliced

In blender or food processor, combine watercress, chives, tarragon, anchovy fillets, and capers. Process until finely minced. Add 2 tablespoons oil, mustard, lemon juice, salt, and egg. Process until mixture thickens, 20–30 seconds. Serve with cut up carrots, celery, and turnip. Makes 1¾ cups.

Super Wheat Germ Zucchini Bread

This made its debut on the Kretschmer jar in 1977, just in time for America's new focus on healthy foods.

1¼ cups wheat germ

3 cups flour

2 eggs

1¾ cups sugar

3 teaspoons baking powder

I teaspoon salt

2 teaspoons cinnamon

I cup chopped nuts

2 teaspoons vanilla

2/3 cups cooking oil

3 cups (about 3 medium-size) grated
zucchini

Preheat oven to 350°F (325°F if using glass pans). In a medium bowl, mix together wheat germ, flour, baking powder, salt, cinnamon, and nuts; set aside. In a large bowl, beat eggs until light-colored and fluffy. Beat in sugar, vanilla, and oil. Stir in zucchini. Gradually stir in wheat germ mixture. Turn into 2 greased and floured 8½-by-4½-by-2½-inch loaf pans. Bake for I hour, or until a pick inserted into center comes out clean. Cool for 5–10 minutes. Remove from pans and cool on rack. Makes 2 loaves.

Crunchy Lemon Squares

This can be made the day before.

I cup quick oats, uncooked

I cup flour

½ cup flaked coconut

½ cup coarsely chopped pecans

½ cup firmly packed light brown sugar

½ cup butter or margarine, melted

I can sweetened condensed milk

2 cups lemon juice

I tablespoon grated lemon rind

I teaspoon baking powder

Preheat oven to 350°F. (325°F if using glass dish). In medium bowl, combine oats, flour, coconut, nuts, sugar, baking powder, and butter; stir to form a crumbly mixture. Set aside. In medium bowl, combine sweetened condensed milk, lemon juice, and rind. Pat half of crumb mixture evenly on bottom of 9-by-9-inch baking pan. Spread sweetened condensed milk mixture on top and sprinkle with remaining crumbs. Bake for 25–30 minutes or until lightly browned. Cool thoroughly before cutting. Makes 9 servings.

Oatmeal Cookies

¾ cup corn oil

1 cup firmly packed brown sugar

2 eggs

1 teaspoon vanilla

1½ cups unsifted flour

1 cup quick cooking oats

1½ teaspoons baking powder

½ teaspoon salt

½ teaspoon ground cinnamon

½ cup coarsely chopped nuts

In large bowl with mixer at medium speed, beat corn oil, sugar, eggs, and vanilla until thick. Add flour, oats, baking powder, salt, and cinnamon. Beat at low speed until blended. Stir in nuts. Drop by level tablespoonfuls 2 inches apart on greased cookie sheet. Bake in 350°F oven 12–15 minutes or until browned. Makes about 3½ dozen cookies.

Martini

What is a twentieth-century party without this classic?

4 ounces gin

2 teaspoons dry vermouth

2 green olives

Chill two martini glasses. In a mixing glass, half-full of ice cubes, combine the gin and vermouth. Stir gently. Strain the mixture into the glasses. Garnish each drink with an olive, speared on a toothpick. Makes 2 cocktails.

Variations on the Theme

✳ **Party of the Year:** Have a party to celebrate every holiday of the year! This works especially well as a bon voyage party for someone who is leaving the country for a while. Bring out all of your leftover theme napkins and paper plates from holidays throughout the year, such as Fourth of July, Halloween, Christmas, or Hanukkah. Hang up holiday decorations, put up banners proclaiming "Happy Birthday," string Christmas lights around your large potted plants, and cook a full Thanksgiving meal. This is Party Girl paradise.

Chic of The Desert:

An Arabian Night to Remember

Stage a shindig celebrating Scheherazade, the Syrian soul sister who spun stories to save her skin. This girl partied all night one thousand and one times in a row, leaving a legacy of torrid and tempestuous tales, not to mention the theme for an exotic party.

Invitations

✳ Get an image of the movie poster of Rudolph Valentino's *The Sheik*. (You can find a digital one at the Internet Movie Database.) Make a master by replacing the actors' photos with your own. Make as many copies as you need and put all of the party details on the back.

Decorating Tips

✳ Create a desert tent atmosphere by draping the ceiling and walls with white fabric. Muslin or sheets are cheap and effective. Use clear pushpins, gummy stickup stuff, or double-sided tape to secure the draperies. Be sure to hang one over the doorway entrance to your party room; you'll want your guests to have the experience of pulling back the drape and entering the exotic setting you've created.

◎ Magic carpets! Cover the floor with oriental rugs. You can find cheap imitation ones at garage sales and thrift stores, or borrow from friends.

★ Pillows Talk! Scatter several large, comfy floor pillows around the room. These go on sale all the time at large linen stores and warehouses. Trim plain ones with pretty buttons, ribbon, or fringe.

◎ Buy or rent a few potted palms; cover the pots with colorful fabric.

★ Light fragrant incense: sandalwood, frankincense, or patchouli.

✳ Set out platters of Camel cigarettes and Sheik condoms.

✳ Have Disney's *Aladdin* on the VCR with the sound off—it's for atmosphere only, not to encourage folks to watch the movie.

Costumes

✳ Turbans for the fellas, veils for the ladies. The more daring can wear belly-dancer garb. Have a couple of sets of finger cymbals available to encourage belly-boogy-ing. Ladies' trousers inspired by harem pants go in and out of style, so there's a good bet your local thrift store will have some version or another.

◎ Have a few towels on hand for instant genie-like turbans.

Games and Activities:

◎ **Three Wishes.** The famous Genie in the lamp granted Aladdin three wishes. You probably can't grant ALL of your guests' wishes, but you can at least find out what they are! Instead of name tags, have each guest wear a tag that lists their three wishes—but don't allow anyone to use the clichés "World Peace" or "More Wishes."

★ **Dance of the Seven Veils.** You'll have to rely on some good music and willing guests for this one! Once the music and dancing get started, distribute seven filmy scarves or pieces of fabric among the dancers. Encourage guests to use the scarves however they like, to rope in more dancers from the sidelines, or as a prop for a sexy shimmy.

Favors and Prizes

◎ Middle Eastern food treats are inexpensive and often come in elaborately decorated packaging. Pick out the prettiest packages of jars of olives, tahini, bottles of rose water, and boxes of falafel mix from the grocery or Middle Eastern market.

✳ A copy of *Arabian Nights* is the perfect prize for the best costume.

Musical Suggestions

You'll want to make a party mix tape of two to see you through the whole party. Be sure to include these ideas:

✳ Troll the ethnic section of the music store for Middle Eastern party music.

◎ Play the soundtrack to *Priscilla, Queen of the Desert*. True, the desert in question is the Australian one, not Arabian, but we'll stretch the theme for the fabulous disco tracks on this CD.

✳ The '50s novelty song "Ahab the Arab" is a must.

✳ Dust off the Christmas music and play the "Arab Dance" from Tschaikovsky's *Nutcracker Suite*.

◎ Not necessarily in the best of taste, but you could play the Cure's song "Killing an Arab" (inspired by Albert Camus' existential novel *The Stranger*).

★ Play "Midnight at the Oasis" by Maria Muldaur at midnight.

Food

Open Sesame Seed Chips

1 package round wonton wrappers
1 cup sesame oil
3 tablespoons sesame seeds

paprika
salt

Preheat oven to 375°F. Lightly film a baking sheet with some of the oil. Arrange the wrappers in a single layer on a lightly oiled baking sheet. Brush with more sesame oil and sprinkle with sesame seeds, paprika, and salt to taste. Bake 8–10 minutes, or until browned. Let cool completely. Can be made one day ahead, store in a tightly covered container. Makes about 6 dozen chips

Olive Melange Mirage

½ pound pitted brine-cured green olives, sliced
½ pound Kalamata olives, pitted and sliced
2 cups chopped tomatoes
⅓ cup olive oil
3 cloves garlic, minced
1 tablespoon tomato paste
½ cup water
3 ¼-inch-thick lemon slices
1 teaspoon paprika
½ teaspoon cayenne pepper

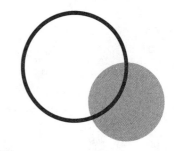

Bring medium pot of water to boil. Add olives and bring to boil. Drain olives.

Combine tomatoes, oil, garlic, and tomato paste in heavy small saucepan; bring to boil. Reduce heat to medium-low and simmer 3 minutes. Add water, lemon, paprika, cayenne, and olives. Boil until liquid is reduced to sauce consistency, stirring often, about 5 minutes. Transfer to bowl and cool. Chill until cold. Can be prepared 3 days ahead. Cover and keep refrigerated. Bring to room temperature to serve. Makes about 3 1/2 cups. (Adapted from *Bon Appetit,* May 1995)

Cool as a Cucumber Soup

4 large cucumbers	2 large cloves garlic, pressed
1 1/2 quarts plain nonfat yogurt	5 tablespoons chopped fresh mint
1 1/2 cups water	salt and pepper to taste

Peel and seed cucumbers, then dice very finely. Mix together with yogurt, water, garlic, mint, and salt and pepper to taste. Refrigerate at least two hours or overnight. You've got 1,001 options for serving. You can spoon it into paper or plastic cups, pop a spoon into each one and bring them out by the trayful, or serve it up punch bowl-style. Makes 10 1/2 cup servings.

Hummus Among Us

3 cups canned garbanzo beans	2 teaspoons ground cumin
1 cup tahini	1 1/2 teaspoons salt
1 cup fresh lemon juice	paprika for sprinklin'
2 cloves, pressed or minced	

Place all of the ingredients except for the paprika into a food processor. Process until smooth. Spread the hummus in a large plate or shallow bowl. Sprinkle the top with paprika. Can be made a day or two ahead, store covered in the fridge, and sprinkle it with paprika just before serving. Serve with pita bread or crudité. Makes about 4½ cups.

Shish Kebab

2½ pounds ground lamb (or beef)	1 medium onion, minced
¼ cup parsley, chopped	1 teaspoon salt

1 generous shake of each:

ground allspice	cardamom
black pepper	ground cloves
cinnamon	ground ginger
nutmeg	2½ tablespoon flour

Garnish

4 onions, peeled and quartered	2 tablespoons olive oil
4 large tomatoes, peeled and quartered	

Soak 15 bamboo skewers in warm water for 30 minutes. Meanwhile, mix all of the ingredients and knead well.

Wet the palms of your hands with water (this will help keep the meat from sticking to them) Take 2- to 3-ounce pieces of the meat mixture and shape into cylinders. Drive skewer lengthwise through the meat sticks. Shape the meat evenly around the skewer; each kebab will be approximately

6–8 inches long. Lay the kebabs on a foil-lined baking sheet and use more plastic wrap between the layers. Chill overnight.

Broil the kebabs 5–10 minutes on each side, turning once. Brush the quartered tomatoes and onions with oil, and broil until just a bit charred, about 10–15 minutes. Serve warm or at room temperature. Makes 15 kebabs.

Land of Milk and Honey Dip with Dried Fruit

3 cups vanilla yogurt
¾ cup honey

2 teaspoons cinnamon

Combine all ingredients and chill. Serve with assorted dried fruits, like apricots, figs, dates, and prunes. Makes 3½ cups.

Baghdad Café Cocktails

5 cups cold coffee
1 cup heavy cream
1 cup Kahlúa or other coffee-flavored liqueur

½ cup vodka
nutmeg

Mix all ingredients in a pitcher or punch bowl. Serve chilled with a shake of nutmeg on top. Makes 15 ½ cup servings.

October

Literary Lunch or A Novel Way To Spend A Day!

Read any good books lately? A good book is a welcome escape from the day-to-day drudgery of life between parties, and Literary Lunch is a great way to get a gaggle of girlfriends together to gab and exchange books. Invite a group of six to eight of your most well-read friends to a casual lunch or dinner. Each guest should bring a copy of a favorite book. After the meal, over coffee, tea, or a sophisticated aperitif, each guest takes turns describing her book and why she loves it. The evening ends with a book exchange. Everyone goes home with a new book to read and suggestions for several more to try!

Invitations

◎ Buy a bunch of cheap paperback books at a thrift shop. Paste a piece of paper over the title page with all of the party information. Send the book in a padded envelope.

✳ Using a blank index card, make a "library card" with your guest's name on it. On the back, write, "Check out some great books at (Name)'s Literary Lunch" and include all of the party details.

Decorating Tips

★ Have your après-meal book discussion in the room of your house with the most bookshelves, even if it's a den, study, or office where you don't usually entertain. Bring in chairs and a low table for coffee cups, or just sprawl out on the floor.

✳ Pile books around the room on floors, and under chairs and tables.

◎ Replace the photos in your frames with pictures of literary figures cut from magazines or copied from books.

✳ Make an impromptu side table by putting a piece of wood or glass on a pile of sturdy coffee-table books

Games and Activities

★ Pass out sheets of paper with famous literary quotes. Award a bookstore gift certificate to the person who can ID the highest number of quote sources.

✳ Shakespearean Show-Down! Set a timer for three minutes and challenge your guests to write down the titles of as many of Shakespeare's plays as they can think of. The one with the most wins!

◎ Write the names of literary characters on slips of paper and put the slips in a basket or bowl. Have each guest draw a name and adopt that character's persona during pre-meal mingling. You can only STOP acting like your character when another guest has guessed who you are.

✳ There are several ways to exchange books at the end of the party. You can draw numbers, and each guest in turn chooses the book she'd like. Or, the person who brought the book can select whom they'd like to pass it to. Or, just toss all the books into a basket or box and have everyone draw at random.

Favors and Prizes

★ Make bookmarks out of construction paper, strips of felt, or wide ribbon. Write (or for the super crafty, embroider), "(Name)'s Literary Art Lunch (DATE) Good Books and Good Friends."

✳ Write down the titles, authors, and publishers of all of the books brought to the party. Make copies and send them to your guests.

◎ Make custom bookplates using blank labels. Create a simple design and print bookplates out on the computer; stamp them with a pretty rubber stamp, or use your best penmanship to write, "From the Library of" on a dozen for each guest. Wrap them in a little bundle with pretty ribbon and set them out in a basket on the coffee table.

Food

DIP INTO A GREAT BOOK—A TRIO OF DIPS!

Set out the following dips in three little bowls on a large platter surrounded by mounds of pita triangles, crackers, baguette slices, and raw veggies. Line the platter with pages torn from a cheap paperback book. (Purists will gasp at ripping out the pages of a book—any book—but if you choose a cheesy romance novel or some other less-than-classic literary tome, they should be easily appeased! If you want to play it safe, make photocopies of a variety of book pages.) If you make the dips a few days ahead, store them in the same bowls you'll be serving in. Then you can just whip off the plastic wrap and go!

Pea Purée

1 16-ounce package frozen peas
1 teaspoon salt
1 tablespoon fresh lemon juice

1/2 cup sour cream or plain yogurt
1/2 cup chopped parsley
1/3 cup chopped onion

Boil the peas in 1 cup of water for 8–10 minutes. Drain well. Process in a food processor with the salt and lemon juice until smooth. Place the purée in a bowl and stir in the rest of the ingredients. Best when made and served the same day. Makes about 3 cups.

Salsa California

1 large red onion, chopped
3 tablespoons olive oil
1 1/3 chopped, seeded tomatoes
1 cup arugula, julienned
1/3 cup black Kalamata olives,
    pitted and chopped

2 teaspoons balsamic vinegar
2 teaspoons red wine vinegar
dash of sugar
salt and pepper to taste

Sauté the onions in one tablespoon of the oil until soft and tender. Put the tomatoes in a medium bowl and stir in the arugula, olives, and cooked onions. Whisk the remaining 2 tablespoons of olive oil, both vinegars, sugar, salt, and pepper in a bowl (or toss them all in a lidded jar and shake) and drizzle over the tomato mixture. Chill, covered, for at least an hour or two, or the night before serving. Serve at room temperature. Makes about 2 cups.

Mushroom Dip

1 pound mushrooms, finely chopped

1 cup dry bread crumbs

2 tablespoons olive oil

¾ cup Parmesan cheese

2 garlic cloves, minced or pressed

salt and pepper to taste

2 tablespoons butter or margarine

Mix all ingredients except butter or margarine and put into ovenproof dish (a glass pie plate works nicely). Dot top with small pieces of butter or margarine. Bake at 350°F for about 20 minutes. Spoon into small bowl to serve.

Can be made the night before, just pop into the oven 15 minutes before guests arrive. Makes approximately 2½ cups

Salad Days Green Salad

The simplest of green salads is delicious all on its own. Most markets now carry bins of premixed greens that make putting out a gourmet salad a snap. If this salad is just too plain for you, add a few croutons, shavings of Parmesan, or some halved cherry tomatoes.

8 large handfuls of mixed greens

8 tablespoons olive oil

2 tablespoons vinegar of your choice
  (red wine, sherry, balsamic)

1 minced garlic clove

½ teaspoon Dijon mustard

salt and pepper to taste

Clean the greens and place in a large bowl. Put all the dressing ingredients in a jar with a tight lid and shake until blended. Toss over the greens just before serving. Serves 8.

This Bread Also Rises—Easy Homemade Poppy Seed Bread

1 package quick-rise yeast
1 teaspoon salt
1 teaspoon sugar
1/2 teaspoon pepper

4 1/2 cups all-purpose flour
1 large clove minced garlic
3 tablespoons olive oil
3/4 cup poppy seeds

In a large bowl, combine yeast, salt, sugar, pepper, and 2 cups flour. In a small saucepan, heat the olive oil and garlic in 1 1/2 cups of water until very warm but not boiling. Using a large, sturdy wooden spoon, stir the liquid into the flour mixture until smooth. Add in another 2 cups of flour to make a soft dough. Turn dough out onto a floured board and knead until smooth and elastic, kneading in about 1/2 cup more flour. Shape the dough into a ball and wrap in plastic wrap. Set aside for 10 minutes. Meanwhile, grease a cookie sheet.

Roll the dough into a 12-by-15-inch rectangle on a floured cutting board. Sprinkle the top with poppy seeds. Starting from one 12-inch end, roll the dough jellyroll style. Pinch the seam and place seam-side down on the greased cookie sheet. Tuck the ends of the roll under.

Preheat the oven to 400°F. Make 4–5 deep, diagonal slashes in the top of the loaf. Cover with a dish towel and set aside in a warm place (the top of the fridge is good) to rise for 15 minutes. Dust the loaf with flour and bake 40–45 minutes until the loaf sounds hollow when tapped and the crust is golden brown.

Cool on a wire rack. Can be made a day or two ahead. Store wrapped tightly in foil. Makes 8 2-slice servings.

EAT YOUR WORDS—THE MAIN PLOT

Pasta with Shrimp and Broccoli

4 tablespoons olive oil	8 large tomatoes, seeded, diced
2 medium onions, chopped	2 tablespoon fresh lemon juice
4 garlic cloves, minced	2 pounds uncooked medium shrimp,
4 cups fresh broccoli florets	peeled and deveined
1/2 cup chopped fresh basil	1 pound spaghetti
4 tablespoons chopped fresh oregano	1 10-ounce package "alphabet" pasta
1/2 teaspoon dried crushed red pepper	additional chopped fresh basil

Heat oil in heavy large skillet over medium heat. Add onion, garlic, and broccoli; sauté until tender, about 5 minutes. Add 1/4 cup basil, oregano, and peppers; stir 1 minute. Add diced tomatoes and lemon juice and cook, stirring until tomatoes are soft, sort of "mushy" and heated through. Stir in shrimp and cook until just cooked through, about 5 minutes. Season to taste with salt and pepper. Can be made a day or two ahead. Store in the fridge and reheat over a medium flame.

Cook the spaghetti in lots of rapidly boiling, salted water until done. Add the alphabet pasta during the last 1/2 of the cooking time. Drain well and toss with a little olive oil.

Add the sauce to the spaghetti and toss to coat. Transfer to large bowl. Sprinkle with additional chopped fresh basil. Makes 8 servings

THE FINAL CHAPTER—A DIZZYING DESSERT DISPLAY!

After dinner, you'll be gathering around a big platter of sweet little treats while you share and discuss the books you brought. Store-bought cookies, candies, and cake slices are fine, mixed in or in place of these recipes. Offer some fresh fruit or berries too, but be careful not to set out anything too gooey or juicy—you don't want to get schmutz on the pages of the books. Use some more of those recycled book pages to line the platter. Serve coffee, tea, or perhaps a snifter of brandy. Add a few shakes of cinnamon to your coffee grounds before you brew—it not only flavors the coffee, but a sweet, spicy aroma will waft from the coffeemaker.

Mock Madeleines

Madeleines are a classic literary food reference, but those lovely shell-shaped pans are expensive and have very limited use. If you've got them or love to collect recipe-specific cookware, by all means use them. For Party Girls with more limited budgets and cupboard space, mini-muffin pans will work just as well.

4 large eggs
2/3 cup granulated sugar
1/2 teaspoon vanilla extract
confectioner's sugar for dusting

1 1/2 cups all-purpose flour
1/2 cup unsalted butter,
    melted and cooled slightly

Preheat oven to 350°F. Beat the eggs and the granulated sugar with an electric mixer until the mixture is thick and pale and forms a ribbon when the beaters are lifted. Beat in the vanilla.

Sift the flour in 4 batches over the mixture, folding it in gently after each addition. Spoon the batter into greased mini-muffin pans, filling each cup about ¾ full. Bake for 12–15 minutes, or until the edges are golden. Turn the Madeleines out on racks, let cool, and sprinkle lightly with confectioner's sugar. (You get a nice, even dusting of sugar if you spoon a bit into a fine mesh strainer, hold the strainer over the cookies, and tap the sides of the strainer lightly.) Store tightly covered at room temperature for up to three days; freeze for longer storage. Makes 24 Madeleines.

Biscotti

2 eggs

¾ cup sugar

1 teaspoon baking soda

2 cups flour

¾ cups coarsely chopped toasted almonds

Preheat oven to 350°F. Line a baking sheet with foil and grease generously. Beat eggs and sugar with an electric mixer for about 2 minutes or until pale. Beat in baking soda and flour until blended. Stir in almonds. With floured hands, form the dough into two long, flat logs, approximately 12-by-3-inches. Bake for 30 minutes.

Remove from the oven, but leave the oven on. Let the cookie logs stand for about 5 minutes. Remove the logs to a cutting board. With a serrated knife, gently cut each log diagonally into 12 slices. Put the slices back on the cookie sheet, on their sides and return to the oven. Bake an additional 20 minutes. Cool completely on a rack.

Biscotti can be kept for about a week in an airtight container, or for months in the freezer. Makes 24.

Java Nuts

¼ cup butter, melted

1 pound pecans, almonds, cashews, walnuts, or a mixture

1½ cups sugar

2 tablespoons instant coffee granules

2 egg whites at room temperature

Preheat oven to 300°F. Toss the nuts with the butter in a large bowl. Combine ⅔ cup sugar and coffee in a small bowl and sprinkle over the nuts. Stir to coat evenly.

Beat the egg whites with an electric mixer until soft peaks form. Add the rest of the sugar gradually, and continue to beat until stiff peaks form. Fold the whites into the nuts, and spread on a rimmed baking sheet or jellyroll pan. Bake for 25–30 minutes, stirring every 10 minutes. For the first few stirs the coating will be syrupy, but it will form into a hard, crunchy coating by the end of the baking time.

Cool to room temperature. Store tightly covered in the fridge. Makes 4 cups.

Variations on the Theme

✳ **Form a Book Club**—it's not just for Oprah anymore! Get a group of six to eight friends together each month for a book discussion club. Your local bookstore will have tips and reading lists for all types of book clubs. Each member of the club takes turns hosting the meeting. Some book clubs serve only nibbles and tea; others do a full meal inspired by that month's book.

※ **Cookie Klatch!** Especially popular around the holidays, every guest brings several dozen cookies, copies of the recipe, and a container for taking some the goodies. Everyone leaves with a sample or two of each guest's baked delights and a pile of sure-fire, tried-and-taste-tested recipes.

◎ **Learning Exchange.** Everyone can do something that she can teach someone else: knitting, cooking, cake decorating, candlemaking. Form a circle of knowledge-able friends and get together for mini-classes. Each month's host sends out an invite and materials list, and teaches her friends a new hobby or skill.

Chicks' Tricks and Treats-So-Chic: *It's Halloween!*

Halloween was probably the Party Girl's first experience with the magic of nightlife. She always felt deliciously decadent, all dolled up in fantastic finery, free to roam the streets demanding what is rightfully hers. Now that she's all grown up, Halloween is still a time for the Party Girl to celebrate her dark side.

Invitations

* Buy thirty-minute audiotapes at a discount store. Get the cheapest ones you can. Record all of the party details in your best creepy voice, while a cohort fills the background with moans, groans, screams, and yells.

* Send each guest a plain black satin half-mask. (Get the ones with the cool pointy eyes for the ladies, plain Lone Ranger types for the men.) Write the party details on the back; ask each guest to decorate their mask and wear it to the party. Have a few extra on hand for the inevitable party poopers.

* Send each guest some Halloween make-up, plastic nose, or other small accessory to help inspire their costume.

Top Ten Reasons Why Trick-or-Treating Is Better Than Sex

10. You're guaranteed to get at least a little something in the sack.

9. If you get tired, you can wait ten minutes and go at it again.

8. The uglier you look, the easier it is to get some.

7. You don't have to compliment the person who gave you candy.

6. It's okay when the person you're with fantasizes you're someone else, because you ARE someone else.

5. Forty years from now, you'll still enjoy candy.

4. If you don't get what you want, you can always go next door.

3. It doesn't matter if the kids hear you moaning and groaning.

2. Less guilt the next morning.

1. You can do the whole neighborhood!!

Decorating Tips

◎ **Party Girls Don't Sweat, They Glow:** Blacklights are available at most drug and hardware stores. They create a groovy, psychedelic glow (and as an extra bonus, hide virtually any facial flaw!). Replace as many bulbs as you can with black lights. Paint posterboard or butcher paper with Halloween icons or abstract shapes and plaster them over much of the room as possible. Buy cheap yardage or on-sale sheets in dark colors, paint with day-glow fabric paint, and drape over furniture. The goal is to create as otherworldly a space as possible.

✳ **Web of Sin:** Spider webbing is cheap, cheap, cheap, yet amazingly effective. Drape tons and tons of it in your party room. Make a big Black Widow (what else?) spider by filling a black trash bag with newspaper; use electrical tape to form a body and legs. Cut out eyes and an hourglass shape for the abdomen from red construction paper. Tape Ms. Spider to a high corner of the room where she can keep an eye out for her next victim.

◎ **Jack, Jill, and Jane O' Lanterns:** Don't stop at the typical triangle-featured Jack o' Lantern. Scatter the house, yard, and buffet tables with dozens of creatively carved pumpkins. Use apple corers, melon ballers, lemon zesters, or even electric drills to create stylish patterns. BEWARE! Carved pumpkins can get moldy quickly. Don't carve them more than a day or two before the party. If you've got an old LP turntable, set a two-faced carved pumpkin on it for 33 rpms of Halloween fun. Set up a table covered with a plastic cloth and plenty of pumpkins and implements of pumpkin destruction, and let your guests go at it. For extra stability, cut out the bottom of the pumpkin, rather than the top, and set it over a candle that's been placed securely in a candleholder or saucer. If you're feeling particularly devilish, carve pumpkins in the likeness of your guests, and see if they can spot their own gourd doppelgänger.

✳ Those teeny, tiny pumpkins also make great candleholders. Carve a hole in the top and stick in a black taper candle.

Games and Activities

◎ **Connect the Corpses!** As people arrive, hand each a nametag with either the name of a famous dead person or their method of death:

Mama Cass/choked on a ham sandwich
Karen Carpenter/starved herself to death
Bob "Hogan's Heroes" Crane/bludgeoned to death
Marilyn Monroe/drug overdose

or murderer and victim:

Charles Manson/Sharon Tate   Lyle Menendez/Kitty Menendez

Guests roam the party to match up the gruesome couplings. The ice will be permanently broken when the victim is reunited with her murderer, or the dead person's final act is recreated.

Costumes

★ Hit the thrift stores with an open mind. You never know when a purse, hat, dress, or other bargain item will inspire a fabulous costume.

◎ Skip the costume shop and head for the lingerie department. You'll find lots of lacy little things that'll be perfect for a variety of costumes like French Maids, Bunnies, Naughty Nurses, and Vampiras.

✳ It's great fun when couples, either romantic partners, best friends, or coworkers, come dressed as each other.

Favors and Prizes

Turn the tables on Trick-or-Treating by passing out goodie bags filled with all of the best candy: mini Snickers bars, M&Ms, Milky Ways, Kit Kats, and even a few of the B- and C-grade candies, like Dum-Dums, Circus Peanuts, and those weird black and orange taffy things.

• **The ancient Druids believed that on October 31 the spirits of the dead roamed the earth, so bonfires were lit to drive them away.**

• **The ancient Roman festival of Pomona was a time of celebrating the harvest, but ghosts and witches were thought to be out prowling around. Bonfires were also lit.**

• **The Celtic festival of Samhain featured bands of guisers (people wearing grotesque masks) carrying lanterns carved from turnips.**

Musical Suggestions

◎ Make sure the music is dark and moody, but with a danceable beat. Choose bands like:

Bauhaus
Siouxsie and the Banshees
The Cure
The Mission
Gene Loves Jezebel
Marilyn Manson

✳ Take a trip to the record store and glance through the CDs. If the band is dressed in black and looks depressed and slightly annoyed, chances are they've got the sound you're looking for.

Food

Creepy Canapés

1 8-ounce package cream cheese,
   room temperature
orange paste food coloring (see note)
1 cup pitted oil-cured black olives, drained
3 anchovy fillets or 1 teaspoon anchovy
   paste

1 tablespoon capers
1 large garlic clove
1 tablespoon lemon juice
2 tablespoons olive oil
salt and pepper

1 16-ounce package cocktail pumpernickel bread

Beat the cream cheese with an electric mixer until fluffy and smooth. Season with salt and pepper. Blend a few drops of orange paste food coloring until a deep, dark, Halloween-y color is achieved. Set cheese aside.

Combine the olives, anchovy, capers, garlic, and lemon juice in a food processor and pulverize. Slowly add the olive oil while continuing to process. Spread the cocktail bread with some of the cheese mixture, then top with 1/4 teaspoon of the olive mixture. Arrange on a platter and serve.

The cheese and olive mixtures can be made a couple of days ahead, store covered in the fridge and bring to room temperature before serving. Makes 45 canapés.

NOTE: *Paste food coloring can be found at cake decorating stores, gourmet cookware stores, and cake decorating departments of craft stores. Liquid food coloring will work okay, but will never give you the vibrant, deep color of paste.*

Halloween Pasta Salad

1 16-ounce package salad pasta
2 4.25-ounce cans chopped black olives, drained
4 medium carrots, grated

Dressing

6 tablespoons olive oil
1 tablespoon red wine vinegar

2–3 cloves garlic, minced or pressed
1/2 teaspoon Dijon mustard

1 tablespoon balsamic vinegar

1 chopped shallot

salt and pepper to taste

Boil pasta according to package directions, drain, and rinse in cold water. Toss the pasta together with the olives and carrots in a large bowl. Put all of the dressing ingredients into a jar with a screw-top lid; cover and shake. Toss the salad with the dressing. Can be made a day ahead. Cover with plastic wrap and chill. You may need to add a bit more dressing to refresh. Serves 8–10.

Blood Orange Salad

8–10 large handfuls of salad greens

1 large sweet, red onion, sliced thin

2–3 blood oranges, peeled and separated into sections

Dressing:

12 tablespoons fruity olive oil

8 teaspoons balsamic vinegar

8 teaspoons red wine vinegar

pinch of ground ginger

salt and pepper to taste

Toss salad greens with onions and oranges. Can be made up to 2 hours ahead; store covered in fridge. For dressing, put all ingredients in a bowl and whisk or put all ingredients in a jar, cover, and shake. Make up to 8 hours ahead; set aside in cool, dark place. Toss salad with dressing just before serving, or serve dressing on the side. Serves 8–10.

Dem Bones

5 pounds chicken wings and drumettes

olive oil spray

1 large onion, finely minced

1 cup molasses

1/2 cup soy sauce

1/2 cup prepared salsa

3 teaspoons Tabasco

1/2 cup lemon juice

2 cloves minced garlic

Preheat oven to 425°F. Line two cookie sheets with aluminum foil, and spray with olive oil. Bake the chicken pieces for 30 minutes. Drain liquid and grease.

Mix all of the remaining ingredients in a large bowl, add the chicken, and toss until coated with sauce. Return chicken to cookie sheets and bake another 30 minutes, or until crispy. Serve immediately if you can, or cool and refrigerate overnight and serve at room temperature. Serves 8–10.

Spicy Pumpkin Praline Squares

Filling

1 cup firmly packed brown sugar

1/4 cup granulated sugar

1 29-ounce can pumpkin (NOT
  pumpkin pie mix!)

1 12-ounce can evaporated milk

4 eggs

1 teaspoon cinnamon

1/2 teaspoon ground ginger

1/4 teaspoon cloves

Preheat oven to 350°F. In large bowl, combine all filling ingredients. Beat at medium speed, scraping bowl often, until smooth, 2–3 minutes. Pour into greased 13-by-9-inch baking pan. Bake for 25–30 minutes, until partially set.

Topping

¾ cup flour

½ cup brown sugar, firmly packed

¼ cup butter, softened

½ cup chopped pecans

In small bowl, combine flour and ½ cup brown sugar. Cut in butter until crumbly, using two knives crisscrossed in a slashing motion, a pastry cutter, or work in with fingertips. Stir in pecans. Sprinkle topping over pumpkin filling. Continue baking 15–20 minutes or until a knife inserted in the center comes out clean. Cool completely.

Cut into squares. Can be made ahead up to 3 days ahead; store wrapped well on the fridge. Makes 24 squares.

Witches' Brew

1 750-ml bottle vodka, chilled

1 2-liter bottle lemon lime soda, chilled

½ gallon orange juice, chilled

green liquid food coloring

Mix first 3 ingredients together in large stockpot or Dutch oven. Add enough food coloring to achieve a truly putrid color. Serve from stovetop or buffet table with a soup ladle. Makes about 25 6-ounce servings.

FOR EXTRA WITCHY FLAIR

※ Pour cranberry juice into a clean latex glove. Secure tightly and freeze until hard. Remove glove and float in punch. Fabulous effect as the hand begins to melt and "bleed."

◎ Float dry ice in punch for the "boil, boil, toil and trouble" treatment.

★ Fill ice cube trays half full of water. Freeze for about 45 minutes or until almost firm. Place a plastic fly, beetle, or spider just under the surface of the ice. Fill the rest of the way with water and freeze until firm. Add the creepy cubes to the punch.

Variations on the Theme

❋ **Dead Movie Stars:** Ask everyone to dress as a dearly departed film favorite. Decorate the party room with photos of stars who have gone on to the big wrap party in the sky. Find newspaper accounts of their demise at the library; copy and post around the room.

★ **Whores from Hell:** Invite your guests to dress their trampy best. Offer cheap, garish make-up as party favors.

◎ **It Came from Mars:** Carry out an outer space theme throughout the party. Use tin-foil, pie plates, and Christmas lights with abandon to crate a spaceship effect. Entertain your visiting Martians and space explorers with songs like "Space Oddity" and "Fly Me to the Moon."

❋ **Masked Ball:** Get inspired by *Romeo and Juliet* or a Venetian carnival for a classic masked ball. Require masks for party admission (have a few extra on hand). Decorate with flowers and fabrics in rich, autumnal colors. Serve a sit-down feast of pasta and roasted meats followed by dancing and a grand unmasking at midnight.

❊ **Monster Mash:** Ask your guests to dress as classic Hollywood monsters, play '60s-era dance music, and have old monster movies playing on the VCR. Try to find inexpensive reproductions of old horror movie posters for decorations.

November

Come as You Were:

Reincarnation Party

Reincarnation is like show business. You just keep doing it until you get it right.

—Shirley MacLaine, **Out on a Limb**

Have you ever noticed that true Party Girls seem to be born that way? Maybe it's because they were Party Girls in another lifetime.

Get in touch with your "inner partier" at a gala event designed to honor any one of your previous incarnations. Forget about the future for the moment—channel the past to reveal the wild, decadent Party Girl you once were. Choose a glittering, glamorous personality from history or fiction. Try Daisy Buchanan from *The Great Gatsby* on for size. Or Scarlett O'Hara in *Gone with the Wind*. Let's see—should it be the rose organdy, lavender-barred muslin, or green plaid taffeta, "frothing with flounces edged in green velvet ribbon"? When Nina "became" Scarlett O'Hara for a trade show one year, theories abounded about whether she was once a Southern Belle. How else do you explain a flawless Southern accent from a born-and-bred New Yorker?

Invitations

◎ **Headline:** *A Celebration of Your Lifetimes: Come as You Were*

✳ **Graphics:** Use computer clip art or cut out pictures of people representing different eras and cultures, such as an ancient Egyptian, Elvis, a Victorian lady, a Pilgrim, or an Asian Empress, and paste them around the border of your invitation. Color copy.

Decorating Tips

- ※ **The Animal Kingdom:** The word *reincarnation* literally means to "come again in the flesh." Could that cat down the street be one of your ancestors? Label animal figurines with nametags. For instance, a plastic horse could be "Uncle Fred." Put a nametag on your dog's collar or on your birdcage.

- ◎ **Shirley's Lives:** Obtain an autographed photograph of Shirley MacLaine. Frame it, and prominently display.

- ✈ **Karmic Debt Insurance:** Karma refers to the debt a soul accumulates because of good or bad actions committed during one's life (or past lives). If one accumulates bad karma, he or she will be reincarnated in a less desirable state. Put out a collection plate for a designated charity. Donations to this worthy cause will help your guests in their journey to a better life (the next one, that is).

- ✳ **Waters of the Ganges:** Once every twelve years, millions of Hindus plunge into the waters of the Ganges in the holy city of Hardwar in Northern India to wash away their sins. These participants in the festival of the Kumb Mela believe that this will accelerate their attainment of nirvana (freedom from the cycle of death and rebirth).

    Create your own exotic plunge by filling up your bathtub with flowers. Post a sign to alert guests of this cosmic opportunity.

- ◎ Rent *Defending Your Life* and run it nonstop on your VCR throughout the evening. A Warner Home Video release, it was written and directed by Albert Brooks and stars Meryl Streep, Albert Brooks, Rip Torn, and Lee Grant, with a cameo appearance by our all-time favorite reincarnated actress Shirley MacLaine. Or rent *What*

Dreams May Come, starring Robin Williams. There are great scenes in which dead people from different periods of time float around in heaven.

✳ Post this adage on your wall from the *Bhagavad Gita* 2:20: "For the soul there is never birth nor death. Nor, having once been, does he ever cease to be. He is un-born, eternal, ever existing, undying, and primeval. He is not slain when the body is slain."

Costumes

◎ **The sky's the limit!** The only requirement is that your guests channel someone who is dead (in body, but not in spirit). It doesn't have to be someone famous. We can't ALL have been Napoleon or Cleopatra. Here's who some celebrities believe they were in their past lives:

Shirley MacLaine: *A maidservant in ancient Egypt; a model for Toulouse Lautrec in France; and lived on Atlantis.*

Stevie Nicks: *An Egyptian high priestess; a concert pianist; a Holocaust victim.*

Glenn Ford: *He recalled five past lives under hypnosis. One of these was Emile Langevin, an expert horseman in King Louis XIV's Horse Cavalry. During his hypnotic recall, Ford was able to speak French with ease, even though his normal French vocabulary consisted of just a few phrases. Not just any ol' French—experts stated that he was using the Parisian French of the 1670s. Wow!*

Henry Mancini: *This composer discovered that he was the reincarnation of Italian composer Giuseppe Verdi. And long before that, he believed he had been an engineer during the building of the Great Pyramid at Giza, and an officer in the court of Montezuma.*

Loretta Lynn: *A powerful, eleventh-century Chinese landowner who ruled over a large estate and whose word was law.*

✳ Hundreds, even thousands of sites on the Internet are devoted to creative costuming. You can rent, buy, or custom-design your own costume for all eras and ethnicities. Start by going to the International Costumers' Guild Web site at **www.costume.org**, which lists local chapters' Web sites.

◎ For medieval and renaissance garb, **www.constumecon.org.** has some great information on making your own costumes. The official Renaissance Faire Web site at **www.renfair.com** can guide you through the process of recreating your Elizabethan persona. Another resource is the Society for Creative Anachronism at **www.sca.org**.

Games and Activities

✳ **Charades!** This party calls for charades. Guests should not reveal who they are—or were—before the party, although some identities will be obvious. When the party begins, ask guests to assemble for a quick game of charades. After each guest's identity is uncovered, he or she should tell a quick story about their life and their fate.

✳ **Past Life Analysis:** Before you start, tape a banner-sized blank strip of paper to your wall. Assemble your guests. Randomly select a lucky guest to be the recipient of a "past life analysis." (Choose someone with a sense of humor.) Pass out slips of paper to everyone else, and instruct each person to describe whom they think the honored guest was in a past life. They can name a famous person like "Cleopatra," or write out a description. They must note the approximate year (or century) when this life was lived. After collecting the submissions, create a chronological timeline by charting these lives on the banner. Read it aloud, and give the chart to the person when he or she leaves.

★ **A Night at the Improv!** Set out modern-day conveniences on your coffee table. The items can include a garlic press, microphone, videotape, stapler remover, portable phone, floppy disk . . . use your imagination when making up your collection. Hand out numbers to everyone in the room. Call out the numbers in turn. Each person should select an item and describe what it was used for in their time. This could get really funny. Afterward, have people vote by a show of hands whose story was the most entertaining. Award this person a prize.

Favors and Prizes

✳ *Dancing in the Light*, by Shirley MacLaine (Bantam Books)
◎ *Autobiography of a Yogi*, by Paramahansa Yogananda (Self-Realization Fellowship)

Musical Suggestions

✳ "Karma Chameleon," Boy George and Culture Club
◎ "Instant Karma," John Lennon, *Greatest*
★ "I'll Come Back as Another Woman," Tanya Tucker, *Greatest Country Hits*
✳ "What Comes around (Goes around)," Dr. John, *Ultimate Dr. John*
◎ "Soul Man," Sam and Dave, *Best of Sam and Dave*

Food

In honor of our ancestors, we are not going to serve anything that once had a "face." We are going to serve delicious vegetarian Indian cuisine.

About the spices: Some of the spices included in the recipes below are available in supermarkets. If you cannot find them, you can check your Yellow Pages for a store near you that sells Indian food ingredients. Trader Joe's is a good source for prepared Indian marinades and chutneys. You can also order ingredients and spices by mail or online. One online source is **www.netbazaar,** which offers a 5 percent discount to students.

Pappadums

These are made of a dal dough. You can purchase these in a specialty store.

12 pappadums   oil for deep frying

Heat oil in a frying pan over medium heat. Fry each side for a few seconds. Drain on paper towels. Serve at room temperature with the two raitas. Serves 12.

Cucumber Raita

This easy dish can be made up to 3 days ahead.

32 ounces plain yogurt   2 cucumbers, peeled and grated

1 teaspoon salt   ⅛ teaspoon cayenne pepper

1 teaspoon roasted, ground cumin   ¼ teaspoon ground cardamom

   seeds (see instructions following)   ¼ teaspoon paprika

To roast whole cumin seeds, fry them in a small, dry skillet until they begin to smoke. Grind them with a mortar and pestle. Empty the yogurt into serving bowl and mix it well with a fork. Add the cucumber, salt, cayenne, cumin, and cardamom. Sprinkle with paprika. Cover and refrigerate. Serves 12.

Spinach Raita

32 ounces plain yogurt

1 1/2 teaspoons roasted, ground cumin seeds

2 cups cooked spinach, washed,
   stemmed, finely chopped

1/2 teaspoon ground coriander

salt and black pepper to taste

Mix the yogurt well. Combine all ingredients. Chill. Serve cold. Serves 12.

Lemon Rice

5 tablespoons vegetable oil

1 teaspoon chana dal

10 curry leaves

3 green chiles, chopped

2 cups long grain rice,
   rinsed well and drained

2 tablespoons coriander leaves,
   chopped

1 teaspoon cumin seeds

1 teaspoon mustard seeds

1/4 teaspoon asafetida

1/2 teaspoon turmeric powder

2 tablespoons grated coconut

2 tablespoons lemon juice

salt to taste

Heat oil in a large pan. Add chana dal, curry leaves, cumin seeds, mustard seeds, asafetida, chiles, turmeric, and rice. Stir-fry for five minutes on a low flame. Add salt to taste. Add 4 cups of hot water and cook until the rice is dry and soft. Turn out on a serving platter. Garnish with coriander and coconut. Sprinkle lemon juice over and serve immediately.

Chana Masala

If you use premade garam masala, this colorful, tasty dish can be made in under a half-hour.
Make it a day ahead, then reheat and garnish before serving.

4 tablespoons vegetable oil

1 onion, chopped

2 cloves garlic, peeled and minced

2 tablespoons garam masala

2 tablespoons tomato paste

2 20-ounce cans of garbanzos,
  partially drained

1 teaspoon salt

In skillet, heat oil over medium flame. Add onion and sauté for 7 minutes. Add garlic and garam masala, and fry, stirring for 2 minutes. Add tomato paste and garbanzos and mix well. Cover and cook on low heat for 10 minutes. Cover and refrigerate. Serve it in a bowl surrounded by quartered tomatoes, raw onion slivers, and green chiles.

Tomato and Onion Chutney

2 medium onions, peeled
  and chopped

2 medium tomatoes, diced

1 1/2 teaspoons salt

1/4 teaspoon black pepper, ground

1/4 teaspoon cayenne

1 teaspoon roasted, ground cumin seeds

1/2 cup plus one tablespoon red
  wine vinegar

Combine all ingredients in a serving bowl. Mix well. Cover and refrigerate. You can make this the day before. Bring to room temperature before serving.

Garlic Naan

Yum, naan bread. Since the rest of this party fare is relatively time intensive, we're going to take a shortcut and use frozen white bread dough. You can find this dough in the frozen food section of your supermarket.

1 loaf frozen white bread dough	2 tablespoons vegetable oil
2 tablespoons water	8 cloves garlic, minced

Follow instructions on package for defrosting bread dough. Preheat broiler to 550°F. Knead the dough a little, and divide into 6 balls. Cover with a damp cloth. Flatten the balls with the palm of your hand, then pull and stretch them into oval shapes, about 1/3-inch thick. Cover with the dough with a damp cloth, and let sit for 15 minutes. Place on two cookie sheets. Brush both sides with oil, and broil one side, until brown. Take the sheet out, turn the bread over, and brush it with additional oil. Place the garlic on top, and broil until lightly browned. Serve warm, if possible.

DRINKS
 ✳ Darjeeling ice tea
 ◎ Indian beer. Try Cobra Lager or the Kingfisher brand.

DESSERT
 Fresh fruit. Have a big bowl filled with bananas, mangos, guavas, oranges, and pomegranates—whatever's seasonally available.

Variations on the Theme

★ **Come as Your Favorite Painting:** Invite guests to come dressed as their favorite painting. Rent paintings from a local museum and purchase poster reproductions of famous works of art. Place large coffee table books featuring the works of famous artists on all flat surfaces. Give away paintbrushes to all. Set up a long table, as depicted in "The Last Supper."

◎ **Medieval Feast:** Have a town crier dressed in medieval garb go to your guests' homes. He should blow on his trumpet, and when the person answers the door, loudly proclaim, "Hear ye, hear ye, you have been summoned to the Queen's (that's you) banquet." Guests should wear medieval attire (see Costumes). Food should be served without utensils. Hire a juggler. Here's a quote from the Queen of the Renaissance Faire: "To pass with goodly sport, Our spirit to revive and comfort; To pipe, to sing, to dance, to spring, With pleasure and delight, To follow sensual appetite!"

Gobble It Up: A Thanksgiving Celebration

T hanksgiving. Hmmm. We are Party Girls, and compared to some other events we can think of, this holiday connotes drudgery more than it does revelry. However, we are going to use all our know-how to throw a fabulous feast and have fun in the process.

We're going to get into the spirit. Get everything ready in advance, and throw a few surprises into the traditional mix. Get ready for Thanksgiving, Party Girl-style.

Invitations

* A simple verbal invitation usually does the trick.
* When selecting your guest list of friends and family, consider inviting someone who has recently moved to the area, or who you know will be alone.
* Ask your guests to each bring a flower with a note attached that denotes something for which they are thankful. Use these flowers to create a centerpiece of thanks.

Decorating Tips

* Roll up your sleeves, Party Girls. It's Arts and Crafts Time! Begin by making your very own wreath. You can dry your own fruit (see note following) and the other supplies should be available at arts and craft stores and floral supply places.

Dried Citrus Wreath

green Spanish moss

sheet moss

12 branches lemon leaves

9 dried orange slices, ¼-inch thick

9 dried lime slices, ¼-inch thick

9 dried miniature pomegranates
  (approximately 2 inches in diameter)

12 dried apple slices

12 dried rosebuds

12 dried sprigs of thyme blossoms

12-inch diameter wire boxed wreath form

floral wire

floral tape

fire cutters

pruning shears or scissors

low-temperature glue gun and glue stick

Fill in the concave surface of the wreath form with Spanish moss. Wrap it with wire to secure. Soak the sheet moss in water to make it flexible. Wrap the wet moss around the entire form and secure it with wire. Let dry thoroughly.

From the lemon branches, cut sprigs of lemon leaves with 3–4 leaves per sprig. Wrap 3–4 sprigs together with floral tape. Using the glue gun, attach the bunches of leaves to the wreath form.

Alternate bunches of leaves with clusters of fruit. Arrange the dried citrus slices into 3 circular clusters of 6 overlapping slices. Add 3 clusters of 3 pomegranates. Still using the glue gun, fill in around the citrus and pomegranate clusters with apple slices, bits of Spanish moss, rosebuds, and thyme blossoms. Fill in any empty spaces with lemon leaves. Hang this masterpiece in a central location.

★ **Tips on drying fruit:** Lemons, limes, oranges, and grapefruits can be air-dried on a cookie sheet placed on a radiator during fall or winter months, or in the oven during the summer. Apples, pears, and other fruits with firm flesh can be air-dried on screens in an area out of direct light and with plenty of air circulation.

In the winter they can be oven-dried at 125° to 150°F. (If the oven does not maintain a low temperature, leave the door ajar to encourage air circulation.) Cut the fruit into slices $1/8$- to $1/4$-inch thick. Lay them on a cake rack, and set the rack on the oven rack. Turn the fruit occasionally. Drying will take $1\frac{1}{2}$ hours or more because fruits contain a lot of moisture. The fruit may not seem completely dry while still warm. Set it in a dry space with good air circulation to cool and dry further.

◎ **Fall Colors:** You can easily and inexpensively decorate fireplace mantels, tabletops, countertops, and buffets throughout your house using gourds, small pumpkins, small pinecones, multicolored dried corn, and pomegranates. You can also use persimmons, but don't place them directly on wood surfaces, and check for decomposition every few days. Place these items—all of which are readily available at most grocery stores—on top of newly fallen green, orange, yellow, and red leaves. If you don't have newly fallen leaves in your neighborhood, take a long drive, or buy fake paper ones at your party supply store.

✳ **Horn of Plenty:** For your Thanksgiving table centerpiece, what better representation of fall than a cornucopia? Purchase a grapevine cornucopia basket from a craft supply shop. Glue any or all of the following around the open end of the cornucopia: sheet moss, white lotus pods, tiny hemlock cones, dried leaves, sprigs of small rosehips, and pepper berries. Place this in the center of your table and arrange a bounty of fruits and unshelled nuts to spill from it. On either side of your cornucopia, place two candlesticks featuring orange (leftover from Halloween?) or green candles.

✳ **The Groaning Board:** Thanksgiving calls for a beautiful table setting. Have your table set before guests arrive. Along with the cornucopia, candles, and a vase for flowers, lay out your best crystal, china, and polished silver.

◎ Purchase plain napkin rings or grapevine rings and attach preserved oak leaves or bay leaves to the inside using a strong glue. Glue a sprig of dried pepper berries to the outside. Place rolled napkins inside.

Games and Activities

✳ As guests arrive, place their flowers and notes inside a vase on your tabletop. Your guests can browse each other's sentiments or each person can read his aloud before dinner.

✦ Create connection: Hold hands and go around in a circle, saying one after another, "May the love that is in my heart pass from my hand to yours."

◎ Read the first Thanksgiving proclamation. On June 20, 1676, the governing council of Charlestown, Massachusetts, held a meeting to determine how best to express thanks for the good fortune that had seen their community securely established. By unanimous vote they instructed Edward Rawson, the clerk, to proclaim June 29 as a day of thanksgiving, our first. That proclamation is reproduced here in the same language and spelling as the original to really get you into the spirit. Try reading it before eating:

> The Holy God having by a long and Continual Series of his Afflictive dispensations in and by the present Warr with the Heathen Natives of this land, written and brought to pass bitter things against his own Covenant people in this wilderness, yet so that we evidently discern that in the midst of his judgments he hath remembered mercy, having remembered his Footstool in the day of his sore displeasure against us for our sins, with many singular Intimations of his Fatherly Compassion, and regard; reserving many of our Towns from Desolation Threatened, and attempted by the Enemy, and giving us especially of late with many of our Confederates many signal Advantages against them, without such Disadvantage

to ourselves as formerly we have been sensible of, if it be the Lord's mercy that we are not consumed, It certainly bespeaks our positive Thankfulness, when our Enemies are in any measure disappointed or destroyed; and fearing the Lord should take notice under so many Intimations of his returning mercy, we should be found an Insensible people, as not standing before Him with Thanksgiving, as well as lading him with our Complaints in the time of pressing Afflictions: The Council has thought meet to appoint and set apart the 29th day of this instant June, as a day of Solemn Thanksgiving and praise to God for such his Goodness and Favour, many Particulars of which mercy might be Instanced, but we doubt not those who are sensible of God's Afflictions, have been as diligent to espy him returning to us; and that the Lord may behold us as a People offering Praise and thereby glorifying Him; the Council doth commend it to the Respective Ministers, Elders and people of this Jurisdiction; Solemnly and seriously to keep the same Beseeching that being perswaded by the mercies of God we may all, even this whole people offer up our bodies and souls as a living and acceptable Service unto God by Jesus Christ.

Favors and Prizes

◎ **Baked with Love:** You can send each guest home with a loaf of homemade Orange-Apricot Sweet Bread (recipe below). It's ready for the oven in just twenty minutes. You can make these ahead of time and freeze them. For extra convenience and a beautiful presentation, bake the loaves directly in oven-safe paper molds. Purchase these inexpensive molds in cookware stores, or by mail from Sur La Table, (800) 243-0852. On Thanksgiving Day, take them out of your freezer and tie a bow around the loaves using raffia string. Cut a 2-by-1-inch square out of a piece of construction paper or card stock and punch a single hole in the corner.

Label your gift and give reheating instructions as follows: Leave bread in paper mold and reheat in a 350°F oven for five to seven minutes.

✳ **Complimentary Condiments:** Send guests home with attractively packaged jars and bottles of condiments, specially selected to their taste. For instance, if your father loves chocolate, a jar of fudge sauce for him; or a bottle of killer hot sauce for your sister who loves spicy food.

Musical Suggestions

◎ Classical music. Play joyful music, such as Beethoven's Ninth Symphony—*Ode to Joy*—and other Beethoven symphonies.

✳ You can also seek out traditional Thanksgiving hymns at your local record store.

Food

Butternut Squash Basket

Add this to your tabletop decor: Serve your fresh vegetables such as strips of red pepper, celery stalks, and cucumber spears in a butternut squash basket. (We know, we know, you've reached the limit of your arts and crafts patience, but this one is easy and very impressive.)

1 large butternut squash	assorted cut raw vegetables

Slice off a thin section from the bottom of the squash to form a stable base. Remove the top stem. For the handle, make two long cuts as shown, 1-inch apart, about halfway down the squash. Cut at least halfway into the squash.

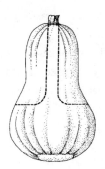

Make two short cuts as shown on the sides, and remove the two sections to be discarded. Carve away the pulp inside the handle with a knife. Hollow out the inside of the basket with a melon baller. Fill the basket with fresh vegetables.

Sweet Potato Aioli

2½ pounds sweet potatoes

16 medium cloves garlic

1½ cups olive oil

2 tablespoons fresh lemon juice

4 teaspoons water

1 teaspoon hot red pepper sauce

salt and pepper to taste

Steam sweet potatoes over a small amount of water until easily pierced with a fork.

Chop the garlic in a food processor. Add peeled sweet potatoes and process until mixture is very smooth. A little at a time, add olive oil, lemon juice, and water, stopping occasionally to scrape down the sides of the bowl. Add hot pepper sauce, salt and pepper, and process until incorporated. Serve as a side dish for 10.

Rosemary Roast Turkey

6 cloves garlic
¼ cup coarsely chopped fresh rosemary leaves
1 13–15 pound turkey
1 tablespoon olive oil
1 lemon, cut in half
5–8 rosemary sprigs

Chop 3 garlic cloves. Mix chopped garlic with chopped rosemary. Get turkey ready to roast. Remove innards (and reserve for gravy), rinse turkey well, and rub oil on skin. Squeeze juice from a lemon half into body cavity, then add the lemon peel. Slide your fingers under turkey skin to gently loosen it (but leave in place) on breast, around outside of thighs, and legs and over back (from the neck end). Push the rosemary–garlic mixture under skin, distributing evenly. Place remaining garlic cloves and the rosemary sprigs inside the bird. Roast turkey as directed on package, then put on platter and let stand up to 30 minutes. Skim and discard fat from pan juices. Reserve juices for Turkey Gravy (recipe follows). Serves 10.

Turkey Giblet Gravy with Mushrooms

Simmer the giblets while the turkey is roasting.

turkey neck
giblets
½ cup Madeira wine

12 button mushrooms, cleaned and sliced
2 tablespoons butter or margarine
2 cups chicken broth

2 tablespoons drippings
(fat and juices from turkey)

2 tablespoons all-purpose flour

Make giblet broth: Bring turkey neck, giblets, wine, and 2 cups chicken broth to boil. Simmer over low heat, covered, for 45 minutes. Pour broth through a fine strainer into a bowl; reserve liquid for gravy. Pull meat from neck bone. Finely chop meat and giblets and add to gravy if desired. In a skillet, sauté sliced mushrooms in butter over low heat for 5 minutes. Place drippings in separate pan. Stir in flour. Cook over low heat stirring constantly until mixture is smooth and bubbly. Stir in giblet broth and add mushrooms. Boil, stirring constantly, for several minutes until desired thickness. Add salt and pepper to taste, pour into a gravy boat, and serve. Makes about 2½ cups.

Traditional Stuffing with Apples

4 cups stale bread cubes in ¼-inch cubes
¼ cup butter, melted
¼ cup butter
2 medium onions, chopped
6 celery stalks, chopped

1 tablespoon dried thyme
1 tablespoon dried sage
1 cup fresh Italian parsley, chopped
2 cups chopped apples, unpeeled
Salt and pepper to taste

Preheat the oven to 350°F. Lightly butter a large baking dish. Mix the bread cubes with the melted butter in a large bowl. Melt the remaining butter in a large skillet over medium heat. Add the onions and celery and sauté for 5 minutes. Mix in the herbs and apples, and season to taste with salt and pepper. Combine the vegetable mixture with the bread cubes and toss together. Add a little water or broth to moisten. Spoon stuffing loosely into the cavity of the turkey just before roasting. Whatever's left over should be put in a small casserole dish and baked alongside the turkey for the last half-hour.

Spicy Cranberry Relish

Author Susannah Seton calls this the "ultimate cranberry relish."

1 tablespoon vegetable oil
1/2 medium onion, diced
1 jalapeño pepper, diced
1 heaping tablespoon grated ginger
1 garlic clove, minced
1/3 cup cider vinegar
1/2 cup dry red wine
1 cup brown sugar
1 teaspoon ground pepper
1 teaspoon cinnamon

1/2 teaspoon ground allspice
1/2 teaspoon ground coriander
1/2 teaspoon ground cloves
1/4 teaspoon ground nutmeg
2 sprigs thyme
1 small bay leaf
3 cups cranberries, washed and
   picked over
2 pears, peeled and diced
1/2 cup raisins

In a large saucepan, heat the oil over medium heat. Add the onion, jalapeño pepper, ginger, and garlic and sauté, stirring often, until the onion is translucent. Add vinegar, wine, brown sugar, herbs, and spices. Simmer, stirring often, until syrupy, about 20 minutes.

Stir in cranberries, pears, and raisins. Simmer until cranberries pop, about 10–15 minutes. Remove the bay leaf and serve at room temperature. Makes 4 cups.

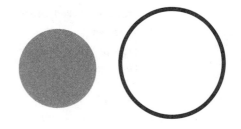

Garlic Mashed Potatoes

Yummy! Unfortunately, this cannot be made in advance.

5 pounds russet potatoes

I cup peeled garlic cloves

¾ cup whipping cream or whole milk

3 tablespoons butter or margarine

salt and white pepper

Peel potatoes and cut into quarters. Boil the potatoes until tender in a covered 5- or 6-quart pan. In a separate pan, over low heat, combine garlic, cream, and butter. Cover and stir occasionally until garlic is tender, about 10 minutes. In a food processor, purée garlic mixture. Drain potatoes, return to pan, and add garlic purée. Mash with a potato masher or mixer until smooth. Add salt and pepper to taste. Makes 10–12 servings.

Orange-Apricot Sweet Bread

Make this up to a week ahead, and freeze it. Double the quantities for two loaves.

½ cup butter or margarine

⅔ cup plus I tablespoon sugar

½ teaspoon hulled cardamom seed, crushed

I tablespoon finely shredded orange peel

I large egg

I large egg yolk

½ cup sour cream

¼ teaspoon baking soda

¾ teaspoon baking powder

I cup all-purpose flour

½ cup diced dried apricots

In a bowl, beat butter, 2/3 cup sugar, and cardamom with a mixer until fluffy. Add orange peel, egg, egg yolk, and sour cream. Mix well. In a separate bowl, stir together soda, baking powder, flour, and diced apricots. Add to butter mixture and stir until evenly blended. Butter and flour-dust a 5- to 6- cup baking pan or paper baking mold. Scrape batter into pan and spread level. Sprinkle batter evenly with 1 tablespoon sugar. Bake on rack slightly below center in a 350°F oven until bread springs back when lightly pressed in center, and just begins to pull from pan sides, 35–40 minutes. Let cool on rack. Serve warm or cool, inverted from pan, then turned topside up. Makes 8–10 servings.

Yam Pudding

2 29-ounce cans cut yams in syrup, well drained	¾ teaspoon salt
2 tablespoons sugar	½ teaspoon ground cinnamon
2 tablespoons honey	¼ teaspoon ground nutmeg
3 large eggs	½ cup half and half
2 tablespoons unsalted butter, melted	¼ cup orange juice
	1 ½ tablespoons grated orange peel

Preheat oven to 350°F. Butter 8-by-8-by-2-inch baking dish. Beat yams, sugar, and honey in large bowl until smooth, about 3 minutes. Beat in eggs one at a time. Beat in orange peel, salt, and spices, then half and half, orange juice, and butter. Transfer yam mixture to prepared dish.

Bake pudding until puffed and set in center, about 75 minutes. Let stand 15 minutes. Serve warm. Serves 8.

Cranberry Wine Punch

Throw this together in the morning, heat before guests arrive, and allow guests to serve themselves.

6 cups cranberry juice cocktail

½ cup orange juice concentrate

2 tablespoons brown sugar

¼ teaspoon almond extract

2 cups red wine such as Merlot or Gamay Beaujolais

Heat all ingredients over very low heat for five to seven minutes. Serves 8–10.

December

Deck The Halls with Matzoh Balls: A Multi-Culti Party

That Keeps the Faiths

You can't please all the people all the time, but a Party Girl will do her darndest to try. She'll open her house and open her mind to all of the holiday possibilities December brings—Christmas, Chanukah, Kwanzaa, and, so as not to offend any practicing pagans, Winter Solstice. This party is a greatest hits of winter holiday food, festoonery, and fun.

(Bonus! See if you can count how many ways *Hanukkah* is spelled in this chapter—the answer is at the end.)

Invitations

◎ Use your computer clip art or cut out images of all of the holidays from magazines, and use them to border a white invitation. Use colored markers or pencils in red, green, black, and blue to address the envelope—alternate colors for each letter. That way you've covered all the colors of the season.

✳ **Headline:** *Merry Hanukkah, Happy Solstice, Joyous Christmas, and Peaceful Kwanzaa—A Pan-Holiday Party to Celebrate the Season*

Decorating Tips

✶ Candles flicker at all winter holiday celebrations; they represent light in the darkest time of the year. Use lots of candles on tables and mantles. For a glittery presentation, buy a bunch of plain, clear glasses and goblets at a thrift store. Fill one small paper plate with a layer of glue and another with glitter. Dip the rims of the glasses in glue and then in glitter. When dry, fill the glasses about half-full with water tinted with a drop or two of food coloring. Float a tea light candle in the water. Gather a bunch of these together and you've got a stunning decoration for your mantle. For an all-Chanukkah look, use silver glitter and blue colored water.

✳ Christmas lights are the cheapest, easiest way to add sparkle and glitz to a holiday party, and best of all, they go on sale and stay on sale all through the holiday season. Start wrappin' 'em 'round your tree and then keep going! Drape them over the buffet table, wind them around banisters, hang them from curtain rods. There are even small strings of battery-powered lights that you can use on dinner tables, doors, and other away-from-a-socket locations.

✴ A Kwanzaa setup is a pretty, easy, and meaningful decoration for a mantle or buffet table. The main attraction is the *Kinara*, a seven-candle candleholder. These can be made or bought. If you make one, it's traditional to use natural materials. Fill the Kinara with three red candles, one black, and three green. Place it on a straw or cloth *Mekka*, a placemat. Surround the Kinara with *Mazao*, veggies and fruit that represent abundant crops; *Kilombe Cha Umoja*, a goblet; and *Vibunzi*, at least one ear of corn or one for each child. Kwanzaa was established in 1966 as an African American celebration of cultural identity and unity. Starting on December 26, families light one candle each night and reflect on the values of Kwanzaa:

Umoja—unity	**Nia**—*purpose*
Kujichagulia—*self-determination*	**Kuumba**—*creativity*
Ujima—*collective work and responsibility*	**Imani**—*faith*
Ujamaa—*cooperative economics*	

✴ Do we even have to mention that a Christmas tree is the paragon of winter holiday decor? Even Jewish Party Girls have to have at least a small one for this cross-cultural party—don't worry, your Bubbe won't really have a heart attack!

◎ A Yule log is a remnant of pagan "bonfire-in-the-woods" type winter rituals. If you've got a fireplace, light it up! If not, you can rent or buy a video Yule Log complete with Christmas carol background music. If your local video store doesn't have one, you can purchase one at Amazon.com (**http://www.amazon.com**).

✳ ***Ring-A-Ding!*** Rings are potent Solstice symbols—they represent the sun and the circle of life. Decorate with purchased wreaths or make your own. To make an easy wreath, cut out a large circle of corrugated cardboard or foamcore, then cut out a smaller circle in the middle. Use a platter and a salad plate as guides if you don't have a protractor. Paint the ring a solid color or wrap with wide ribbon or fabric. Get out the hot glue gun and pile on your choice of decor. Make one for each holiday: Multicolored ball ornaments for Christmas; small fresh fruits and nuts-in-the-shell for Kwanzaa; dried flowers, leaves, and other garden-gatherings for Solstice; and chocolate coins, cutout Stars of David and candles for Hanuka. Or, make paper ring chains using construction paper in Christmas (red and green), Kwanzaa (red, green, and black), and Hannukah (blue and white) colors. Cut out lots of construction paper strips 8½-by-1-inches long. Start with one loop, secured with tape or a glue stick. Loop another one through the first and keep going until you have a long chain. Swag around the room.

✳ **Did You Think I Was Kidding?** Make Matzoh Ball ornaments! You'll need a dozen 3-inch Styrofoam balls, tacky craft glue, matzoh meal, wax paper, long straight pins, and blue ribbon. Pour some of the matzoh meal onto a paper plate. Coat one of the foam balls in glue, then roll it around in the meal until it's well covered. Set the coated ball on a sheet of waxed paper to dry. Coat rest of the balls (you'll probably have to wash your hands between balls—it gets a bit messy). When the balls are dry, pin a loop of ribbon to them with two or three pins. Hang the balls from your Christmas tree, or from a houseplant you've designated as a "Channuka Bush."

Games and Activities

✳ **Dreidel, Dreidel, Dreidel!** Go ahead and make one out of clay, but don't expect it to spin. To play the dreidel game, you'll need a store-bought one. If you're not familiar with the names of the Hebrew letters on the dreidel, buy one that has them spelled out. Gather the players 'round a table or on a hard floor. Give each player five betting chips: gold candy coins, jelly beans, or pennies. Each player antes up with one chip. The first player spins the top and, depending on the side it lands on:

> **Gimel** (think "gimmie")—*takes all of the chips in the pot*
> **Hey** (think "half")—*takes half of the chips in the pot*
> **Nun** (think "next!")—*skips his turn and passes the dreidel to the next player*
> **Shim** (think "schlemiel")—*puts a chip into the pot*

Spinning continues until one player has all of the chips. If you're playing with candy, that's prize enough—just give the winner a baggie for the loot. If you're playing with pennies, give the winner a prize. The dreidel itself can also be a prize.

For the record, here are the words to the dreidel song:

> Dreidel, dreidel, dreidel, I make it out of clay,
> And when it's dry and ready,
> Oh dreidel I shall play!

So, why a dreidel? The letters on the dreidel are initials for words that mean, "A Great Miracle Happened Here," and refer to the miracle of one day's worth of oil lasting for eight days during the rededication of the Temple at Jerusalem by the Maccabees. So why were the Maccabees rededicating the temple? Because it had been desecrated by the Syrians and reclaimed by the Maccabees in a successful skirmish.

✳ **Gift Exchange:** One Naughty and One Nice! Ask each guest to bring a wrapped gift costing no more than $5 (or $10 if the economy is going well). For the "Naughty" exchange, put all the gifts in a pile and gather everyone in a circle around them. Have each guest draw a number from a hat. For the first round, each guest in sequence chooses a gift from the pile. In the second round, Guest Number 1 opens her gift and shows it to the crowd. Guest Number 2 can then either open the wrapped gift in her hand, or "steal" the open gift from Guest Number 1 in exchange for the wrapped one she's holding. If she steals, the person she has stolen from opens the wrapped gift and shows it to the crowd. The game then goes on through the numbers, with all of the open gifts available for stealing. In the "Nice" version, all of the guests put their names in a hat. Draw the names in pairs and have the two who are drawn exchange gifts. You can add an element of matchmaking to this if you've got a lot of unattached singles at your party by putting the men's and women's names in separate bowls and drawing one from each. Hmm, the "nice" version may turn out "naughty" after all. . . .

◎ **Share the Spirit!** Ask your guests to bring either new, unwrapped toys or canned food. Pile the generous contributions under the tree or on a table. After the party, donate them to a homeless shelter, food bank, or toy drive.

Favors and Prizes

★ **Scent Home Smiling!** Make cinnamon scented cutouts—they can be hung on the tree as ornaments or in the closet as a sachet. Mix unsweetened applesauce with one bottle (4.25 oz) ground cinnamon to make a stiff dough. Roll out to about 3-inch thick. Cut out shapes with cookie cutters. Make a hole at the top of each cutout with a toothpick. Lay the ornaments on a rack and let them dry for a few days, turning every so often. When they're dry, tie a ribbon loop through the hole. Wrap in plastic or pop into a cello gift bag and tie with a "Thank You" tag.

✳ **Give 'Em a Gelt Complex!** A mesh bag of Hanukah gelt (those gold chocolate coins—gelt means "gold" or "money"—is a ready-made favor. Tie a bow and add a "Thank You" tag and you're done!

✳ **...And a Happy New Year!** The new year is right around the corner! A new desk, wall, or pocket calendar is a great holiday party favor.

Musical Suggestions

Mix up swingin' versions of traditional Christmas carols with alternative sounds of the season:

★ Kwanzaa Party, Various Artists

◎ A Winter's Solstice, Volumes I–VI

✳ Mazel Tov! Popular Songs for Jewish Celebrations, Various Artists
★ Jazz for Joy: A Verve Christmas Album, Various Artists
✺ Christmas Cheers from Motown, Various Artists
◎ A Very Special Christmas, Volumes 1–3, Various Artists

Food

Rings of Fire

Rich, flavorful pastry rounds that honor the pagan symbol of the sun

3 cups flour

2 cups shredded sharp Cheddar
   cheese

2 teaspoons paprika

1 teaspoon salt

1 cup butter or margarine,
   at room temperature

6 tablespoons milk

1 egg, slightly beaten with
   1 tablespoon water

Preheat oven to 350°F. Mix all of the dry ingredients together in a large mixing bowl. With a pastry blender, your fingertips, or two knives, cut the butter into the flour mixture until the whole thing looks like coarse meal. Add the milk and mix onto a dough. Divide the dough into 48 pieces. Roll each piece into a 5-inch log. Form each log into a ring on an ungreased cookie sheet. Brush each ring with the beaten egg. Bake for 20–25 minutes or until golden brown.

    Can be made a day or two ahead. Store cooled rings in a tightly sealed container at room temperature. Makes 48 rings.

Lotsa Latkes!

Latkes used to be an all-day ordeal. Hours of grating—the inevitable blood in the batter—followed by slavery over a bubbling frying pan of oil. These blender babies are much easier—but just as tasty! We've added a Christmas touch to these latkes—a shot of sweet potato. Double, triple, or quadruple the recipe, but blend in batches. After each batch is blended, pour the batter into a large mixing bowl. Pull a chair up to the stovetop—you'll be there a while! While you're frying the pancakes, reddish-brown liquid may rise to the top of the batter in the bowl. Just skim this off the top with a large metal spoon.

2 eggs
1 small or $1/2$ large onion, cut into chunks
1 teaspoon salt
2 tablespoons flour or matzoh meal
$1/4$ teaspoon baking powder
2 tablespoons chopped fresh parsley
$1/2$ cup raw, cubed unpeeled sweet potato
$2^{1}/2$ cups raw, cubed unpeeled russet potato
applesauce and sour cream

Toss the first 6 ingredients and a large handful of the potatoes into a blender and whir until liquid. Add the rest of the potatoes and blend until smooth. Fry the pancakes (about 2 tablespoons of batter per pancake) in a skillet in about 3 inches of hot oil. Be patient and wait for each side to get brown and crispy. Drain the pancakes on a paper-lined plate.

Can be made a day ahead. Store in one or two layers on a baking sheet covered with foil. Can be refrigerated or left at room temperature. Reheat in a 400°F oven for about 15 minutes. Serve with applesauce and sour cream on the side. Makes about 18 pancakes.

Kwanzaa Collard Greens

African American families often eat down-home "soul food" during Kwanzaa. This vegetarian version also tastes great piled on top of a latke.

2 tablespoons olive oil

2 large red onions, chopped

3 cloves garlic, minced or pressed

3 pounds collard or other sturdy greens, trimmed, rinsed and torn into pieces.

¼ cup white wine or vegetable broth

1 teaspoon salt

black pepper to taste

Heat the olive oil in a large lidded stockpot. Add the onions and garlic and cook for about 5 minutes. Add the greens to the pot—you may have to do this in batches. Add the wine or broth and cover the pot. Cook the greens for about 10 minutes, stirring once or twice. Add salt and pepper and cook another 3–4 minutes. Serve immediately or cool and store in the fridge overnight. Zap in the microwave to reheat before serving. Serves 10–12.

Black-Eyed Pea and Ham Salad

This recipe combines a soul food staple with traditional Christmas ham.

2½ cups dried black-eyed peas, rinsed and picked over

1¼ teaspoons salt

5 tablespoons cider vinegar

1½ cups finely chopped celery

1¼ cups finely chopped red onion

1 1/2 tablespoons olive oil

1 1/4 pounds smoked cooked ham, cut into 2-inch chunks

1 teaspoon honey

1/4 teaspoon ground cloves

In a saucepan, combine peas with salt; cover with water by 2 inches and simmer, uncovered, until just tender, 25–30 minutes (do not overcook). Drain peas into a bowl; toss with vinegar, vegetables and 1 tablespoon oil.

In a small skillet, heat remaining 1/2 tablespoon oil over moderately high heat until hot but not smoking, and sauté ham, stirring, 1 minute. Add honey and cloves; sauté for 1 minute. Add ham to salad and toss well.

Can be made a day ahead. Cover and chill. Bring to room temperature before serving.

Serves 10–12.

Ever-Green Salad

10 cups fresh salad greens

1/2 cup chopped toasted pecans

3/4 cup dried cranberries

1 large red onion, thinly sliced

1 tart green apple, cored, seeded, and
chopped

1/2 cup toasted pine nuts

Dressing

1/2 cup cider vinegar

2 teaspoons Dijon mustard

1/4 cup orange juice

3/4 cups canola oil

1 tablespoon honey

salt and pepper to taste

Toss all of the salad ingredients together in a bowl. To make the dressing, put all of the ingredients into a screw-top jar and shake. Toss the salad just before serving. Serves 1012.

Turkey Yule Log

This bird comes to the table lookin' like fuel for a pagan bonfire.

2 teaspoons olive oil
2 small onions, chopped
1/2 pound mushrooms, coarsely chopped
2 cloves garlic, minced or pressed
2 tablespoons chopped fresh sage or 1 teaspoon dried
1 1/2 pounds ground turkey
1 1/2 cups bread crumbs
1 egg, beaten
1/3 cup milk
sprigs of parsley to garnish

Preheat oven to 375°F. Heat the oil in a skillet. Add the onions and cook until soft, about 5 minutes. Add the mushrooms and garlic and cook until the mushroom liquid evaporates.

In a large bowl, mix the onion-mushroom mixture with all of the ingredients except parsley. Season with salt and pepper and mix well. Line a baking sheet with tin foil. Form the turkey mixture into a log shape on the foil. Bake until done, 50–60 minutes. Garnish with parsley and serve immediately, or, to make ahead, cool and store overnight in the fridge. Heat in a 350°F oven for 15 minutes before serving. Serves 10–12.

Tri-Holiday Trifle!

Trifle is a traditional English Christmas dessert. To end this feast of many fests, we're including the jam usually found in Hanukkah safgayot or jelly doughnuts, and the peaches from soul food's peach cobbler.

Cake

1 16-ounce frozen pound cake or
    Spicy Almond Pound Cake
3 tablespoons milk
3 large eggs
1 teaspoon vanilla
1 teaspoon almond extract
Fruit Filling (recipe follows)
Cream (recipe follows)
fruit liqueur or rum (optional)

1 1/2 cups flour
3/4 cup sugar
3/4 teaspoon baking powder
1/4 teaspoon salt
1 1/2 teaspoons pumpkin pie spice
3/4 cups unsalted butter, softened

Fruit Filling

2/3 cup plus 3 tablespoons water
1/4 cup brown sugar
1/2 cup sugar

4 tablespoons fresh lemon juice
9 ounces dried peaches
1 teaspoon pumpkin pie spice

Cream

2 cups apricot jam, heated and
    pressed through a metal strainer
1 1/2 tablespoon water or fruit liqueur

1 envelope gelatin
3 cups whipping cream

Preheat oven to 350°F. Grease and flour a 6-cup loaf pan.

Combine the milk, eggs, and extracts in a medium bowl. In a large mixing bowl, combine the dry ingredients. Add the butter and half of the egg mixture, and combine at low speed. Mix at medium for 2 minutes. Add the rest of the egg mixture in two batches, blending well after each addition. Pour into the prepared pan and bake for about an hour, or until a cake tester comes out clean. Can be made ahead, store tightly wrapped at room temperature for up to 3 days, in the fridge for a week, or frozen for 2 months.

To make the Fruit Filling, combine ⅔ cup water, sugars, and 2 tablespoons lemon juice in heavy medium saucepan. Stir over high heat until sugar dissolves. Add peaches and bring to boil. Reduce heat, cover, and simmer 10 minutes. Add pumpkin pie spice. Place peach mixture in a food processor with 3 tablespoons water and 2 tablespoons lemon and puree. Can be prepared 1 day ahead. Cover and store at room temperature.

To make the Cream, mix the jam with the water or liqueur in a bowl or 2-cup measuring cup. Place the jam in a small bowl and sprinkle the gelatin over the top. Let it sit for 5 minutes. Heat the jam in the microwave for 20 seconds or until the gelatin is melted. Set aside to cool. Whip the cream in a chilled bowl with chilled beaters until you can see the beater marks in the cream. Add the room-temperature jam and beat until stiff peaks form.

Assemble the dessert the day before the party. Cut the cake into 1-inch slices. Cut each slice into 1-inch squares. Put half of the cake squares into the bottom of a glass bowl with a flat bottom. Spread half of the Fruit Filling over the cake, and top with half of the Cream. Make one more layer of cake, Fruit, and Cream. Chill overnight. Remove from the fridge about half an hour before serving. To serve, spoon the trifle into bowls.

To booze it up, sprinkle a few tablespoons of fruit liqueur or rum over the cake before adding fruit layer. Serves 10–12.

Variations on the Theme

⭑ **Cope with Christmas Party!** Right after Thanksgiving a holiday panic can set in. Major holidays are coming and there's no stopping 'em—you've got a lot to do, girl! Shopping, cooking, baking, wrapping, decorating, wassailing (wassailing?) are all showing up on the "to do" list. If you could use a little help, you can bet your friends could too. Invite your burdened buddies for an afternoon pre-holiday reality check. Serve cookies and tea, and ask everyone bring their holiday "to do" lists to share. Exchange gift-giving ideas and recipes, pool resources for buying bulk baking supplies or gift wrap, and running errands. Or challenge each other to make holiday card lists right then and there!

◎ **Christmas with the King!** Recreate Christmas at Graceland with a pink-flocked Christmas tree, cover tables with gold lamé, serve fried peanut butter and banana sandwiches and other treats from an Elvis Presley cookbook (there are at least three in print!), and play an Elvis Christmas album. Call 1-888-ELVIS-ROCKS for a full-color catalog of Elvis merchandise, including books, music, and decorative tchochkes.

ANSWER: *Hanukkah is spelled seven ways in this chapter—and each and every one of them is kosher. There's no wrong way to spell Chanuka!*

Crystal Balls and Fortune Tellers: *A New Year's Eve*

Fortune-Telling Party

Party Girls want—no, need—to know what's going to happen next: "When will I meet Mr. Right?" "When will I get that raise?" and especially . . . "When is the next party?"

That's why, standing at the brink of a New Year, no Party Girl would leave her fortunes purely to chance. Throw a New Year's Eve Fortune-Telling Party and make sure you're prepared for a future full of fun.

Invitations

✳ Design a flyer using clip art images of psychic forecasters, playing card decks, astrological symbols, stars, celestial bodies, and dice. The invitation should promote psychic readings, fortune-telling, and special surprises. On the outside of the envelope, use one of the following headlines in boldface type:

◎ **Headlines:**

> Prediction: You Will Have a Great Evening!
>
> You're About to Forecast Your Future!
>
> Your Destiny Is in Your Hands
>
> We Predict Good Fortune in the New Year!

★ Enclose a lottery ticket in the invitation.

Decorating Tips

◎ Hand-letter signs that boldly declare "Psychic Readings Inside." Prominently place in front windows. Exchange your porch light bulb with a red light.

✳ **Gypsies, Tramps, and Thieves:** Beg, borrow, or steal oriental rugs and pillows to scatter around the house. Buy '60s-style beaded door hangings that you can pin to the top of doorframes. The effect works best on doors that guests have to pass through, such as the hallway or the kitchen entry. Buy inexpensive top sheets in bright purple, yellow, red, and green to drape over your furniture, and to create instant tablecloths. Look for inexpensive chains and fake coins—the chains can be pinned around the table edge, and the coins can be scattered on the tabletop. Decorate your walls with zodiac posters.

★ **It's in the Cards:** Tarot cards and even regular playing cards are cheap, easy insta-decor. Tape them up on any wall, doorway, or dull-looking surface. Spread them around the buffet table.

◎ Don't forget to place candles throughout your house, especially in the bathrooms.

✳ On your television screen, run a video loop of Dionne Warwick and Kenny Kingston advertising their psychic services.

Costumes

Guests should be encouraged to dress like Gypsies. Scout thrift stores for out-of-fashion paisley clothes. Men can don blowzy shirts and leather boots and wrap their heads in bandannas. Women can wear scarves, coin necklaces, big hoop earrings, and long skirts.

Games and Activities

★ **Look into the Future:** Set up a skirted round table in a corner with a "crystal ball." These can be purchased at specialty stores, or you can improvise with a large round light bulb, purchased at your local hardware store. Place it screw-end down into something hollow, such as a roll of packing tape covered with a scarf. Cut out an image of a "spirit" from black construction paper. Tape it to the light end of a strong, large flashlight. Black out the room. After gazing into the crystal ball, summon up the "spirit" by surreptitiously shining the flashlight onto the wall.

◎ If you have any friends who can interpret tarot cards or read palms, put 'em to work! If not, you may want to look in your Yellow Pages and hire someone who at least claims he or she has the ability to forecast the future. You can also set out books on palmistry, numerology, and tarot card reading that your friends can refer to at the fortune-telling station. Surf the Web for do-it-yourself fortune-telling kits.

✳ **Numerology:** Use only the numbered cards from a deck of cards. Shuffle and cut the deck, then remove any three cards at random from the face-down pack. Add their values together and note the meaning of their total from the following:

> **3.** You must get around to writing that letter.
> **4.** Trust in your intuition and be bold.
> **5.** Beware of flattery.
> **6.** Spare a thought for your partner's feelings.
> **7.** Forget about that worrying letter.
> **8.** Your determined struggle will reap results.

9. Your actions could cause trouble for your friends or relatives.

10. Bad news will cause you much sorrow.

11. Accept the business proposal.

12. Beware of a false friend.

13. You will need to be broad-minded to remain calm.

14. Pleasant news and a great reward are heading your way.

15. Remember to keep a smile on your face this week.

16. Stick to your plans; don't waver.

17. A long journey could be dangerous.

18. Forgive and forget. It is not worth holding a grudge.

19. Avoid the company of someone that you already do not trust completely.

20. Stop brooding about the past—live for today!

21. Turmoil on the home front could be possible.

22. Take a second look at an offer coming to you.

23. Absent friends will get in contact with happy news.

24. A happy week is ahead of you.

25. An unexpected windfall is coming your way.

26. Act now—don't delay! Success will be yours.

27. Trust in your friend. Don't rock the boat.

28. Search for more answers. Don't rest on your laurels!

29. Don't abuse your success.

30. Your charitable act will be rewarded tenfold!

✳ Set up games of blackjack. You can also purchase a Ouija board.

A trinity of goddesses, Fors Fortuna or the Three Fates, rules chance. The Triple Goddess, the ruler of fate, consists of Lachsis, who controls the length of the threads of life; Clotho, her older sister who spins and weaves the tapestry of our lives into a beautiful work of art; and Atropos, the oldest, who controls endings with her shears and cuts the threads of life when she feels it's time. When the fates are not honored, they become the Furies Alecto, Tesiphone, and Megaera. They are pictured often as old maids spinning in a dark cave sharing one eye among them; thus the saying "The fates are blind." Light three candles and pray to the Fates for good luck.

Favors and Prizes

- ✳ Rabbit's foot keychains
- ◎ Magic Eight balls
- ✴ Tarot card deck
- ✦ A set of dice

Musical Suggestions

- ◎ Music from Albania, Romania, and other Eastern European countries. Hungarian gypsy music is a style played mostly by Rom people originally from Transylvania or by settled Rom. It is a mixture of Hungarian folk songs and Transylvanian influences with a touch of Viennese music. Various percussion instruments such as milk cans, spoons, utensils, and even rubbing wet hands on a table can accompany the vocals.
- ✳ Spanish Gypsies enjoy Flamenco music. Try the Best of the Gypsy Kings.
- ✦ "Love Potion No. 9," Clovers, Very Best of the Clovers

◎ "Gypsies, Tramps and Thieves," Sonny and Cher, *Greatest Hits* (UNI/MCI)
✳ "Destiny," Gloria Estevan, *Destiny* (Sony)

Food

◎ Set out bowls of flavorful nibblies, such as green and black olives, seeded bread-sticks, and store-bought sun-dried tomato and basil pesto spread on sturdy crackers, alongside heartier buffet fare.

Romanian Eggplant Dip

You can make this recipe up to one week ahead!

1 medium eggplant
¼ cup olive oil
2 tablespoons fresh lemon juice
2 medium cloves garlic, or to taste, smashed, peeled and minced
2 teaspoons kosher salt
freshly ground black pepper, to taste
¼ cup chopped fresh parsley
6 pieces of pita bread, cut into quarters.

Bake or microwave the eggplant. To bake, heat oven to 400°F. Roast on a heavy ungreased baking sheet until it bursts and becomes very tender. This should take approximately 1 hour. Remove baking sheet from oven. Using two forks, immediately tear the eggplant open. Scrape out the pulp onto the hot baking sheet. Let it sizzle and brown. This will help some of the liquid to evaporate. Discard the dry skin. Transfer the pulp to a bowl.

Shred eggplant, or purée in food processor. Beat in all remaining ingredients except pita bread. Store, covered, in refrigerator at least overnight to let flavors develop. Serve with quartered pita bread or mini pitas. Serves 6.

Dolmades

2½ cups water

1 teaspoon salt

1½ cup long grain rice, uncooked

2 jars grape leaves, rinsed

3 cups onions, minced

½ cup olive oil

1 teaspoon dried mint

1½ cups pine nuts

1½ cups currants

freshly ground black pepper, to taste

¾ cup fresh lemon juice

Bring water and salt to a boil. Add rice and simmer 18 minutes. Remove stem ends from rinsed and dried grape leaves. Sauté onions in olive oil for 5 minutes, or until transparent. Stir in mint. Roast pine nuts for 7 minutes at 325°F until light brown. Mix together rice, onions, pine nuts, and currants. Remove from heat and allow to cool slightly. Form rolls, using 1 rounded teaspoon of the rice mixture for each grape leaf by placing filling near stem end. Fold the stem end over, fold sides in and roll. Sprinkle lemon juice on top, and refrigerate until ready to serve. Makes 120 packages.

Chicken Paprikash

4 skinless boneless chicken breast halves,
   cut crosswise into 1/2-inch-wide strips
3 tablespoons paprika, preferably Hungarian sweet
3 tablespoons butter
1 large onion, chopped
2 large plum tomatoes, seeded, chopped
2 cups canned low-salt chicken broth
   1/2 cup regular or reduced-fat sour cream
12 ounces noodles, cooked and buttered

Season chicken with 1 tablespoon paprika, salt, and pepper. Melt 2 tablespoons butter in large non-stick skillet over medium-high heat. Add chicken and sauté until just cooked through, about 3 minutes. Using slotted spoon, transfer chicken to plate. Add remaining butter to same skillet. Add onion and sauté until beginning to soften, about 3 minutes. Add remaining paprika; stir 10 seconds. Add tomato and stir until beginning to soften, about 1 minute. Add broth. Increase heat to high and boil until sauce thickens enough to coat spoon thinly, about 5 minutes. Mix in chicken and any collected juices. Reduce heat to low. Add sour cream and stir just until heated through (do not boil). Season to taste with salt and pepper and serve over buttered noodles. Makes 5 servings.

Gypsy Lamb Skewers

Food that is skewered and roasted over an open fire is a favorite among nomadic people. This is a traditional Gypsy recipe for lamb. Get everything prepared in advance, and barbecue just before serving.

¼ cup plain yogurt

2 tablespoons fresh oregano, chopped

4 cloves garlic, minced

2 tablespoons fresh lemon juice

2 pounds lean lamb, cut into cubes

10 cherry tomatoes

10 squares bell pepper

10 mushroom caps

10 small white onions

Mix yogurt, oregano, garlic, and lemon in a large bowl. Add lamb cubes and marinate overnight in the refrigerator. Take 10 metal skewers and spear lamb and vegetables one at a time, alternating vegetables. Use two lamb chunks per skewer. Barbecue until lamb is cooked through. Remove from skewers and place on a serving tray. Makes 10 skewers.

Magic Eight Nut Balls

Easy and fun to make.

16 ounces semisweet chocolate

1 cup evaporated milk

1 cup walnuts, finely chopped

½ cup raisins

½ cup dried apricots, finely chopped

½ cup unsweetened cocoa powder

In a double boiler or microwave oven, gently melt the chocolate together with the milk. Stir until smooth. Stir in the walnuts, apricots, and raisins. Spread evenly on an ungreased cookie sheet. Refrigerate overnight, covered.

Spread the cocoa on a plate. Cut the chilled mixture into 40 equal squares. Remove a square from the cookie sheet with a spatula, quickly roll it between your palms into a walnut-sized ball, and evenly coat each ball in the cocoa.

Keep the magic eight nut balls separate by layering on wax paper. These can be frozen, or kept in the refrigerator for 2 weeks before serving. Makes 40 balls.

A Date with Destiny Bars

You can make these a few days before the party. Store in airtight containers.

I cup butter, softened

2 cups sugar, plus more for garnish

3 eggs

I teaspoon baking soda

2 teaspoons water

I 10 ounce package chopped pitted dates

3 cups all-purpose flour

I teaspoon cinnamon

I teaspoon ground nutmeg

¼ teaspoon salt

I cup chopped walnuts

With an electric mixer, cream butter and 2 cups sugar. Beat eggs in one at a time. In a small dish, dissolve baking soda in water and combine with creamed mixture. Add dates. Sift flour and spices together and beat into cream mixture. Stir in chopped walnuts.

Cover the dough with waxed paper and chill several hours or overnight. Preheat oven to 350°F.

Divide chilled dough into 6 equal portions for easier handling. On a lightly floured surface, work dough with palms into 10-inch ropes, about ¾-inch in diameter. Then flatter the ropes with fingers to form a ½-inch-thick ribbon.

On an ungreased baking sheet, place 2 ribbons far enough apart so they do not touch. Sprinkle tops with sugar. Bake on the center rack of the oven 20–25 minutes until light brown, dry on top, and barely moist on the inside. Cool about 2 minutes. While still hot, gently cut in half lengthwise, then slice crosswise diagonally into 1-inch bars. Remove bars to wire rack to cool. Cookies will harden as they cool. Makes about 12 dozen small bars.

DRINKS
Champagne, of course.

Variations on the Theme

◎ This concept also lends itself to anniversary celebrations. We planned a special event using this theme for a company celebrating ten years in business. Instead of looking back, we all looked forward . . . and bestowed good fortune on the company for many years to come.

✳ **Fortune Cookies:** If there is a Chinatown in your city, look in the Yellow Pages for custom fortune cookie stores. Or, you can e-mail **wonton@worldnet.att.net.** for Wonton Food, located in Brooklyn, New York. They offer fortune cookies individually wrapped in three varieties: Citrus, Vanilla, and Chocolate. And you can customize your fortunes.

Afterword

by Anneli Rufus

Look back over your life.

Sparkling like stars between the freeways and the meatloaf, the dental appointments and the Stairmaster, were parties. However brief, these glittering moments offered respite from your daily round, a sense of having been transported—rescued, even, to another realm where sizzling barbecues and ice clinking in glasses sounded like musical anthems.

There were parties—and then there were *parties*. Some stand out: those perfect afternoons and evenings whose every last paper lantern, every toothpick parasol, and every pig-and-blanket you remember perfectly.

The best parties, where everything just *clicked*, were those whose givers clearly had the most fun planning them: cooking the strudel that was difficult but worth it, making invitations, decorations, games. With the right hors d'oeuvres, the right record, they could turn living rooms into oases, basements into castles, backyards into outer space.

A vanished art?

Not anymore.

Guiding you so that you have every bit as much fun as your guests, the Party Girls offer all the blueprints you need. Drawing on considerable skill and boundless energy, they show how a baby-bottle-as-a-flower-vase, a well-placed crystal ball, or a wonton-skinned "Spliff" can elevate your fêtes above the rest. The Party Girls are determined to have fun, and it's contagious. Who could resist serving a luscious "Uncle Salmon Spread" on July Fourth? Inviting grownups to a slumber party, turning bridal showers into *Jeopardy*, recapturing the senior prom? Asking guests on St. Patrick's Day to compose limericks using the words *roadkill, anteater,* and *shoehorn*?

And what in the world is worth celebrating? Everything, on any day. Not only birthdays but also reincarnation (come as you *were*). Not just New Year's Eve but also Bastille Day and Oscar Night. You would do well to celebrate the beach, the desert, comic books, big cities. Anything and everything. Turn an attic wall into a city skyline. Build sandcastles in a studio apartment.

Since the best parties have a way of glowing in guests' memories forever—who could forget her first baby shower?—to give an unforgettable party is to make history. That's a huge responsibility, enough to make you tremble over the bundt pan. But it's an honor, too, so go for it. Make daiquiris. Make history.

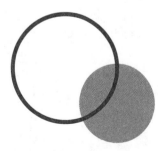

Party Girl Resource Guide

Here is just a partial listing of places to order specialty foods, kitchenware, and baking supplies.
You can order a catalog and order by phone, or via the Internet.

Balducci's

424 Sixth Avenue
New York, NY 10011
(800)225-3822
http://www.balducci's
Specialty foods; catalog available

Ballard Designs

1670 DeFoor Ave. NW
Atlanta, GA 30318
(800) 367-2775
http://www.ballard-designs.com
Catalog features seasonal and theme home decor

Bed, Bath & Beyond

650 Liberty Avenue
Union, NJ 07083
(908) 688-0888
More than 150 stores throughout the United
States; kitchen supplies, sheets, towels, and
more

Chef's Professional Restaurant Equipment for the Home Chef Catalog

(800) 338-3232
http://www.chefscatalog.com

Cost Plus

201 Clay Street
Oakland, CA 94607
(510) 893-7300
73 stores throughout the United States

Costco

800 Lake Drive
Issaquah, WA 98027
(800) 220-6000
http://www.costco.com
More than 280 warehouses throughout the
United States; call for locations

Crate & Barrel

725 Landwer Road

Northbrook, IL 60062

(847) 272-2888

http://www.crateandbarrel.com

75 stores throughout the United States

Dean & Deluca

560 Broadway

New York, NY 10012

(800)221-7714

http://www.dean-deluca.com

Catalog available; specialty foods, baked goods, kitchenware, truffles, caviar, estate-bottle olive oils, varietal vinegars, and more

Digital Chef

A comprehensive source of online shopping for gourmet food and kitchenware

http://www.digitalchef.com

Drew's Famous Party Music

P. O. Box 508

Kenilworth, NJ 07033

(888) HEYDREW (439-3739)

http://www.drewsfamous.com

Premixed party music including disco, Halloween, wedding, and more

Headlines

838 Market Street, Suite 400

San Francisco, CA 94102

(415) 989-8240, ext. 0

Six stores throughout the United States; lava lamps and more

King Arthur Flour Baker's Catalog

P. O. Box 876

Norwich, VT 05055

(800) 827-6836

http://www.kingarthurflour.com

Baking supplies, flour, baking stones, and more

Oriental Trading Company

(800) 228-2269

A great source for inexpensive party favors and decorations

Party 411

Sherri Foxman, a true Party Girl and professional party planner in Cleveland, has a great Web site.

http://www.party411.com

Pier 1 Imports

301 Commerce Street, Suite 600

Fort Worth, TX 76102

(817) 878-8000

750 stores throughout the United States

Sur La Table

1765 Sixth Avenue South

Seattle, WA 98134

(800) 243-0852

Kitchen equipment; call for a catalog

Stumps

(800) 348-5084

http://www.stumpsparty.com

Lots of party supplies, plus props, scenes, and backdrops

Williams-Sonoma

P. O. Box 7456

San Francisco, CA 94120

(800) 541-2233

http://www.williamssonoma.com

Windsor Vineyards

P. O. Box 368

Windsor, CA 95492

(707) 285-7770

Personalize your own wine label

Acknowledgments

From Lara Starr

To my main Party Boy, John, for patience, inspiration, and being the co-host with the most.

To Brenda Knight, for the idea and encouragement.

To Mary Jane Ryan, for guidance and expert advice.

To Sue Miller and Sandy Minella, for showing up at all of my parties, and staying to help clean up afterward!

From Nina Lesowitz

To my Party Soul Mate Martin Eggenberger, for his unwavering support and party prowess.

To Party Goddess Brenda Knight, for her inspiration and enthusiasm.

To the Queen of Themes, Barrie Kerper, for epitomizing the Party Girl esprit.

To Party Priestess Ellen Goldstein, for showing me how it's done.

To my Cooking Comrade Ruthanne Lui-Johnston, for sharing life's themes with me.

To Steve Hueston, a Party Hero, for his excellent suggestions.

To my parents Tomoko and Arthur Lesowitz, for their great taste, and to my brothers Jay and Gary for being life-of-the-Party-Boys.

To Mary Jane Ryan, Will Glennon, and everyone associated with Conari Press: I can't wait to throw a big party for all of you!

From Both

To all of you who shared recipes, tips, ideas, and invitations, thank you from the bottom of our hearts.

Who Are We?

Nina Lesowitz, who has planned and executed many special events for companies and agencies, absolutely loves to party. Although she has very definite ideas about what constitutes a fabulous fête, she can have fun virtually anywhere. Her party persona takes over whenever she's at a gathering of people where liquor is being served. Brunch, holiday parties, company picnics, bar mitzvahs. . . whatever the venue, Nina always wants to turn up the music and get people involved. The more frenzied, the better. She's received acclaim for many of the themes in this book, and cannot wait to throw her next smashing bash.

No one ever leaves one of Lara Morris Starr's parties hungry! Her tendency to "over-cater" has earned her the reputation among family and friends as the hostess with the mostest! With expertise at throwing the biggest of bashes in the smallest of apartments, Lara lets no event go uncelebrated. She has thrown dozens of personal and professional parties with great success, and loves to show off her latest high-drama pastry creations.

Index fo Recipes

Spreads, Relishes, and Seasonings

Alphabetical Index of Recipes

If you enjoyed *The Party Girl Cookbook*, chances are you'll like these other tasty books published by Conari Press:

• *Wild Women in the Kitchen: 101 Rambunctious Recipes & 99 Tasty Tales*
by The Wild Women Association
• *Goddess in the Kitchen: 201 Heavenly Recipes, Spirited Stories & Saucy Secrets*
by Margie Lapanja

Look for them in your local bookstore, on the Internet at **http://www.conari.com**
or call Conari Press at (800) 685-9595.

Conari Press, established in 1987, publishes books on topics
ranging from psychology, spirituality, and women's history to sexuality,
parenting, and personal growth. Our main goal is to publish quality books
that will make a difference in people's lives—both
how we feel about ourselves and how
we relate to one another.

Our readers are our most important resource, and we
value your input, suggestions, and ideas. We'd love to hear
from you—after all, we are publishing books for you!

To request our latest book catalog, or to be added
to our mailing list, please contact:

CONARI PRESS
368 Congress Road, 4th Floor
Boston, MA 02210
ph: 617-542-1324 fax: 877-337-3309
orders@redwheelweiser.com